Catholicism

GREAT RELIGIONS OF MODERN MAN

Richard A. Gard, *General Editor*

BUDDHISM
Edited by Richard A. Gard

CHRISTIANITY: CATHOLICISM
Edited by George Brantl

CHRISTIANITY: PROTESTANTISM
Edited by J. Leslie Dunstan

HINDUISM
Edited by Louis Renou

ISLAM
Edited by John Alden Williams

JUDAISM
Edited by Arthur Hertzberg

Catholicism

EDITED BY

George Brantl

GEORGE BRAZILLER

NEW YORK   1962

NIHIL OBSTAT: JOHN A. GOODWINE, J.C.D.
CENSOR LIBRORUM

IMPRIMATUR: ✠ FRANCIS CARDINAL SPELLMAN
ARCHBISHOP OF NEW YORK

The nihil obstat and imprimatur are official declarations that a book or pamphlet is free of doctrinal or moral error. No implication is contained therein that those who have granted the nihil obstat and imprimatur agree with the contents, opinions or statements expressed.

September 12, 1961

Library of Congress Catalog Card Number: 61-15501

First Printing, October 1961
Second Printing, December 1961

Printed in the United States of America

FOR

ROBERT, MARY AND WINAFRED

Estote imitatores Dei
sicut filii carissimi:
et ambulate in dilectione
sicut et Christus dilexit nos
et tradidit semetipsum pro nobis.

Ephesians 5:1–2

Contents

CHAPTER ONE

The Absence of God

Our time is as the passing of a shadow.[1]

"God is dead," cried Nietzsche. "Do we not wander through an endless nothingness?" In proclaiming the death of God for the modern world, Nietzsche foretold as well its fate. Destroy God and there opens before men a void of nothingness, an abyss upon which man must construct the vain structures of his meaningfulness.

Religion begins in the anguish of a man who faces the abyss of nothingness and who wanders through a broken world made desolate in the absence of God. From the abstract reasonings of the metaphysicians and the nostalgic plea of the poet to the passionate logic of the absurd universe in a work by Sartre or Camus and the anxious questionings of twentieth-century Everyman about "the meaning of it all," we encounter the stark fact that the death of God can lead finally but to the anxiety of the godless or to a rebirth of the desire for God. Deprive man of his God, and he will either create one or die of meaninglessness.

The roots of religion must be sought in a human need, its fruit in a personal response. It is only from the matrix of existential need that reason can move, as it is only in the waiting, thirsting spirit that revelation can find reply. The man who does not need God will not find God, and it is his vital need alone which can be transfigured into the response in which the essence of religion consists.

Contingency is many-faced. Generally it is an absence

of self-explanation or self-sufficiency, the inability of a being to give meaning or sustenance to itself. Men experience this radical contingency in many ways: in the precariousness of their situation, their mere "thereness" without a whence, a why or a whither; in the imminence of death in every choice, every project, every personal relationship; in the absence of foundation for their logic, of ultimate values for their moral life; in their finitude, their inescapable limitations, which are the essential counterpart of their existential contingency. In his desire for meaning, man of himself finds meaninglessness; in his wish for infinite fulfillment, man is limited in every way; in his thirst for life, man finds death a stark intruder in every act and every relationship. He may substitute infinity of longing for fulfillment, limitless having for being, but ultimately he must revert to the reality of himself, call himself by his proper name: man the contingent, man the finite.

ALL THINGS PASS AWAY : ECCLESIASTES

All things have their season: and in their times all things pass under heaven.

A time to be born, and a time to die. A time to plant, and a time to pluck up that which is planted.

A time to kill, and a time to heal. A time to destroy, and a time to build.

A time to weep, and a time to laugh. A time to mourn, and a time to dance.

A time to scatter stones, and a time to gather. A time to embrace, and a time to be far from embrace.

A time to get, and a time to lose. A time to keep, and a time to cast away.

A time to rend, and a time to sew. A time to keep silence, and a time to speak.

A time to love, and a time of hatred. A time of war, and a time of peace.

What hath man more of his labour?[2]

THE CONTINGENCY OF THINGS : ST. AUGUSTINE

These days have no true being; they are gone almost before they arrive; and when they come they cannot continue; they press upon one another, they follow the one the other, and cannot check themselves in their course. Of the past nothing is called back again; what is yet to be expected is something which will pass away again; it is not as yet possessed, whilst as yet it is not arrived; it cannot be kept when once it is arrived. The Psalmist therefore asks, "what is the number of my days" (Ps. xxxviii, 5), what *is,* not what is *not;* and (for this confounds me by a still greater and more perplexing difficulty) both *is* and *is not.* For we can neither say that that *is,* which does not continue, nor that is *is not* when it is come and is passing. It is that absolute IS, that true IS, that IS in the strict sense of the word, that I long for, that IS which is in the Jerusalem which is the bride of my Lord, where there shall be no death, where there shall be no failing, where the day shall not pass away but shall endure, a day which no yesterday precedes nor a morrow ousts. This number of my days, which *is,* I say, make Thou known to me.[3]

Do we not carry our destruction about with us in this flesh? Are not we more brittle than if we were made of glass? Yet even though glass is brittle it lasts a long time if looked after; and thou findest cups which had belonged to grand-fathers and great-grandfathers out of which their grandchil-dren and great-grandchildren are drinking. Such brittleness as this has been kept safe for many years. But we men, brittle as we are, go about subject to such great accidents, that, even if the immediate mischance does not strike us, we cannot live for very long.[4]

The paradox of man, his misery and his grandeur, is found in the ultimate aloneness of man with himself. If we strip away his possessions, his distractions and his accomplishments, we uncover beneath the texture of his "having" the raw center of his being, that abyss of the self where in the most crucial moments of his life a man must ultimately face himself, be alone with himself. Here it is that man must name himself for himself in despair or hope. And it is here alone that religion takes root.

Man is to himself an eternal paradox. Finite in every sense, mortal from birth, he is infinite in his striving, immortal in his longing. Inexplicable to himself in his "thereness," he feels the right to claim an absolute foothold, a foundation for his ontological meaning. He may negate traditional absolutes; still he establishes and embraces new necessity for his living. Whatever label he gives it, an inalienable something remains for man without which he must cease to be man. However he reject transcendents, he starves without a cause which can demand his sacrifice. Take away from man his necessity, the fixed roots of his meaning, and he fulfills Nietzsche's prediction: he wanders through fields of nothingness in search of a being to give his life its meaning. Man is ever a contingent being in search of necessity.

THE ABYSS OF MAN : ST. AUGUSTINE

If by "abyss" we understand a great depth, is not man's heart an abyss? For what is there more profound than that abyss? Men may speak, may be seen by the operation of their members, may be heard speaking; but whose thought is penetrated, whose heart is seen into? What he is inwardly engaged on, what he is inwardly capable of, what he is inwardly doing, or what purposing, what he is inwardly wishing to happen or not to happen, who shall comprehend? . . . Do not you believe that there is in man a deep so profound as to be hidden even to him in whom it is?[5]

THE VANITY OF MAN : ECCLESIASTES

Vanity of vanities, said Ecclesiastes: vanity of vanities, and all is vanity.

What hath a man more of all his labour that he taketh under the sun?

One generation passeth away, and another generation cometh: but the earth standeth for ever.

The sun riseth, and goeth down, and returneth to his place: and there rising again,

Maketh his round by the south, and turneth again to the north: the spirit goeth forward, surveying all places round about, and returneth to his circuits.

All the rivers run into the sea, yet the sea doth not overflow: unto the place from whence the rivers come they return, to flow again.

All things are hard: man cannot explain them by word. The eye is not filled with seeing, neither is the ear filled with hearing.

What is it that hath been? The same thing that shall be. What is it that hath been done. The same that shall be done.

Nothing under the sun is new, neither is any man able to say: Behold this is new. For it hath already gone before in the ages that were before us. . . .

I have seen all things that are done under the sun: and behold all is vanity and vexation of spirit.

The perverse are hard to be corrected: and the number of fools is infinite.[6]

How do men face up to this awareness of meaninglessness, the absurd condition of man? There would seem to be no escape for him who would not evade life: he must not only adopt an attitude, but pursue the logic of his attitude. He must go beyond the rational categories upon which optimism and pessimism were founded; both were intellectual attitudes which rarely touched the nerve centers of life itself. He goes beyond the ordered structures of his life, his language, his reason to the existential core of the human situation from which expression rises and where an attitude demands commitment, where action is irrevocable. This is not the path for him who would reject the need for meaning or who would restrict the scope of meaning. It is rather the unavoidable path for him who recognizes at once the vital thirst and the logical need for a meaning beyond contingency and his own painful need to survive in the absence of such meaning. This is by no means a place for bourgeois complacency or Bohemian irresponsibility.

THE ABSENCE OF GOD : JOB

Can the rush be green without moisture, or a sedge-bush grow without water?

When it is yet in flower, and is not plucked up with the hand, it withereth before all herbs.

Even so are the ways of all that forget God: and the hope of the hypocrite shall perish.

His folly shall not please him: and his trust shall be like the spider's web.

He shall lean upon his house, and it shall not stand. He shall prop it up, and it shall not rise.

Man, born of woman, living for a short time, is filled with many miseries.

Who cometh forth like a flower, and is destroyed, and fleeth as a shadow, and never continueth in the same state.[7]

THE MISERY OF MAN WITHOUT GOD : WISDOM

For he that rejecteth wisdom, and discipline is unhappy: and their hope is vain, and their labours without fruit, and their works unprofitable.

For they have said, reasoning with themselves, but not right: The time of our life is short and tedious, and in the end of a man there is no remedy, and no man hath been known to have returned from hell.

For we are born of nothing, and after this we shall be as if we had not been: for the breath in our nostrils is smoke, and speech a spark to move our heart.

Which being put out, our body shall be ashes, and our spirit shall be poured abroad as soft air, and our life shall pass away as the trace of a cloud, and shall be dispersed as a mist which is driven away by the beams of the sun and overpowered with the heat thereof.

And our name in time shall be forgotten, and no man shall have remembrance of our works.

For our time is as the passing of a shadow, and there is no going back of our end: for it is fast sealed, and no man returneth.[8]

THE VANITY OF THE WORLD : ST. JOHN CHRYSOSTOM

"Vanity of vanities, all is vanity"—it is always seasonable to utter this, but more especially at the present time. Where are now the brilliant surroundings of the consulship? where are the gleaming torches? where is the dancing, and the noise of dancers' feet, and the banquets and the festivals, where are the garlands and the curtains of the theater, where is the applause that greeted thee in the city, where the acclamation in the hippodrome and the flatteries of the spectators? They are gone—all gone: a wind has blown upon the tree, shattering down all its leaves, and showing it to us quite bare, and shaken from its very roots: for so great has been the violence of the blast that it has given a shock to all these fibers of the tree and threatens to tear it up from the roots. Where now are your feigned friends, where are your drinking parties, and your suppers, where is the swarm of parasites, and the wine that used to be poured forth all day long, and the manifold dainties invented by your cooks, where are they who courted your power and did and said everything to win your favor? They were all mere visions of the night, and dreams that have vanished with the dawn of day: they were spring flowers, and when the spring was over they all withered: they were a shadow that has passed away—they were a smoke that has dispersed, bubbles that have burst, cobwebs that have been rent in pieces.

Therefore we chant continually this spiritual song—"Vanity of vanities, all is vanity." For this saying ought to be continually written on our walls and garments, in the market place and in the house, on the streets and on the doors and entrances and above all on the conscience of each one, and to be a perpetual theme for meditation. And inasmuch as deceitful things and maskings and pretense seem to many to be realities, it behooves each one every day both at supper and at breakfast, and in social assemblies, to say to his neighbor and to hear his neighbor say in return: "Vanity of vanities, all is vanity."[9]

Catholicism understands the need for meaning as a desire for God. From the discovery of God in nature, the revelation in reason and nature, to the direct revelation of God in Christ and in His Church, Catholicism acknowledges that before there can be human response there must be the dispositions for response: there must be need; desire must grow from need and from desire, search. Gabriel Marcel has suggested that pessimism and despair are often the necessary passage towards spiritual affirmation, that a man must be stripped down to the painful point of ultimate ontological awareness and aloneness before he can affirm value and meaning. Certainly in a matter so central in human life, a decision which can make tremendous demands on a man in his thinking and his behavior, there must be a readiness, a "good will," a sincerity, before there can be desire, even desire for desire. This is the moral, aesthetic, and rational purification which precedes the healthy use of the human powers in those matters that make a difference to man.

Given this preparedness of spirit to accept reality whatever be its demands, man's need for meaning is transformed into a desire for God. The dynamics of religious experience then transport a man on an infinite journey of discovery and response: from desire to discovery, from discovery to the response of faith, from faith to the renewal of search and ever-deepening response.

Catholicism sees human experience as an all-embracing growth in the awareness of and the response to God. It leaves no area of human experience apart from the transformation which it promises. Prepare the spirit for sincere search, kindle human desire for meaning, and God is everywhere, answering every fundamental need of man in every area of his life and inspiring a response which takes man far beyond his needs to a personal response which draws nature to and beyond the limits of its powers. Need will be transformed into response; "eros" becomes "agape." Reason will find God, but reason will find, too, the need to transcend reason, the promise of more than reason can offer. Reason discovers the need for and the reality of revelation. In seeming to leave reason, man finds in revelation that his reason is strengthened; he has entered upon a new life which transcends in its present reality and its future promises the life of nature and reason, a life which transfigures, without destroying, that which it transcends.

THE THIRST FOR GOD : PSALM 41

As the hart panteth after the fountains of water; so my soul panteth after thee, O God.

My soul hath thirsted after the strong living God. When shall I come and appear before the face of God?

My tears have been my bread day and night, whilst it is said to me daily: Where is thy God?

These things I remembered, and poured out my soul in me; for I shall go over into the place of the wonderful tabernacle, even to the house of God. . . .

Why art thou cast down, O my soul? and why dost thou disquiet me?

Hope thou in God, for I will still give praise to him: the salvation of my countenance and my God.[10]

THE INQUIETUDE OF THE SPIRIT : ST. AUGUSTINE

Thou has created us for Thyself, and our heart knows no rest until it may repose in Thee.

With a hidden goad Thou didst urge me, that I might be restless until such time as the sight of my mind might discern Thee for certain.

Too late am I come to love Thee, O thou Beauty, so ancient and withal so new; too late am I come to love Thee. And behold, Thou wert within me, and I without; and there made

I search for Thee, and in a deformed manner I cast myself upon the things of Thy creation, which yet Thou hadst made fair. Thou wert with me indeed, but I remained not with Thee. Those things withheld me from Thee, which yet, if they had not their being in Thee, would not be at all. Thou didst call and cry out, and so didst break through my deafness. Thou didst shine forth and glow refulgent, and so didst chase away my blindness. Thou didst breathe thy fragrance upon me, and I drew in my breath, yet do I pant after Thee. I tasted Thee, and still I hunger and thirst for more. Thou didst but touch me, and I do even burn with a desire to enjoy Thee.[11]

CHAPTER TWO

Theophany

The heavens show forth the glory of God.[1]

Man can find meaning for himself only in finding God, and to find God he must desire to find God. It soon becomes apparent, however, that God is not an object which man can find and clutch to himself as the key to all his problems. God is transcendent, personal: a person must reveal himself to be understood and loved; the transcendent is infinitely beyond finite comprehension. The discovery of God must be a response to the revelation of God.

Revelation is God's making Himself and His intentions known to man. He does this in many ways. Christian experience, as we have said, is the coming to awareness of the fullness of divine revelation and the response of the total man, in love and knowledge, to the full implications of the divine revelation. Three phases of the revelation of God to man form central tenets of Catholic belief: the natural revelation of God through reason, the supernatural revelation of God in Christ, and the revelation in the Church. The actual sequence in which these come to awareness for the Catholic is not our concern here. What is essential is to realize the organic relation of the various stages of revelation as they constitute the integrity of Catholic belief.

GOD AND REASON

Nature, and reason as the interpreter of nature, are the primordial ground of the revelation of God. All things in nature are for Catholics in the likeness of God to some degree and are impelled, as St. Thomas Aquinas claimed, by an appetite for the divine. But, it is in man that the likeness becomes image: man alone among beings of nature can evoke from the structure of nature the fact of its God. All nature is regulated by law which reflects the nature of God; but only man comes to conscious awareness that the lawful structure of nature reflects the creative act of God. For man is governed in his thinking and willing by the laws which bind the nature of God Himself. Everywhere he turns, nature speaks to him of God. If he ignores the voice, nature and human nature fall into meaninglessness. Man cannot think without implicitly evoking God; he cannot seek the good or the beautiful without accepting by implication at least, the Good and the Beautiful. He cannot discover and improve the structure of nature without discovering God; his projects become cooperation with Divine Expression, for nature is the matter of the divine creative act. To extricate the form of Nature is to unveil the structure of divine discourse. Nature is revelation, a book to be read (*intuslegere*) by eyes which wish to see.

There is gratuity in the divine revelation in nature. True, by the fact that man has reason by nature, he has the right to discover. But, nature is stubborn and man's reason does not enjoy the immediacy of vision. Neither nature nor God reveals itself to the proud man. Man cannot tear God from nature, but God speaks to the man who is attentive. There is, therefore, a natural humility of reason which is the prerequisite for the natural discovery of God.

Catholicism maintains, therefore, that man by his reason, however feeble its power of penetration, reads into nature to the ultimate point of nature's being; reason is governed by and discovers the operations of the laws of being. And as such a power, reason can discover the fact and something of the nature of the Supreme Being. "Reason is a faculty of being because it is a faculty of the divine." This statement of Père Rousselot, S.J., is provocative in its sequence; but it is a capsule statement of the fullest reaches of the Catholic philosophical commitment.

INVOCATION FOR LIGHT : ST. ANSELM

O Lord, my God, teach my heart how and where to seek Thee, where and how to find Thee. If Thou art absent, Lord, where can I seek Thee? But if Thou art present everywhere, why do I not see Thee. . . . By what signs, under what guise shall I seek Thee? I have never seen Thee, my Lord God, I do not know Thy face. . . . I do not try to penetrate Thy mystery, O Lord, for in no way is my intelligence commensurate with it. But I desire to find Thy Truth which I believe and love in my heart. I do not seek to understand in order to believe; I believe in order to understand. For I believe that I cannot understand unless I believe.[2]

Certainly one of the distinguishing marks of Catholicism is its refusal to invalidate reason or to exile it from religious belief. It is maintained that although Christian faith far exceeds the powers of reason, it does not destroy reason. On the contrary, Catholicism maintains that the pre-conditions for the commitment of faith may be validated by reason. The act of faith which is supernatural is grown in the soil of nature and is strengthened by natural belief.

What can reason, therefore, know of God? Reason can establish the existence of God by proof and can make certain statements concerning the nature of God and His operation in nature. As we shall see later, reason is called upon also to establish certain statements upon which faith rests and to enter into the dynamics of faith in the explication of its content, the building of a theology.

THE EXISTENCE OF GOD

The proofs of the existence of God require a commitment that nature is meaningful, or that it must be made meaningful. This commitment takes several forms, all of which culminate in the commitment to reason in its ability to extricate that which is required to give meaning to nature and experience. Basically, all proofs are reducible to the following statements, if these are understood in the widest definition of the terms: Nature (this object, fact, activity, etc.) is incapable of constituting its own explanation or meaningfulness; nature must in the last analysis be meaningful; therefore, I can with certainty postulate the existence of a Being (however hidden and beyond the senses) which can give meaning to the being of nature.

The interpretation of meaninglessness and the areas stressed vary with the various authors of proofs in the Catholic tradition. In writers like Augustine, Anselm and Pascal, the emphasis is on the total, personal commitment to meaningfulness. For them the need for meaning is so diffused through the personality and its experience that their proofs often suggest an independence from experience; they are the authors of what have traditionally been called "a priori proofs"—proofs which seemed to postulate God before experience. Meaning for these writers is existential; it is the heart, the guts even, as much as reason, which clamors for meaning. Their tendency is to "prove" God from the fact that *no* experience, whether rational, emotional, or moral, is possible unless God is implicated in the very origin of the experience. They *live* the contingency which makes the spirit cry out for God. They would say that it is this cry of affirmation which is echoed in the proofs of reason.

On the other hand, writers like St. Thomas Aquinas isolate reason and its logical processes and prove God by applying the principles of reason (being) to contingent data of nature to show that they require the existence of God in order that they may have meaning. These are the "a posteriori" proofs of God.

Each of these approaches has had its critics within the Catholic tradition. The first group, in emphasizing the vital need for God in order that there be meaningful human experience, seem at times not to "prove" God but to postulate Him. The second group are often criticized as being overly clinical, cold-blooded, vitally meaningless. Aquinas' proofs are, it is true, scientific proofs, intricate applications of reason to experiential data. In answer, it must be understood that reason in religious matters may appear isolated from vital concerns, but it never is actually so. Each of Aquinas' proofs may readily be translated into areas in which human feeling and emotion are intricately involved. No one, it has been said, prays to a Prime Mover or a Necessary Being. These attributes, however, are the rational counterparts of aspects of the Divinity which make it right that man pray.

Before outlining the traditional proofs it will be helpful to indicate briefly the position of the Catholic Church on proofs of God. In 1870, the Vatican Council stated: "Whoever says that the one and only true God, our

Creator and Lord, cannot be known with certainty by the natural light of the human reason by means of created things, let him be anathema."[3] The Church has opposed such trends as Fideism (God must be known by faith), Traditionalism (the idea of God must come from tradition), and Ontologism (the idea of God must be gotten in immediate vision of God). She does not deny that the idea of God may be derived from faith or tradition; but she opposes diligently any approach to the question which refuses to admit the possibility of a proof from nature. As for other proofs, the Church allows any which do not infringe on the validity of reason or which do not destroy the distinction of the natural and the supernatural modes of knowledge.

The Ontological Argument of St. Anselm is the most well known of the priori proofs. Although it has been refuted over and over again from Anselm's own day to the present, it recurs, is modified, is reinterpreted and misinterpreted in writer after writer. The only explanation which can make this history intelligible is that based on a distinction between the verbalization of the proof and its actual intent. As the proof is worded in Anselm or as it was reworked in Descartes, it is readily refutable: since it is based in every case on the statement that the idea of God is a metaphysically valid idea, a "possible" for Descartes, before any experiential proof, it is open to Aquinas' valid charge that prior to proof we haven't the slightest idea whether the idea of God is the idea of a possible being, whether it is contradictory or non-contradictory. To Anselm's wording, Aquinas merely says: "I can't go along with your reasoning since I have no idea whether the idea of God is a valid idea." The opponents of Anselm and Descartes recognize that once the metaphysical possibility of God is admitted, His existence follows immediately: a necessary Being which would be a mere possibility would be a contradiction. Of course, this entire question hinges, too, on the derivation of metaphysical ideas: the Anselmian proof suggests, as the Cartesian does, that ideas can be derived and formed in combinations without recourse to experience. To such an idea, of course, Aquinas answers as the good empiricist, that ideas are only known as possible on the basis of experience.

THE ONTOLOGICAL ARGUMENT : ST. ANSELM

Thou, o Lord, who granteth understanding to faith, grant, insofar as it is good, that I may understand that Thou dost exist as we believe Thou dost exist and that I may understand that Thou art such as we believe Thee to be. We believe that Thou art a Being greater than which none can be conceived. Is it possible that such a Being should not exist even though "the fool hath said in his heart: God does not exist"? Certainly when the fool hears what I say—"a being greater than which none can be conceived"—he understands what he hears; and whatever he understands is in his intelligence even if he does not understand that this being exists in actuality. To conceive of a being in the mind is not the same as to understand that that being exists in actuality. When, for example, a painter reflects on a painting which he plans to make, the painting is in the mind; but he does not believe that it actually exists, for he has not made it yet. When, however, he has actually painted it, the painting is in his mind and he understands as well that it exists in actuality.

Now, the fool must agree that he has before the mind an idea of a being greater than which none can be conceived; after all, he understands the expression when he hears it. Anything understood must be in the intelligence. Certainly, too, the being greater than which none can be conceived cannot exist in the intellect alone; for if it were only in the intellect, it could be conceived as existing also in reality and this would be to conceive a still greater being. In such a case, if the being greater than which none can be conceived is merely in the intelligence [and not in reality], then this same being is something than which one could still conceive a greater [i.e., one which exists both in the intelligence and in reality]. This is a contradiction.

Consequently, there can be no doubt that the being greater than which none can be conceived must exist both in the intelligence and in reality.[4]

THE TESTIMONY OF TRUTH : ST. BONAVENTURE

The intelligence understands a proposition when it knows with certitude that the proposition is true. To know this is to know that the intelligence is not deceived, that this truth cannot be otherwise, that it is an unchangeable truth. But our spirit is subject to change: it could not see truth in an unchangeable way without recourse to an unchangeable light, which can be nothing created. If the intelligence knows truth, then, it knows in the light which illumines every man who comes into the world, the true Light, the Word which was with God from the beginning. . . . St. Augustine says, therefore, in his treatise *De Vera Religione* that the light which illumines our reasoning is derived from the eternal Truth and leads us thence. We conclude, therefore, that our intelligence is united with the eternal Word, since without the aid of His Light we could know nothing with certitude.

You yourself may contemplate the Truth which teaches you, if passions and material images do not hinder you and interpose themselves as a cloud between you and the rays of the Truth.[5]

What is actually behind the arguments of the apriorists? They seem to say that the very fact of proving God must presuppose an affirmation of God: the tools of proof, the principles by which reason must argue, implicitly contain the affirmation of God. Man desires meaning; he commits himself to a meaningful universe. The principles by which reason must operate express this commitment. God is the source of ultimate meaning. Therefore, in every rational act, implicitly "prior" to every act, at the fine point of the human spirit where the rational act originates, God is affirmed. Man commits himself to Truth "before" affirming truths; he embraces the Good "before" seeking goods; he senses Beauty "before" he creates beautiful things. For an Augustine, Truth is the Magister in the first act of knowing, Good, of the first act of loving. The God Who is the ultimate term of all human affirmation and willing presides at the very initiation of every human act. Reason translates this fact, these writers would say, into the principles by which it reasons. Reason explicates in finite nature, using these principles, the need to affirm God; it proves God's existence but its proof is founded upon principles which themselves implicitly contain the affirmation of God which presides over all proof.

The human reason and the human will, in other words, are themselves finite and subject to the awareness of contingency within themselves. Yet they are uniquely vibrant with the responsiveness to Necessity. They move outward towards the finite in search of the infinite; they would not seek the infinite, St. Augustine and Pascal would say, unless they first desired; they would not desire the Infinite, had they not first affirmed Him. We return finally to Rousselot's dictum: "The human intelligence is a faculty for knowing being because it is a faculty for knowing the divine." These "proofs" are best interpreted as a priori not because they are not founded in experience, but because they make the commitment to God the very condition for meaningful experience. All other proofs are, for the apriorists, elaborations upon this first and crowning fact.

The a posteriori proofs, most often represented by St. Thomas Aquinas' *Five Ways,* have been more readily understood. They are a posteriori in that they claim to arrive at the fact of God's existence from prior experience of nature. From this approach there can result as many proofs as there are data of natural experience which cannot adequately explain their own existence. Although they grant the ontological priority of God in nature, these proofs are based on the assertion that the knowledge of contingent beings must be logically prior to the knowledge of the necessary being. The logical tool which governs all such proofs is what the philosophers call the Principle of Sufficient Reason or Explanation: Every being must have adequate reason, ontological and logical, for its existence; if this reason is not adequately found in the being itself, it must be found in another being. This is the principle of meaningfulness. Using this principle, the a posteriori arguments proceed generally as follows. X is a fact of nature. X is a contingent fact, i.e., it does not have adequate reason for existence within itself. Now, any being requires adequate explanation (Principle of Sufficient Reason); therefore, the adequate reason for X is sought in Y or Z or in the series $X, Y \ldots n$. The same reasoning is applied to Y and Z and any series which partially explains X until ultimately it is shown that a being must be postulated which is beyond such a series and which supplies ultimate and adequate explanation for X and which itself does not require another being for its explanation; this final being is, then, a necessary being; and this is what men call God.

It will be noticed in each of the a posteriori proofs that the contingent fact from which the proof begins determines the aspect of God to which the proof leads. One proof will prove God exists as an uncaused cause, another as a supreme good, another as a necessary being, another as a supreme legislator of order in the universe.

Each of these terminal attributes of God can be predicated of the infinite necessary being alone so that it becomes a simple corollary for the philosopher to prove that all ways lead to the same one God, each revealing some one aspect by which He is known.

GOD CAN BE FOUND : WISDOM

But all men are vain, in whom there is not the knowledge of God: and who by these good things that are seen could not understand him that is. Neither by attending to the works have acknowledged who was the workman:

But have imagined, either the fire, or the wind, or the swift air, or the circle of the stars, or the great water, or the sun and moon, to be the gods that rule the world.

With whose beauty, if they being delighted, took them to be gods: let them know how much the Lord of them is more beautiful than they. For the first author of beauty made all those things.[6]

THE EVIDENCE OF GOD : ST. PAUL

For the invisible things of him from the creation of the world are clearly seen, being understood by the things that are made. His eternal power also and divinity: so that they are inexcusable.

Because that, when they knew God, they have not glorified him as God or given thanks: but became vain in their thoughts. And their foolish heart was darkened.

For, professing themselves to be wise, they became fools.[7]

THE TESTIMONY OF BEAUTY : ST. AUGUSTINE

Ask the loveliness of the earth, ask the loveliness of the sea, ask the loveliness of the wide airy spaces, ask the loveliness of the sky, ask the order of the stars, ask the sun making the day light with its beams, ask the moon tempering the darkness of the night that follows, ask the living things which move in the waters, which tarry on the land, which fly in the air; ask the souls that are hidden, the bodies that are perceptive; the visible things which must be governed, the invisible things which govern: ask all these things, and they will all answer thee, Lo, see we are lovely. Their loveliness is their confession. And these lovely but mutable things, who has made them, save Beauty immutable?[8]

THE FIVE WAYS : ST. THOMAS AQUINAS

The fact that God exists may be proved in five ways.

The first way, which is also the most immediately apparent, is the *argument from motion*. It is evident from the testimony of our senses that certain things in the world are in motion. Now, whatever is moved must be moved by another being; for nothing can be moved unless it be in a state of potentiality for that toward which it is moved: a being moves only insofar as it is actual. To move something is to bring it from a state of potentiality to a state of actuality. Nothing, however, can be reduced from potentiality to actuality without the influence of a being in actuality. In this way, fire, which is actually hot, makes wood, which is potentially hot, become actually hot; the fire moves and changes the wood. Now, it is impossible for a being to be simultaneously and in the same respect both in act and potency, although it may be so under diverse respects. That which is actually hot cannot be potentially hot; it is, however, potentially cold. It is, therefore, impossible for something to move itself, to be the mover and the moved in respect to the same term of motion. Anything which is moved, therefore, must be moved by another. If that by which the first being is moved be likewise moved, then this mover, too, must be moved by another; and so, too, of this third being. There can be no infinite regress here in things which move and things which are moved, for then there would be no first mover of the series; consequently, there would be no mover at all in the series, for the secondary movers do not move except insofar as they are moved by the primary mover. A cane does not move unless it be first moved by the hand. It is therefore necessary to arrive ultimately at some first mover which is moved by no other being. Such a Being is understood by all men to be God.

The second argument is derived from the fact of *efficient causality*. In the data of the senses we discover an order among efficient causes. Nothing is found, nor would such be possible, which is the efficient cause of itself; for such a being would be anterior to itself, and this is impossible. Still, it is not possible that we proceed to infinity in the series of efficient causes; for in any ordered series of efficient causes, the first is the cause of the intermediary, the intermediary the cause of the last, and this whether the intermediaries be one or several. If the cause is removed, so too is the effect removed. Therefore, if there be not a first in the series of efficient causes, there is no ultimate and no intermediary cause. If we were to admit an infinite regress in efficient causes, then there would be no first efficient cause and consequently no final effect and no mediate efficient cause. This, of course, cannot be. Therefore, it is necessary that we posit a first efficient cause. All men call this Cause God.

The third way is based on *possibility and necessity* in beings. The argument runs as follows. We discover certain things for which both existence and non-existence are possibilities: this may be shown in those things which are generated and corrupted and which, therefore, are capable of existence and non-existence. It is impossible that all beings be possibles in this way; for a being which is capable of non-existence must at some time not have existed. If, therefore, all things were beings for which non-existence is possible, at some time nothing would have been. If this were true, then nothing would now exist: for what does not exist, cannot begin to exist except through that which is existent. If there had been nothing, it would have been impossible for anything to begin to exist; and there would now be nothing. Evidently this is not the case. Therefore it cannot be that all beings are mere possibles; there must be a necessary being in nature. A necessary being either has the reason for its necessity from elsewhere or not. As in the case of efficient causes, it is not possible to admit an infinite series of necessary beings which require a cause for their necessity. Therefore, we must admit a being which is necessary of itself, which does not have an extraneous cause of its necessity and which is the cause of all other necessary beings. All men call this Necessary Being God.

The fourth way is derived from *the degrees of perfection* which can be found in things. The greater and the less good, the more or less true, the more or less noble can be found in nature; so, too, degrees of other qualities. But "more" or "less" are attributed to things insofar as they approximate in varying degrees that which is perfection in a particular quality. Thus, that is more hot which more closely approximates the absolute hot. There must be, therefore, something which is supremely true, supremely good, supremely noble and, consequently, perfect being: for what is supremely true is supremely being, as Aristotle has said in *II Metaphysics*. Whatever is supreme in any line of perfection is the cause of all degrees within that line of perfection: so fire, which is most hot, is the cause of all heat, as Aristotle says in the same work. Therefore, there must be a being which is the cause, for all things, of their being, their goodness, in fact of their every perfection. And we call this Supreme Being God.

The fifth argument is taken from the fact of *the order which governs nature*. We see that things which lack the power of knowledge, e.g. natural bodies, still act towards purposes. We can observe this in the fact that always, or most often at least, they operate in the same manner in such a way as to achieve the best result. From this it is evident that they do not achieve such results from chance but from intention. Now, whatever lacks the power of knowledge cannot tend to an end unless it be directed by a being with knowledge and intelligence. The arrow must be directed by the archer. Therefore, there is an intelligent being by which all natural things are directed towards their purpose. This Being we call God.[9]

GOD FOUND IN THE HUMAN CONSCIENCE :
JOHN HENRY CARDINAL NEWMAN

. . . Conscience has a legitimate place among our mental acts; as really so, as the action of memory, of reasoning, of imagination, or as the sense of the beautiful; that, as there are objects which, when presented to the mind, cause it to feel grief, regret, joy, or desire, so there are things which excite in us approbation or blame, and which we in consequence call right or wrong; and which, experienced in ourselves, kindle in us that specific sense of pleasure or pain, which goes by the name of a good or bad conscience. This being taken for granted, I shall attempt to show that in this special feeling, which follows on the commission of what we call right or wrong, lie the materials for the real apprehension of a Divine Sovereign and Judge.

The feeling of conscience (being, I repeat, a certain keen sensibility, pleasant or painful,—self-approval and hope, or compunction and fear,—attendant on certain of our actions, which in consequence we call right or wrong) is twofold:— it is a moral sense, and a sense of duty; a judgment of the reason and a magisterial dictate. Of course its act is indivisible; still it has these two aspects, distinct from each other, and admitting of a separate consideration. Though I lost my sense of the obligation which I lie under to abstain from acts of dishonesty, I should not in consequence lose my sense that such actions were an outrage offered to my moral nature. Again; though I lost my sense of their moral deformity, I should not therefore lose my sense that they were forbidden to me. Thus conscience has both a critical and a judicial office, and though its promptings, in the breasts of the millions of human beings to whom it is given, are not in all cases correct, that does not necessarily interfere with the force of its testimony and of its sanction: its testimony that there is a right and a wrong, and its sanction to that testimony conveyed in the feelings which attend on right or wrong conduct. Here I have to speak of conscience in the latter point of view, not as supplying us, by means to its various acts, with the elements of morals, such as may be developed by the intellect into an ethical code, but simply as the dictate of an authoritative monitor bearing upon the details of conduct as they come before us, and complete in its several acts, one by one.

Let us then thus consider conscience, not as a rule of right conduct, but as a sanction of right conduct. This is its primary and most authoritative aspect; it is the ordinary sense of the word. Half the world would be puzzled to know what was meant by the moral sense; but every one knows what is meant by a good or bad conscience. Conscience is ever forcing on us by threats and by promises that we must follow the right and avoid the wrong; so far it is one and the same in the mind of every one, whatever be its particular errors in particular minds as to the acts which it orders to be done or to be avoided; and in this respect it corresponds to our perception of the beautiful and deformed. As we have naturally a sense of the beautiful and graceful in nature and art, though tastes proverbially differ, so we have a sense of duty and obligation, whether we all associate it with the same certain actions in particular or not. Here, however, Taste and Conscience part company: for the sense of beautifulness, as indeed the Moral Sense, has no special relations to persons, but contemplates objects in themselves; conscience, on the other hand, is concerned with persons primarily, and with actions mainly as viewed in their doers, or rather with self alone and one's own actions, and with others only indirectly and as if in association with self. And further, taste is its own evidence, appealing to nothing beyond its own sense of the beautiful or the ugly, and enjoying the specimens of the beautiful simply for their own sake; but conscience does not repose on itself, but vaguely reaches forward to something beyond self, and dimly discerns a sanction higher than self for its decisions, as is evidenced in that keen sense of obligation and responsibility which informs them. And hence it is that we are accustomed to speak of conscience as a voice, a term which we should never think of applying to the sense of the beautiful; and moreover a voice, or the echo of a voice, imperative and constraining, like no other dictate in the whole of our experience. . . .

If, as is the case, we feel responsibility, are ashamed, are frightened, at transgressing the voice of conscience, this implies that there is One to whom we are responsible, before whom we are ashamed, whose claims upon us we fear. If, on doing wrong, we feel the same tearful, broken-hearted sorrow which overwhelms us on hurting a mother; if, on doing right, we enjoy the same sunny serenity of mind, the same soothing, satisfactory delight which follows on our receiving praise from a father, we certainly have within us the image of some person, to whom our love and veneration look, in whose smile we find our happiness, for whom we yearn, towards whom we direct our pleadings, in whose anger we are troubled and waste away. These feelings in us are such as require for their exciting cause an intelligent being: we are not affectionate towards a stone, nor do we feel shame before a horse or a dog: we have not remorse or compunction on breaking mere human law: yet, so it is, conscience excites all these painful emotions, confusion, foreboding, self-condemnation; and on the other hand, it sheds upon us a deep peace, a sense of security, a resignation, and a hope, which there is no sensible, no earthly object to elicit. "The wicked flees, when no man pursueth"; then why does he flee? whence his terror? Who is it that he sees in solitude, in darkness, in the hidden chambers of his heart? If the cause of these emotions does not belong to this visible world, the Object to which his perception is directed must be Supernatural and Divine; and thus the phenomena of Conscience, as a dictate, avail to impress the imagination with the picture of a Supreme Governor, a Judge, holy, just, powerful, all-seeing, retributive, and is the creative principle of religion, as the Moral Sense is the principle of ethics. . . .

. . . whatever be the actual history of the first formation of the divine image within us, so far at least is certain, that, by informations external to ourselves, as time goes on, it admits of being strengthened and improved. It is certain too, that, whether it grows brighter and stronger, or, on the other hand, is dimmed, distorted, or obliterated, depends on each of us individually, and on his circumstances. It is more than probable that, in the event, from neglect, from the temptations of life, from bad companions, or from the urgency of secular occupations, the light of the soul will fade away and die out. Men transgress their sense of duty, and gradually lose those sentiments of shame and fear, the natural supplements of transgression, which, as I have said, are the witnesses of the Unseen Judge. And, even were it deemed impossible that those who had in their first youth a genuine apprehension of Him, could ever utterly lose it, yet that apprehension may become almost undistinguishable from an inferential acceptance of the great truth, or may dwindle into a mere notion of their intellect. On the contrary, the image of God, if duly cherished, may expand, deepen, and be completed, with the growth of their powers and in the course of life, under the varied lessons, within and without them, which are brought home to them concerning that same God, One and Personal, by means of education, social intercourse, experience, and literature.

To a mind thus carefully formed upon the basis of its natural conscience, the world, both of nature and of man, does but give back a reflection of those truths about the One Living God, which have been familiar to it from childhood. Good and evil meet us daily as we pass through life, and there are those who think it philosophical to act towards the manifestations of each with some sort of impartiality, as if evil had as much right to be there as good, or even a better, as having more striking triumphs and a broader jurisdiction. And because the course of things is determined by fixed laws, they consider that those laws preclude the present agency of the Creator in carrying out of particular issues. It is otherwise with the theology of a religious imagination. It has a living hold on truths which are really to be found in the world, though they are not upon the surface. It is able to pronounce by anticipation, what it takes a long argument to prove—that good is the rule, and evil the exception. It is able to assume that, uniform as are the laws of nature, they are consistent with a particular Providence. It interprets what it sees around it by this previous inward teaching, as the true key of that maze of vast complicated disorder; and thus it gains a more and more consistent and luminous vision of God from the most unpromising materials. Thus conscience is a connecting principle between the creature and his Creator; and the firmest hold of theological truths is gained by habits of personal religion. When men begin all their works with the thought of God, acting for His sake, and to fulfil His will, when they ask His blessing on themselves and their life, pray to Him for the objects they desire, and see Him in the event, whether it be according to their prayers or not, they will find everything that happens tend to confirm them in the truths about Him which live in their imagination, varied and unearthly as those truths may be. Then they are brought into His presence as that of a Living Person, and are able to hold converse with Him, and that with a directness and simplicity, with a confidence and intimacy, *mutatis mutandis*, which we use towards an earthly superior; so that it is doubtful whether we realize the company of our fellow-men with greater keenness than these favoured minds are able to contemplate and adore the Unseen, Incomprehensible Creator.[10]

What of the significance of such abstract proofs for the religious life? Many have criticized the Catholic emphasis on philosophy and rational proofs of God. One does not go to God by proofs, it is said. "God speaks of God," said Pascal.

In the abstract form in which such proofs are provided, it can certainly not be claimed that they are such as to "touch" a man, to bring about a conversion of spirit, unless he be that rare individual for whom rational or mathematical consistency are a supreme value. Still, the traditional proofs in their abstract form do actually reflect the concrete experiential paths by which men realize the existence of God in nature. Difficult as they might become to recognize, each of these proofs may be found incarnate in the experience of someone who has found meaning in God. Place side by side the proofs and the narrations of natural conversion to God and the difference will not be as great as usually it is said to be.

Further, it must be emphasized that Catholicism recognizes that man comes to proof with a desire for proof. A moral and emotional precondition for reasoning is the necessary seedbed in which the conviction of God grows. A rational proof is more than an abstract mathematical theorem; it is a structure to be received into the vital core of man's experience to become a power dominating his choices, his thoughts, his desires. He can, therefore, resist any proof when he finds its uncomfortable to accept it. A truth to become acceptable as a truth must first be seen as a good.

THE NATURE OF GOD

Implicit in the proofs of God's existence are both the possibilities and the limits of rational knowledge of the nature of God. The Five Ways of St. Thomas Aquinas, for example, lead to affirmations that God is personal (Way 4 and 5); necessary (Way 3); transcendent cause of all finite being (Way 2); source of and cooperator with all action (Way 1); perfect being and goodness, identified with infinite perfection (Way 4); providential legislator (Way 5). Yet, by the very fact that God is proved necessary being, He is proved transcendent: God must infinitely surpass the cognitive powers of the finite man, and any concept man forms of the nature of God will require correction on this basis.

To the basic facts shown in the proofs that God is Necessary Being and that He is the sufficient explanation of all contingent beings correspond the two general characteristics of the Divine Nature: transcendence and immanence. God is transcendent (beyond, different, absent, other, etc.); God is immanent (in nature; similar to nature; present, etc.). These terms constitute the poles between which the many theories of the knowledge of God must move both in Catholic and other philosophies.

God is Transcendence. The transcendent can be approached only as mystery, the "great unknown," the One beyond the chasm of infinite unapproachability, infinite otherness. God, in other words, cannot be considered "another" being; in the proper sense of the words, He has absolutely nothing in common with finite creatures.

On the other hand, God is Immanence. He is the sufficient explanation of nature, the prime mover of finite activity and causality, the first cause of finite being, the orderer of finite systems. As such, God must act in nature, be in nature. Then, too, as seen in Aquinas' Fourth Way, God is the primary Exemplary Cause, the supreme Perfection in every line of perfection.

From these facts of divine transcendence and immanence follow the various cognitive approaches to the divine nature. If God is pure transcendence, our knowledge of Him must be negative knowledge: we affirm of God only the negation of limitation. God, in this sense, is nothing, other than all beings we know, infinitely beyond any possible concept we can form. This is the path of what in Catholic thought has been called negative theology; it is the path of the mystic; and it is always a necessary corrective to any tendency towards pantheism or any system which might tend to destroy the mystery of God.

Insofar as God is immanent and the infinite source of finite perfection, there must be similarity of creature to God. Knowing the perfections of creatures, we must know something of the perfection of God, for God is the exemplary cause of all creaturely perfection.

For Catholic thought, God is at once transcendent and immanent: His transcendence cannot be affirmed independently of His immanence, nor His immanence independently of His transcendence. He is the transcendent/immanent. Catholic thought rests, then, between theories of pure transcendence as in Deism or in many contemporary Protestant theologies and theories of pure immanence which are characteristic of pantheist philosophies. Allowing within her tradition for the perennial corrective influence of the negative theologies, the Catholic Church is firm in insisting that man can have natural knowledge of the nature of God because of Divine Immanence-in-Transcendence.

The fine point on which Catholic thinking balances here is that of the "analogy of being" which is the conceptual counterpart of the ontological identity-in-difference of God and nature (transcendence/immanence). It maintains that perfections found in nature may be attributed to God in a sense which is neither univocal

(Pantheism), nor equivocal (Deism), but analogous, that is, simultaneously similar but totally other. In brief, God and nature are neither totally same nor totally other; they are at once same-infinitely-other. God is, for example, personal; but in a sense infinitely other than that in which a creature is personal.

What, then, can reason know of the nature of God? God is transcendence: He is infinitely beyond nature and contingency. God is infinite: He is all perfection, actual or possible, in perfect identity of being. God is omnipotent: whatever is possible can be done by God (the impossible is such because it contradicts the nature of God; therefore, God himself cannot perform the impossible). God is personal: He is spirit with knowledge and will, but infinitely (note that we do not say *person,* for revelation of the Trinity acts as negative norm here for such an affirmation). God is necessary: He is without beginning and lacks the metaphysical structure which would even make a cessation of existence possible. God is free: all that He is, He is necessarily; but the necessary act of God towards contingents is a free act (a God who is not necessary would not be God, but a God who would not be free towards creatures would cease to be God). God is one: as infinite, He cannot have an equal. God is good: He is perfection and the source of all perfection. God is truth: He is both ontological truth and the Truth which makes all finite truths true. God is beauty: He is that infinity of perfection in unity which alone can give ultimate delight.

THE TRANSCENDENCE OF GOD : ST. AUGUSTINE

All things can be said of God, yet is nothing worthily said of God. Nothing is wider than this utter want. Thou seekest a name befitting Him and findest none; thou seekest in what way soever to speak of Him and thou findest Him all things.[11]

What then, brethren, shall we say of God? For if thou hast been able to understand what thou wouldest say, it is not God. If thou hast been able to comprehend it, thou hast comprehended something else instead of God. If thou hast been able to comprehend Him as thou thinkest, by so thinking thou hast deceived thyself. This then is not God, if thou hast comprehended it; but if this be God, thou hast not comprehended it. How therefore wouldest thou speak of that which thou canst not comprehend?[12]

But yet, when I love Thee, what is it that I love? Not the beauty of any body, not the order of time, not the clearness of this light that so gladdens our eyes, not the harmony of sweet songs of every kind, not the fragrancy of flowers, or spices of aromatical odours, not manna, nor honey, nor limbs delightful to the embrace of flesh and blood. Not these things do I love, in loving my God. Yet do I love a kind of light, a kind of voice, a kind of odour, a kind of food, a kind of embracing, when I love my God, who is the light, the voice, the odour, the food, the embracing of my inward man; when that light shineth into my soul which is not circumscribed by any place, when that voice soundeth which is not snatched away by time, when that odour pours forth which is not scattered by the air, when that food savours the taste which is unconsumed by eating, when that embracement is enjoyed which is not divorced by satiety. This it is which I love, when I love my God.[13]

THE ATTRIBUTES OF GOD : VATICAN COUNCIL

The Holy, Catholic, Apostolic, and Roman Church believes and confesses that there is one only true and living God, Creator and Lord of Heaven and earth, all-powerful, eternal, immense, incomprehensible, infinite in intelligence, in will, and in every perfection, who, being a unique spiritual substance by nature, absolutely simple and unchangeable, must be declared distinct from the world in fact and by essence, happy in Himself and by Himself, and lifted above all that is and can be conceived outside of Him.[14]

THE PERFECTIONS OF GOD : ST. BONAVENTURE

Contemplate, if you can, pure Being. It will necessarily be evident that pure being does not receive its existence from another and is, consequently, the absolutely first being. It comes neither from nothingness nor from another being. What could constitute Being-of-Itself if pure being is not of-itself and from-itself.

... the Perfect and Absolute Being, which is simply being, the first and the last, is principle and end of all creatures. Being eternal and omnipresent, it embraces and penetrates all durations: it is at once center and circumference. Being simple and great, it is entirely in all things and entirely beyond all things. It is like an intelligible sphere whose center is everywhere and whose circumference nowhere.[15]

THE ETERNITY OF GOD : ST. AUGUSTINE

Thou dost precede all times past by the sublimity of Thy ever present eternity; and Thou dost pass all future times, because they are future now, and when they shall have come they will be past. "But Thou art always the selfsame, and Thy years shall not fail" (Ps. ci, 28). Thy years neither go nor come; but ours do both go and come, that they may come in their order. Thy years stand all at the same time because they stand; neither are they that pass excluded by others that come, because they do not pass; but these years of thine shall be ours, when time shall be no more. Thy years are one day (cf. 2 Pet. iii, 8); and Thy day is not every day, but to-day; because Thy to-day neither gives place to to-morrow, nor comes it in place of yesterday. Thy to-day is eternity.[16]

THE OPERATIONS OF GOD

The dependence of creatures on God for their being leads to a definition of the three operations of God relative to creatures: creation, conservation and concurrence. The first two of these pertain to the being and existence of creatures, the third to their action.

Creation, *productio rei ex nihilo sui et subjecti* (the production of something out of absolute nothingness, both nothing of the substance of the producer and nothing as matter), was brought into Western thinking by *Genesis*. This concept was a scandal to the Greek mind;

yet, once revealed, it became for Christians that kind of logical explanation which seemed absolutely inescapable. Creation was seen as the only logical consequence of the fact of contingency, the denial of pantheism and the maintenance of the simplicity of God.

Conservation is the sustenance of a being in existence. Existence is seen as a creative gift and just as the creature is dependent on God for the beginning of his existence, he continues to depend in continuing existence. God alone can give being; so God alone can sustain a being in existence. If the conserving power of God were withheld, a creature would simply cease to be: it would be annihilated.

As contingency in origin requires creation as an explanation and contingency in being requires conservation, so too creaturely activity requires cooperation in activity. This cooperation by God with every act of the creature is called divine concurrence. The logic by which it is postulated can clearly be found in the First Way of St. Thomas Aquinas. The theory of concurrence postulates that the creature cannot act unless God act with him.

One of the most difficult areas of Catholic thought, the theory of divine concurrence is fundamental to the historical debates over the problem of evil, predestination, divine foreknowledge, grace and free will. Both in the natural order of concurrence and in the supernatural order, where Grace is the counterpart of natural concurrence, the problems have arisen from the attempt to conserve, on the one hand, divine goodness, knowledge, and power and, on the other, human freedom and the reality of evil. Although the theories are many and the debate heated, all have firmly aimed at preserving both elements in the problem. The Church has tolerated, even encouraged the debate: ultimately, of course, all recognize that in the last analysis the problem is insoluble by the human mind, for it is one of the supreme mysteries of God. The best that the human can do is to continue to protect the established truths involved in the problem and to preserve the mystery involved in a seeming contradiction.

The immanent role of God in nature is summarized in the term Divine Providence. God is personal, knowing and willing. God creates finite natures, gives them their possibilities of fulfillment and thus establishes the law unto their natures. He conserves them in being and concurs with their actions. The totality of the divine plan for nature and the singular activity of God in the life of the individual as part of this plan are the broad canvas of Divine Providence.

GOD THE CREATOR : ST. AUGUSTINE

But why did God choose then to create the heavens and earth which up to that time He had not made? If they who put this question wish to make out that the world is eternal and without beginning, and that consequently it has not been made by God, they are strangely deceived, and rave in the incurable madness of impiety. For, though the voices of the prophets are silent, the world itself, by its well-ordered changes and movements, and by the fair appearance of all visible things, bears a testimony of its own, both that it has been created, and also that it could not have been created save by God, whose greatness and beauty are unutterable and invisible. As for those who own, indeed, that it was made by God, and yet ascribe to it not a temporal but only a creational beginning, so that in some scarcely intelligible way the world should always have existed a created world they make an assertion which seems to them to defend God from the charge of arbitrary hastiness, or of suddenly conceiving the idea of creating the world as a quite new idea, or of casually changing His will, though He be unchangeable. But I do not see how this supposition of theirs can stand in other respects. . . .

Next, we must see what reply can be made to those who agree that God is the Creator of the world, but have difficulties about the time of its creation. . . .

. . . For if eternity and time are rightly distinguished by this, that time does not exist without some movement and transition, while in eternity there is no change, who does not see that there could have been no time had not some creature been made, which by some motion could give birth to change, —the various parts of which motion and change, as they cannot be simultaneous, succeed one another,—and thus, in these shorter or longer intervals of duration, time would begin? Since then, God, in whose eternity is no change at all, is the Creator and Ordainer of time, I do not see how He can be said to have created the world after spaces of time had elapsed, unless it be said that prior to the world there was some creature by whose movement time could pass. And if the sacred and infallible Scriptures say that in the beginning God created the heavens and the earth, in order that it may be understood that He had made nothing previously,—for if He had made anything before the rest, this thing would rather be said to have been made "in the beginning,"—then assuredly the world was made, not in time, but simultaneously with time. For that which is made in time is made both after and before some time,—after that which is past, before that which is future. But none could then be past, for there was no creature by whose movements its duration could be measured. But simultaneously with time the world was made, if in the world's creation change and motion were created, as seems evident from the order of the first six or seven days. For in these days the morning and evening are counted, until, on the sixth day, all things which God then made were finished, and on the seventh the rest of God was mysteriously and sublimely signalized.[17]

THE EVOLUTIONARY THEORY : POPE PIUS XII

. . . the teaching authority of the Church does not forbid that, in conformity with the present state of human sciences and sacred theology, research and discussions on the part of men experienced in both fields take place with regard to the doctrine of evolution in as far as it inquires into the origin of

the human body as coming from pre-existent and living matter—for Catholic faith obliges us to hold that souls are
immediately created by God. However, this must be done in
such a way that reasons for both opinions, that is those favor-
able and those unfavorable to evolution, be weighed and
judged with the necessary seriousness, moderation and measure, and provided that all are prepared to submit to the judgment of the Church, to whom Christ has given the mission
of interpreting authentically the sacred scriptures and of defending dogmas of faith. Some, however, highly transgress
this liberty of discussion when they act as if the origin of the
human body from pre-existing and living matter were already
completely certain and proved by facts which have been discovered up to now and by reasoning on those facts and as if
there were nothing in the sources of divine revelation which
demands the greatest moderation and caution in this question.

When, however, there is a question of another conjectural
opinion, namely polygenism, children of the Church by no
means enjoy such liberty. For the faithful cannot embrace
that opinion which maintains either that after Adam there
existed on this earth true men who did not take their origin
through natural generation from him as from the first parent
of all, or that Adam represents a certain number of first
parents. Now it is in no way apparent how such an opinion
can be reconciled with that which the sources of revealed
truth and the documents of teaching authority of the Church
propose with regard to original sin, which proceeds from sin
actually committed by an individual Adam and which through
generation is passed on to all and is in everyone as his own.[18]

DIVINE PROVIDENCE : ST. MATTHEW

Therefore I say to you, be not solicitous for your life, what
you shall eat, nor for your body, what you shall put on. Is
not the life more than the meat and the body more than the
raiment?

Behold the birds of the air, for they neither sow, nor do
they reap, nor gather into barns: and your heavenly Father
feedeth them. Are not you of much more value than they?

And which of you by taking thought can add to his stature
one cubit?

And for raiment why are you solicitous? Consider the lilies of the field, how they grow: they labour not, neither do they spin.

But I say to you that not even Solomon in all his glory was arrayed as one of these.

And if the grass of the field, which is today and tomorrow is cast into the oven, God doth so clothe: how much more you, O ye of little faith?[19]

DIVINE PROVIDENCE : ST. JOHN DAMASCENE

Providence, then, is the care God takes of all existing things. And again, Providence is the will of God through which all existing things receive their fitting issue. But if Providence is God's will, according to true reasoning, all things that come into being through Providence must necessarily be most fair and most excellent and such that they cannot be surpassed. For the same person must of necessity be creator of and provider for what exists; for it is not meet nor fitting that the creator of what exists and the provider be separate persons. For in that case they would both be deficient, one in creativity, the other in providence. God, therefore, is both Creator and Provider and His creative and preserving and providing power is simply His good-will. . . .

That He provides and that He provides excellently, one can most readily perceive thus. God alone is good and wise by nature. Since then He is good, He provides; for He who does not provide is not good. For even men and creatures without reason provide for their own offspring according to their nature, and he who does not provide is blamed. Again since He is wise, He takes best care over what exists. . . .

Now the works of Providence are partly according to the good-will of God and partly according to permission. Works of good will include all those that are undeniably good, while works of permission are of many forms of concession. For Providence often permits the just man to encounter misfortune, in order that he may reveal to others the virtue that lies concealed within him, as was the case with Job (Job 1,11). At other times it allows something strange to be done in order that something great and marvellous might be accomplished through the seemingly strange act, as when the salvation of men was brought about through the Cross. In another way it allows the pious man to suffer sore trials in order that he may not depart from a right conscience nor lapse into pride on account of the power and grace granted to him, as was the case with Paul (2 Cor. 7:7).

One man is forsaken for a season with a view to another's restoration, in order that others when they see his state may be taught a lesson, as in the case of Lazarus and the rich man (Luke 16:9). Another is deserted by Providence in order that another may be glorified, not for his own sin or that of his parents, just as the man who was blind from birth ministered to the glory of the Son of Man (John 9:1).

. . . Moreover, it is to be observed that the choice of what is to be done is in our own hands; but the final issue depends, in the one case when our actions are good, on the cooperation of God, who in His justice brings help according to His fore-knowledge to such as choose the good with a right conscience and, in the other case when our actions are evil, on the desertion by God, who again in His justice stands aloof by His foreknowledge.

. . . The ways of God's Providence are many and they cannot be explained in words nor conceived by the mind. Remember that all the assaults of dark and evil fortune contribute to the salvation of those who receive them with thankfulness and are assuredly ambassadors of help.

Also one must bear in mind that God's original wish was that all should be saved and come to His kingdom (1 Tim. 2:4). For it was not for punishment that He formed us, but to share His goodness, inasmuch as He is a good God. But inasmuch as He is a just God, His will is that sinners should suffer punishment.

The first then, is called God's antecedent will and pleasure and springs from Himself, while the second is called God's consequent will and permission and has its origin in us.[20]

From what precedes, it can be explained how Catholic tradition understands the word "miracle." When understood in terms of Divine Providence (creation, conservation, concurrence), a miracle which is a supernatural event in nature becomes naturally intelligible.

A miracle is, by definition, an event perceptible to the senses which is beyond the power or order of nature and which can be attributed to God alone. The explanation of the possibility and justification for miracle must be found in the fact that nature and its laws are contingent; God alone is necessary. In order for a natural being to continue in existence or for a natural law to continue to be operative, it requires conservation and concurrence on the part of God, and these are free activities on the part of God. Natural law, like natural beings and activities, consists of a dual element: the law in existence and the cooperative act of God in its fulfillment. If nature were necessary, its law would be necessary; but in the case of contingents, there is no contradiction in the withholding by God of conservation or concurrence. Such a miracle comes within the comprehension of Divine foreknowledge and does not, therefore, introduce an element of change into God. So, too, it is not a "playfulness" on the part of God: a miracle is always an act of God in special providence for creatures. In the case of the miracles of Christ, the miracle was precisely a testimony on Christ's part as God that He is God.

MAN, THE IMAGE OF GOD

The creative process in nature is the imaging of God, an outpouring of divine Goodness such that beings in nature achieve their fulfillment in realizing that degree of perfection which is their nature as an imitation of the divine Nature. The fulfillment of nature is a return of all things to God which reaches its culmination in the loving response of man as the image of God. The calling of man in nature is to restore all things to God, to bring forth the imagery of divine Perfection in nature and ultimately in the human community which is the highest natural image of the inner life of God.

Catholicism is firmly committed to certain rational affirmations concerning man, his nature, origin, and destiny. Man is first of all a creature of God: he owes his origin in being to God, is dependent on God in both being and action. He is a creature "composed of body and soul and made to the image and likeness of God," as the standard Catholic catechisms teach. The soul, the inner principle of life for all living beings, is for man the one principle of his total life, biological and spiritual. However much during history certain Catholic writers have appeared to treat of soul and body as two entities, often at war with each other, Catholicism has ever held officially that the soul and body do not form two separate, dualistic substances, but that they are united (even better, in Thomistic terminology, soul and matter are united) in one composite substance. The soul of man, spiritual though it be in some of its operations, is still a human soul, not that of an angel. It is so radically rooted in and related to the matter with which it forms a composite that the best of Catholic tradition has held that in a separate state it would stand in metaphysical need of its body. The Catholic does not indulge in a mystique of the soul; he is realistic about the fact that a living thing has a principle which makes it living and this, in man, is his soul. What is unique for the Catholic about the human soul is the higher potentialities which it enjoys by virtue of its spirituality and which serve as the seedbed for the supernatural calling in which Catholicism finds its ultimate meaning.

Natural composites have a tendency to disintegrate, to "die." Death is the ultimate term of natural decomposition which reaches its term in the metaphysical separation of ultimate principles, form and matter. Insofar as they are composite beings, all men have the seeds of death within them. The death of a man, however, is not the death of his soul: death is the separation of soul and matter so that if, as in the case of man, the soul is spiritual and has capacity for activity independently of matter, it is capable of continued existence after death if its creator freely grant such continued existence. The soul, in other words, is immortal: it does not of itself corrupt (die) and may continue in existence after the corruption of the composite of which it was a member.

From the spirituality of the human soul, its transcendence of the laws of matter, flows the freedom of the human will. Various meanings of freedom have vied for priority throughout history: the freedom of choice and the freedom for good of the Pauline tradition. The Catholic tradition has asserted both the freedom of choice, the freedom to act or not act, to act this way or that, as well as the freedom for good which is the reflection at the philosophical level of the Pauline freedom in grace from the slavery of sin.

In freely bringing to fulfillment the image of God in himself, man realizes his destiny and achieves happiness. Happiness consists in the realization of the fullness of which the human powers are capable, ultimately in the attainment of God in knowledge and love. The moral duty of man to respond to the good in the law of God ultimately is equated with the happiness of man since the good to which he responds is the good of his nature which alone can fully satisfy the appetites which he has by being human. God in Himself and God as realized in created nature is the necessary and sufficient object of natural human happiness. All other things can bring authentic happiness to man only insofar as they are known and loved in God. From the contact of his intellect and the embrace of his will with God and their quiescence in this experience, man immanentizes his awareness in action. Human action becomes a cooperation with the creative expression of God: to realize in nature and the human community the fullest imaging of the divine Nature and the divine Community. In becoming an instrument of divine creation, man achieves his own happiness.

If the attainment of God is the term of human happiness, it is God who becomes both end and normative principle for human action. As source of the normative, God is Lawgiver and His laws for nature as applied to human activities constitute the moral law for man. The Catholic position on moral law is a vastly intricate whole. From the fact of God's personal Nature and His creative Will is derived a definition of law as intelligence and will directing things to their ends and promulgated to the subjects of the law. We begin with the divine Nature which is the perfection to be shared with creatures and which contains implicitly the limitations to be imposed on creaturely action in the form of law. The divine Nature is eternal law in a fundamental or material sense. The creative act by which God communicates His Perfection to nature is a knowing and willing act: the act of creation is the promulgation of the Eternal Law in the formal sense. The nature which is created with its various powers and its immanent teleologies is the counterpart of the divine Nature which God images in creation: it is the natural law in a material sense. In knowing his nature, its possibilities and that which will fulfill them, man expresses to himself the ground of this natural law. In his practical judgments is to be found the formal promulgation of the natural law. To know the moral law for man is, then, to know the Eternal Law as promulgated in the act of creation: for human reason nature is the Word of God.

From this proceeds the entire development of the morality based on natural law. God wills human happiness and gives man a natural complex of powers and appetites with immanent directives toward attainment of happiness. The discovery of the nature of human tendencies or appetites with the end which will naturally fulfill each tendency and maintain its proper relation to the integral structure of the human person constitutes a discovery of the law of God for nature, the natural law for man.

It is from this theory that the moral commitments of Catholicism in the natural order are derived. The adherence of Catholics to certain conclusions from the natural law and their insistence that these tenets cannot change should not be surprising in the light of the foregoing explanation. Morality and its principles are not for Catholics isolated from the wider metaphysical structure of their belief. The fundamental tenets of Catholic morality are rooted in the nature of God and His creative act and must remain as unchangeable as the nature and will of God.

CHAPTER THREE

Advent

And there shall come forth a rod out of the root of Jesse.[1]

If man had been created to attain natural happiness alone, the fulfillment of the potentialities of his nature, his reason would have been able theoretically to lead him to the truths necessary for the attainment of this happiness. There is no conclusion outlined in the preceding sections which cannot be grasped by human reason. Still, in the concrete the human reason has a habit of stumbling even in the most serious decisions of life; and when it deals with the invisible world beyond sense, its frailty is even more evident. Still more is this the case when reason must track down realities and principles whose demands may well be uncomfortable to the established pattern of a man's life. For this reason, the Catholic Church affirms that even if man had been created in a state of pure nature, a revelation by God of the truths necessary for the attainment of happiness would have been morally necessary: that is, the difficulty men would experience in achieving the truth would be so great for the general run of men and the results would be so imperfect, that a revelation by God would be necessary that men might arrive at the security of knowledge necessary for the pursuit of the moral life.

MORAL NECESSITY FOR DIVINE REVELATION : POPE PIUS XII
Disagreement and error among men on moral and religious matters have always been a cause of profound sorrow to all

good men, but above all to the true and loyal sons of the Church, especially today, when we see the principles of Christian culture being attacked on all sides.

It is not surprising that such discord and error should always have existed outside the fold of Christ. For though, absolutely speaking, human reason by its own natural force and light can arrive at a true and certain knowledge of the one personal God, who by His Providence watches over and governs the world, and also of the natural law, which the Creator has written in our hearts, still there are not a few obstacles to prevent reason from making efficient and fruitful use of its natural ability. The truths that have to do with God and the relations between God and men, completely surpass the sensible order and demand self-surrender and self-abnegation in order to be put into practice and to influence practical life. Now the human intellect, in gaining the knowledge of such truths, is hampered both by the activity of the senses and the imagination, and by evil passions arising from original sin. Hence men easily persuade themselves in such matters that what they do not wish to believe is false or at least doubtful.

It is for this reason that divine revelation must be considered morally necessary so that those religious and moral truths which are not of their nature beyond the reach of reason in the present condition of the human race, may be known with a firm certainty and with freedom from all error.[2]

NATURAL RELIGION ANTICIPATES REVELATION :
JOHN HENRY CARDINAL NEWMAN

One of the most important effects of Natural Religion on the mind, in preparation for Revealed, is the anticipation which it creates, that a Revelation will be given. That earnest desire of it, which religious minds cherish, leads the way to the expectation of it. Those who know nothing of the wounds of the soul, are not led to deal with the question, or to consider its circumstances; but when our attention is roused, then the more steadily we dwell upon it, the more probable does it seem that a revelation has been or will be given to us. This presentiment is founded on our sense, on the one hand, of the infinite Goodness of God, and, on the other, of our own extreme misery and need—two doctrines which are the primary constituents of Natural Religion. It is difficult to put a limit to the legitimate force of this antecedent probability. Some minds will feel it to be so powerful, as to recognize in it almost a proof, without direct evidence, of the divinity of a religion claiming to be the true, supposing its history and doctrine are free from positive objection, and there be no rival religion with plausible claims of its own.[3]

THE SUPERNATURAL

This moral necessity for revelation applies to nature and natural religion. The actual situation of man in history, however, was such that he was in *absolute* need of revelation. Man, according to Catholic belief, never was in a state of pure nature; he was created in the state of supernature with a destiny beyond and above his nature, a calling which surpassed both his needs and his capacities. For such a state, in distinction from the state of pure nature, a divine revelation is an absolute necessity.

Adam required divine revelation that he might achieve his destiny; his heirs share this need. Still more, by the sin of Adam, to the need of supernatural revelation was added the need of a redemptive act which might free man from the slavery of sin to which Adam had committed the race. From the need of nature for God and its moral need for revelation, we have arrived, therefore, at the need of man for a Revealer and a Redeemer. It is in the Incarnation of Christ as the Redeemer of man from sin and as the Revealer of the Way of Salvation, a Redemption and a Revelation which restored to man the possibility and the awareness of his supernatural destiny, that Catholicism recognizes the central event of human history. From Adam to Christ it finds the age of absence and longing; in Christ and His Sacrifice, the redemption and the triumph.

Human history began, Scripture narrates, with the creation of the first man and the first woman. These were the masterwork of God: in all other things the artistry of God could be read, but in the first humans God Himself reflected His own image. Their powers of intelligence and will alone would suffice to make them natural images of God, persons in the full sense of the word; but this was not all. God endowed men with the finest of natural gifts, the keenest powers of insight and sensitivity so that with no further gifts, theirs would have been human nature in its highest realization. But God went further. He called man into a special relationship with Himself, a friendship which involved sharing of communion in the life of God by Grace. This was the supernatural calling of man.

For Catholicism, the supernatural is beyond and above nature, not contrary to nature. It is beyond nature in that unaided nature could never achieve it of its own power, nor would nature require it for its fulfillment. It is pure gratuity on the part of God. The supernatural is not contrary to nature because it builds on nature, transforms the powers of nature and extends them towards objects and modes of action of which it in itself would not be capable.

By nature man is *capax dei:* he can attain knowledge and love of God. His knowledge, however, is discursive, piecemeal, progressive, infinitely unfulfilled. He is capable, too, of love; but so often it is a love of need, a love of servant for master. The supernatural elevation is the gratuitous offering by God of Himself to man, of a power ultimately to see God immediately and to love as God loves. Man is called beyond servitude to the friendship of God. The principle by which the supernatural life is realized is the principle of Grace which is the indwelling of the Spirit and the elevating assistance by God in the human (supernatural) act. From the *capax dei* of nature, supernature leads man to become *filius dei*.

Adam was created in this supernatural state of divine favor over and above the extraordinary natural gifts which were his. Never would man, Adam or his heirs, be in the state of pure nature. The historical need of man for God is the need for the friendship of God, for fulfillment of his supernatural destiny. Were Adam to sin, he would not return to a state of nature but to what some writers call a "transnatural state." The consequence of his sin would be greater, infinitely so, than the misery which human nature of itself would experience; it would be the misery of the sinner. In the historical context, then, the need for God becomes a need for Christ.

The [supernatural] goods which surpass greatly our mortal nature because of their grandeur and their elevation beyond the power of man, gifts which cannot be understood by our feeble reason, the great and multiple grace which God spread among men and rendered men capable of possessing.[4]

Those ineffable gifts which are super-essential and supernatural to every creature . . . These gifts are natural to the divinity because they flow from the divine nature and they are supernatural to man because they are identical with the divine nature.[5]

The Supreme Builder created this member of mankind a male imparting to him His divine grace and through this communicating His very Self to him.[6]

THE SIN OF MAN

In the dispensation of Divine Providence, Adam was tempted. He sinned the primordial sin and sacrificed the gifts and fulfillment of his supernatural state. This sin of Adam lost Grace not only for Adam but for his descendants. It introduced sinfulness as a condition and a tendency in man. All men after Adam would be born with the taint of the Original Sin, inherited guilt; the race would be blighted and live centuries of longing for a Redeemer.

Sin is a simple concept, however awful its meaning and its consequences. From the fact that God is the creator of man, the logical consequence is the total submission of man to God in all things. Sin is any violation of the will of God whether this be found immanent in the natural law or in a positive law expressed by God Himself or through those who have authority to command in his stead. Three elements are found in any sin: the *matter* of the sin, the act which violates the will of God; *reflection*, the consideration by the human practical reason of the dictates of conscience regarding the matter; and *consent* of the will to act. In addition to the Original Sin, Catholicism distinguishes two types of Actual Sin: Mortal and Venial. Mortal sin is any act in which the matter is grievous, the reflection sufficient, and the consent of the will to the act complete. A deficiency in any of the three characteristics constitutes a sin as Venial.

When Adam sinned, he reversed the supernatural destiny of the race of man. His disobedience merited for men an eternal punishment and brought to men the miseries that accompany a "fallen" nature. Human nature after Adam was, according to Catholic belief, not intrinsically changed, but weakened. Man became subject to a weakening of his natural powers, and he was deprived of the special natural gifts which had been Adam's. Man was subsequently turned from God, subject to death, to physical ills from which he had been protected, and worst of all, to an unbalance of the appetites in his nature. Adam had had integrity: his powers were organized without conflict. His sin introduced duality, war within the human person, lack of direction and inter-relatedness: the weakness which is called concupiscence. Man became a victim of his own powers.

THE FALL OF MAN : GENESIS

And he said: Behold Adam is become as one of us, knowing good and evil: now, therefore, lest perhaps he put forth his hand, and take also of the tree of life, and eat, and live for ever.

And the Lord God sent him out of the paradise of pleasure, to till the earth from which he was taken.

And he cast out Adam; and placed before the paradise of pleasure Cherubims, and a flaming sword, turning every way, to keep the way of the tree of life.[7]

ORIGINAL SIN : THE THEOLOGIANS

This sin which I call original I cannot understand in infants to be anything else than the stripping of that due justice, a loss caused by the disobedience of Adam.[8]

The mere fact that a thing is without grace does not make it sinful. For in that case a stone would be sinful.[9]

The disorderly character of the other powers of our soul is especially noticeable in this, that they incline in a disorderly way towards a perishable good; and this disorderliness can be called by the common name of concupiscence. And so original sin materially considered is concupiscence, but formorally it is the loss of original justice.[10]

ORIGINAL SIN A UNIVERSAL CONDITION OF MAN : COUNCIL OF TRENT

If anyone asserts that the sin of Adam injured him alone and not his descendants, or that only in regard to himself alone did he lose the holiness and justice which he had from God and did not lose it for us as well; or that stained as he was by the sin of disobedience Adam transmitted death and afflictions of body to all the human race but did not also transmit sin which is the death of the soul, let him be anathema; since he contradicts the words of the Apostle, "Wherefore as by one man sin entered into this world, and by sin death; and so death passed upon all men, in whom all have sinned" (Romans 5:12).[11]

EVIDENCE OF AN ORIGINAL FALL :
JOHN HENRY CARDINAL NEWMAN

To consider the world in its length and breadth, its various history, the many races of man, their starts, their fortunes, their mutual alienation, their conflicts; and then their ways, habits, governments, forms of worship; their enterprises, their aimless courses, their random achievements and acquirements, the impotent conclusion of long-standing facts, the tokens so faint and broken of a superintending design, the blind evolution of what turn out to be great powers or truths, the progress of things as from unreasoning elements, not towards final causes, the greatness and littleness of man, his far-reaching aims, his short duration, the curtain hung over his futurity, the disappointments of life, the defeat of good, the success of evil, physical pain, mental anguish, the prevalence and intensity of sin, the pervading idolatries, the corruptions, the dreary hopeless irreligion, that condition of the whole race, so fearfully yet exactly described in the Apostle's words, "having no hope and without God in the world,"—all this is a vision to dizzy and appal; and inflicts upon the mind the sense of a profound mystery, which is absolutely beyond human solution.

What shall be said to this heart-piercing, reason-bewildering fact? I can only answer, that either there is no Creator, or this living society of men is in a true sense discarded from His presence. Did I see a boy of good make and mind, with the tokens on him of a refined nature, cast upon the world without provision, unable to say whence he came, his birthplace or his family connexions, I should conclude that there was some mystery connected with his history, and that he was one, of whom, for one cause or another, his parents were ashamed. Thus only should I be able to account for the contrast between the promise and the condition of his being. And so I argue about the world:—*if* there be a God, *since* there is a God, the human race is implicated in some terrible aboriginal calamity. It is out of joint with the purpose of its Creator. This is a fact, a fact as true as the fact of its existence; and thus the doctrine of what is theologically called original sin becomes to me almost as certain as that the world exists, and as the existence of God.[12]

THE MISERY OF MAN

The sin of Adam introduced new misery and anxiety into the history of man. Turned away from God in sin, man experiences agony, a very special agony of spirit. He becomes a slave of his own self, is in bondage to another self within him and longs for a freedom which he himself cannot give. His vision becomes self-centered; in his bondage he cannot turn from self. The contingency of man in the natural state is now increased by the anguish of guilt. The natural man knows the contingency of things; it requires the experience of a creative God to awaken awe before the abyss of pure nothingness over which man is suspended by the merciful hand of God. And the sinner knows that he does not have sufficient power even to annihilate himself.

Infinite offense requires infinite retribution: after Adam a redeemer had to be found whose merits or payment could equal the gravity of Adam's sin: a second Adam had to make infinite retribution.

THE MISERY OF THE SINNER : LAMENTATIONS OF JEREMIAS
Remember, O Lord, what is come upon us: consider and behold our reproach. . . .

Our fathers have sinned and are not: and we have borne their iniquities. . . .

The joy of our heart is ceased: our dancing is turned into mourning.

The crown is fallen from our head. Woe to us, because we have sinned!

Therefore is our heart sorrowful: therefore are our eyes become dim.

For mount Sion, because it is destroyed: foxes have walked upon it.

But thou, O Lord, shalt remain for ever: thy throne from generation to generation.

Why wilt thou forget us for ever? Why wilt thou forsake us for a long time?

Convert us, O Lord, to thee, and we shall be converted: renew our days, as from the beginning.

But thou hast utterly rejected us: thou art exceedingly angry against us.[13]

THE LAW OF SIN : ST. PAUL

For we know that the law is spiritual. But I am carnal, sold under sin.

For that which I work, I understand not. For I do not that good which I will: but the evil which I hate, that I do.

If then I do that which I will not, I consent to the law, that it is good.

Now then it is no more I that do it; but sin that dwelleth in me.

For I know that there dwelleth not in me, that is to say, in my flesh, that which is good. For to will is present with me; but to accomplish that which is good, I find not.

For the good which I will, I do not: but the evil which I will not, that I do.

Now if I do that which I will not, it is no more I that do it: but sin that dwelleth in me.

I find then a law, that when I have a will to do good, evil is present with me.

For I am delighted with the law of God, according to the inward man:

But I see another law in my members, fighting against the law of my mind and captivating me in the law of sin that is in my members.

Unhappy man that I am, who shall deliver me from the body of this death?[14]

THE PROMISE OF REDEMPTION

This redeemer God promised. Man should wander for many years, He said, but a Redeemer would come, a Messiah, who alone could buy man back from sin and restore him to his destiny. The history of man now entered into the period of longing. The Catholic Church finds in the history of the Jewish people before Christ the drama of the consequences of sin and the intensity of longing for redemption. The Prophecies foreshadow the coming redemption; the texts are laden with symbols of the Messiah. The world stood in need of Christ, the new Adam, the God-Man whose supreme vision and infinite love would restore to man the power to see and to love.

THE REDEEMER SHALL COME : ISAIAS

And there shall come forth a rod out of the root of Jesse: and a flower shall rise up out of his root.

And the spirit of the Lord shall rest upon him: the spirit of wisdom and of understanding, the spirit of counsel and of fortitude, the spirit of knowledge and of godliness.

And he shall be filled with the spirit of the fear of the Lord. He shall not judge according to the sight of the eyes, nor reprove according to the hearing of the ears.

But he shall judge the poor with justice, and shall reprove with equity for the meek of the earth. And he shall strike the earth with the rod of his mouth: and with the breath of his lips he shall slay the wicked.

And justice shall be the girdle of his loins: and faith the girdle of his reins.[15]

The land that was desolate and impassable shall be glad: and the wilderness shall rejoice and shall flourish like the lily. . . .

Say to the fainthearted: Take courage, and fear not. Behold your God will bring the revenge of recompense. God himself will come and will save you.[16]

Therefore the Lord himself shall give you a sign. Behold a virgin shall conceive and bear a son: and his name shall be called Emmanuel.[17]

Behold the Lord God shall come with strength: and his arm shall rule. Behold his reward is with him and his work is before him.

He shall feed his flock like a shepherd. He shall gather together the lambs with his arm and shall take them up in his bosom, and he himself shall carry them that are with young.[18]

Drop down dew, ye heavens, from above: and let the clouds rain the just. Let the earth be opened and bud forth a saviour: and let justice spring up together. . . .[19]

THE PRAYER OF THE SINNER : *De Profundis*

Out of the depths I have cried to thee, O Lord: Lord, hear my voice.

Let thy ears be attentive to the voice of my supplication.

If thou, O Lord, wilt mark iniquities: Lord, who shall stand it?

For with thee there is merciful forgiveness: and by reason of thy law, I have waited for thee, O Lord.

My soul hath relied on his word: my soul hath hoped in the Lord.

From the morning watch even until night, let Israel hope in the Lord.

Because with the Lord there is mercy: and with him plentiful redemption.

And He shall redeem Israel from all his iniquities.[20]

THE PREACHING OF JOHN THE BAPTIST : ST. LUKE

. . . the word of the Lord was made unto John, the son of Zachary, in the desert.

And he came into all the country about the Jordan, preaching the baptism of penance for the remission of sins.

As it was written in the book of the sayings of Isaias the prophet: *A Voice of one crying in the wilderness: Prepare ye the way of the Lord, make straight his paths.*

Every valley shall be filled and every mountain and hill

*shall be brought low: and the crooked shall be made straight,
and the rough ways plain.*

And all flesh shall see the salvation of God.[21]

THE APPROACH OF THE REDEEMER : THE LITURGY FOR ADVENT

O Lord, arouse thy power and come! Come that by your protection we may be rescued, by your Redemption we may be saved from the dangers which threaten us because of our sins.

O Lord, arouse our hearts that we may prepare the way for your only begotten Son: that through His coming we may be worthy to serve thee with purified spirits.

Lift up your gates, O ye princes, and be ye lifted up, O eternal gates: and the King of Glory shall enter in.

The Glory of the Lord shall be revealed: and all flesh shall see the saving Gift of God.

And she shall bring forth a Son, and thou shalt call His name Jesus: for He shall save His people from their sins.[22]

CHAPTER FOUR

Incarnation

In the beginning was the Word: and the Word was with God: and the Word was God.

The same was in the beginning with God.

All things were made by him: and without him was made nothing that was made.

In him was life: and the life was the light of men.

And the light shineth in darkness: and the darkness did not comprehend it.

There was a man sent from God whose name was John.

This man came for a witness, to give testimony of the light, that all men might believe through him.

He was not the light, but was to give testimony of the light.

That was the true light, which enlighteneth every man that cometh into this world.

He was in the world: and the world was made by him: and the world knew him not.

He came unto his own: and his own received him not.

But as many as received him, he gave them power to become the sons of God, to them that believe in his name.

Who are born, not of blood, nor of the will of the flesh, nor of the will of man, but of God.

And the Word was made flesh and dwelt among us (and we saw his glory, the glory as it were of the only begotten of the Father), full of grace and truth.[1]

The Incarnation—the tremendous fact of God becoming man by the union of a divine and a human nature in the Person of Christ—is the mystery which lies at the heart of all Catholic belief. The moment of incarnation when "the Word became Flesh and dwelt amongst us" is for Catholics a unique moment, a focal point from which all human history from Adam to the last man derives its meaning. It is the moment of the redemption of man, the birth of a new life and a new destiny for man through the sacrifice of the new Adam. Old Testament history anticipated the event, the New Testament bears witness to its reality, all history after the event is transfigured by the continuing presence of the spirit of Christ among men.

This sense of history is magnificently realized in Catholic liturgy. At the end of the Advent season, which anticipates the coming of the Redeemer, the Church solemnly intones the Martyrology for the Feast of the Nativity, in which the intense drama of historical fulfillment is expressed:

MARTYROLOGY FOR THE FEAST OF THE NATIVITY

In the year from the creation of the world, when in the beginning God Created Heaven and Earth, five thousand one hundred and ninety-nine; from the flood two thousand nine hundred fifty-seven; from the birth of Abraham, two thousand fifteen; from Moses and the coming of the Israelites out of Egypt, one thousand five hundred and ten; from the anointing of King David, one thousand and thirty-two; in the sixty-fifth week according to the prophecy of Daniel; in the one hundred and ninety-fourth Olympiad; in the year seven hundred and fifty-two from the founding of the city of Rome, in the forty-second year of the empire of Octavius Augustus, when the whole earth was at peace, in the sixth age of the world, Jesus Christ, eternal God and son of the eternal Father, desirous to sanctify the world by His most merciful Coming, having been conceived of the Holy Ghost and nine months having elapsed since His conception, is born in Bethlehem of Juda, having become man of the Virgin Mary. *The Nativity of our Lord Jesus Christ, according to the Flesh.*[2]

THE HOLY TRINITY

The Incarnation of Christ and His teachings reveal the supreme mystery of the nature and life of God—the

Holy Trinity. Jesus Christ is the second Person, the Son, incarnate: begotten, not made, consubstantial with the Father without beginning. The Holy Spirit, the third Person of the Trinity, the Spirit of Love, proceeds from Father and Son. One God, Three Persons: a mystery infinitely unfathomable to the human mind is the condition without which an incarnation of God would be unthinkable. By appropriation, Catholic tradition considers the Son, the Word, as the infinite relation of divine Knowledge in the inner life of God, the Spirit as the bond of divine Love uniting Father and Son; these, of course, are human modes of speaking since the nature of God is wholly present in each Person, yet each is distinct from the Other. It is not surprising that theologians are wont to say that if there is *any* mystery, the Trinity is a mystery. Yet, it is for Catholics a firmly revealed truth in Christ and an absolutely necessary belief for membership in the Church. Once revealed, the Trinity becomes a source of great insight, as in St. Augustine, for understanding the nature of the human person and human community.

The fundamental theological beliefs of the Catholic Church concerning the Trinity are summed up in the great creed which follows:

THE ATHANASIAN CREED

Whoever will be saved: before all things it is necessary that he hold the Catholic Faith. Unless he keep this Faith whole and undefiled, without doubt he shall perish everlastingly.

And the Catholic Faith is this: we worship one God in Trinity, and Trinity in Unity, neither confounding the Persons, nor dividing the Substance. For there is one Person of the Father, another of the Son, another of the Holy Ghost. But the Godhead of the Father, of the Son, and of the Holy Ghost is all one: the Glory co-equal, the Majesty co-eternal. Such as the Father is, such is the Son, and such is the Holy

Ghost. The Father uncreated, the Son uncreated, and the Holy Ghost uncreated. The Father incomprehensible, the Son incomprehensible, and the Holy Ghost incomprehensible. The Father eternal, the Son eternal, and the Holy Ghost eternal. And yet they are not three eternals, but one Eternal. As also there are not three incomprehensibles, nor three uncreated, but one Uncreated and one Incomprehensible. So likewise the Father is almighty, the Son almighty, and the Holy Ghost almighty; and yet they are not three almighties, but one Almighty. So the Father is God, the Son is God, and the Holy Ghost is God; and yet they are not three gods, but one God. So likewise the Father is Lord, the Son Lord and the Holy Ghost Lord; and yet not three lords, but one Lord. For like as we are compelled by the Christian truth to acknowledge every Person by Himself to be God and Lord, so are we forbidden by the Catholic religion to say, there are three gods or three lords.

The Father is made of none, neither created nor begotten. The Son is of the Father alone, not made, nor created, but begotten. The Holy Ghost is of the Father and of the Son, neither made, nor created nor begotten, but proceeding. So there is one Father, not three Fathers, one Son, not three Sons, one Holy Ghost, not three Holy Ghosts.

And in this Trinity none is before or after the other; none is the greater or less than another; but the whole three Persons are co-eternal together, and co-equal; so that in all things the Unity in Trinity, and the Trinity in Unity is to be worshipped. He therefore that will be saved must thus think of the Trinity.

Furthermore, it is necessary to everlasting salvation that he also believe rightly in the Incarnation of our Lord Jesus Christ. For the right Faith is, that we believe and confess, that our Lord Jesus Christ, the Son of God, is God and Man: God, of the Substance of the Father, begotten before the worlds: and Man, of the Substance of His mother, born in the world: Perfect God and perfect Man: of a reasonable soul and human flesh subsisting: equal to the Father, as touching His Godhead, and inferior to the Father, as touching His Manhood. Who although He be God and Man, yet He is not two, but one Christ: One, not by conversion of the

Godhead into flesh, but by the taking of the Manhood into God. One altogether is Jesus Christ, not by confusion of Substance, but by unity of Person. For as the reasonable soul and flesh is one man, so God and Man is one Christ. He suffered for our salvation, descended into hell, rose again the third day from the dead. He ascended into heaven, sitteth at the right hand of the Father, God Almighty, from whence He shall come to judge the living and the dead. At his coming all men shall rise again with their bodies and shall give account for their own works. They that have done good shall go to life everlasting, and they that have done evil into everlasting fire.

This is the Catholic Faith. Unless a man believe it faithfully, he cannot be saved.[3]

St. Augustine reveled in the mystery of the Trinity, finding in it the supreme reality of which the inner life of man is an image. In the following selection from one of his letters, he summarizes the mystery of the Trinity.

There is One invisible, from whom as the Creator and prime cause all things seen by us derive their being; and he is supreme, eternal, immutable, and comprehensible by none save Himself alone. There is One by whom the supreme Majesty reveals and proclaims Himself, namely, the Word, not inferior to Him by whom it is begotten and revealed. There is One who is Holiness, the sanctifier of all that becomes holy, who is the inseparable and undivided communion between this immutable Word through whom that Prime Cause is revealed and that Prime Cause which reveals Himself by the Word which is His equal. But who is able with perfectly calm and pure mind to contemplate this whole essence—whom I have attempted to describe without naming, instead of naming without describing—and to draw blessedness from that contemplation, and losing himself in such contemplation to become, as it were, oblivious of self, and to press on to that of which the sight is beyond our perception, in other words, to be clothed with immortality and obtain eternal salvation?[4]

The great Papal explication of Catholic belief on the Trinity is found in Leo XIII's encyclical, *Divinum Illud*[1] from which the following selection is taken.

This dogma is called by the Doctors of the Church "the substance of the New Testament," that is to say, the greatest of all mysteries, since it is the fountain and origin of them all. In order to know and contemplate this mystery, the angels were created in heaven and men upon earth. In order to teach more fully this mystery, which was but foreshadowed in the Old Testament, God Himself came down from the angels unto men: *No man hath seen God at any time; the only begotten Son, who is in the bosom of the Father, He hath declared Him.** . . . The danger that arises is lest the divine persons be confounded one with the other in faith or worship, or lest the one nature in them be separated: for "This is the Catholic faith, that we should adore one God in Trinity and Trinity in Unity." Therefore Our predecessor Innocent XII absolutely refused the petition of those who desired a special festival in honor of God the Father. For, although the separate mysteries connected with the Incarnate Word are celebrated on certain fixed days, yet there is no special feast on which the Word is honored according to His divine nature alone. And even the Feast of Pentecost was instituted in the earliest times, not simply to honor the Holy Ghost in Himself, but to commemorate His coming, or His external mission. And all this has been wisely ordained, lest from distinguishing the persons men should be led to distinguish the divine essence . . . The Church is accustomed most fittingly to attribute to the Father those works of the divinity in which power excels, to the Son those in which wisdom excels, and those in which love excels to the Holy Ghost. Not that all perfections and external operations are not common to the divine persons; for "the operations of the Trinity are indivisible, even as the essence of the Trinity is indivisible"** because as the three divine persons "are inseparable, so do they act inseparably."†

* Summ. Th. la., q. xxxi. De Trin. 1. i., c. 3.
** St. Aug. *De Trin.*, 1. i., cc. 4, 5.
† *Ibid.*

But by a certain comparison, and a kind of affinity between the operations and the properties of the persons, these operations are attributed or, as it is said, "appropriated" to one person rather than to the others. "Just as we make use of the traces of similarity or likeness which we find in creatures for the manifestation of the divine persons, so do we use their essential attributes; and this manifestation of the persons by their essential attributes is called *appropriation*."†† In this manner the Father, who is "the principal of the whole Godhead," is also the efficient cause of all things, of the Incarnation of the Word, and the sanctification of souls; "of Him are all things," *of Him* referring to the Father. But the Son, the Word, the Image of God, is also the exemplary cause, whence all creatures borrow their form and beauty, their order and harmony. He is for us the way, the truth, and the life: the reconciler of man with God. "By him are all things," *by Him* referring to the Son. The Holy Ghost is the ultimate cause of all things, since, as the will and all other things finally rest in their end, so He, who is the divine goodness and the mutual love of the Father and the Son, completes and perfects, by His strong yet gentle power, the secret work of man's eternal salvation. "In Him are all things," *in Him* referring to the Holy Ghost.

. . . Among the external operations of God, the highest of all is the mystery of the Incarnation of the Word, in which the splendor of the divine perfections shines forth so brightly that nothing more sublime can even be imagined, nothing else could have been more salutary to the human race. Now this work, although belonging to the whole Trinity, is still appropriated especially to the Holy Ghost, so that the Gospels thus speak of the Blessed Virgin: She was found with child of the Holy Ghost and that which is conceived in her is of the Holy Ghost. And this is rightly attributed to Him who is the Love of the Father and the Son, since this *great mystery of piety* proceeds from the infinite love of God towards man, as St. John tells us: "God so loved the world as to give His only begotten Son." Moreover, human nature was thereby elevated to a personal union with the Word; and this dignity

†† St. Th. Ia., q. xxxix., 7.

is given, not on account of any merits, but entirely and absolutely through grace, and therefore, as it were, through the special gifts of the Holy Ghost.[5]

THE VIRGIN MARY

The veneration of Mary as mother of Christ has always been an important part of Catholic devotion. Her praise has been sung in every age of the Church; her example is offered as an example of the ideal Christian life. The devotion and the honor paid the Virgin is the highest that the Church recognizes possible for a creature of God, while Mariology (the theological study of Mary) is today reaching its greatest development in explicating from Catholic tradition the role of Mary as symbol of the Church.

Mary is the new Eve foretold in Genesis. As the first Eve was instrumental in the fall of man, Mary would destroy sin by giving birth to the Redeemer of fallen man. A virgin, conceived without the sin of Adam (the Immaculate Conception), she would mother the New Adam.

MARY : GENESIS

And Adam said: The woman whom thou gavest me to be my companion, gave me of the tree, and I did eat.

And the Lord God said to the woman: Why hast thou done this? And she answered: The serpent deceived me, and I did eat.

And the Lord God said to the serpent: . . . I will put enmities between thee and the woman, and thy seed and her seed: she shall crush thy head and thou shalt lie in wait for her heel.[6]

The narrative of the conception by Mary of Christ is one of the most beautiful in Scripture. The angel Gabriel was sent to the virgin, a Jewish maiden who was espoused to Joseph, a carpenter of Nazareth. By her consent she would conceive a son through the power of the Holy Spirit, and would give birth to the promised Messiah.

The simplicity of the narrative conceals the tremendous significance of her role. At the moment of her acceptance Mary became mother of Jesus (Christokos) and mother of God (Theotokos). She became mother of the Redeemer and temple of the Holy Ghost. As such, she became mother of all men, for as mother of the Head of the Mystical Body she became mother of the Church. Thus did Christ present her to John on Calvary: "Son, behold thy Mother."

The humility of the virgin in accepting this awful role is recalled throughout the Church by the daily recital of her prayer of acceptance in the Angelus: "Be it done to me according to thy word." And her awareness of her calling is echoed in the recitation of her Magnificat.

THE MAGNIFICAT OF MARY : ST. LUKE

And Mary said: My soul doth magnify the Lord.

And my spirit hath rejoiced in God my Saviour.

Because he hath regarded the humility of his handmaid: for behold from henceforth all generations shall call me blessed.

Because he that is mighty hath done great things to me: and holy is his name.

And his mercy is from generation unto generation, to them that fear him.

He hath shewed might in his arm: he hath scattered the proud in the conceit of their heart.

He hath put down the mighty from their seat and hath exalted the humble.

He hath filled the hungry with good things: and the rich he hath sent empty away.

He hath received Israel his servant, being mindful of his mercy.

As he spoke to our fathers: to Abraham and to his seed for ever.[7]

The importance of Mary in the life of the Church and her role in Catholic piety can be found in the following selections.

MARY AS TYPE OF THE CHURCH : THE APOCALYPSE

And a great sign appeared in heaven: A woman clothed with the sun, and the moon under her feet, and on her head a crown of twelve stars.

And being with child she cried travailing in birth; and was in pain to be delivered. . . .

And she brought forth a man child, who was to rule all nations with an iron rod. And her son was taken up to God and to his throne.

And the woman fled into the wilderness, where she had a place prepared by God, that there they should feed her, a thousand two hundred sixty days.

And there was a great battle in heaven: Michael and his angels fought with the dragon [Satan], and the dragon fought, and his angels.

And they prevailed not: neither was their place found any more in heaven.

And that great dragon was cast out, that old serpent, who is called the devil and Satan, who seduceth the whole world. And he was cast unto the earth: and his angels were thrown down with him. . . .

And when the dragon saw that he was cast unto the earth, he persecuted the woman who brought forth the man child.

And there were given to the woman two wings of a great eagle, that she might fly into the desert, unto her place, where she is nourished for a time and times and half a time, from the face of the serpent.

And the serpent cast out of his mouth, after the woman, water, as it were a river: that he might cause her to be carried away by the river.

And the earth helped the woman: and the earth opened her mouth and swallowed up the river which the dragon cast out of his mouth.

And the dragon was angry against the woman: and went to make war with the rest of her seed, who keep the commandments of God and have the testimony of Jesus Christ.[8]

MARY, STAR OF THE SEA : ST. BERNARD OF CLAIRVAUX

O thou who findest thyself tossed by the tempests in the midst of the shoals of this world, turn not away thine eyes from the Star of the Sea, if thou wouldst avoid shipwreck. If the winds of temptation blow, if tribulations rise up like rocks before thee, a look at the star, a sigh to Mary, will be thy aid. If waves of pride, ambition, calumny, jealousy threaten to swallow up thy soul, look toward the star, pray to Mary. If anger, avarice, or love of pleasure shiver thy frail vessel, seek the eyes of Mary. If horror of thy sins, trouble of conscience, dread of the judgments of God, commence to plunge thee into the gulf of sadness and the abyss of despair, attach thy heart to Mary. In thy perils, thy anguish, thy doubts, think of Mary, call on Mary. Let the name of Mary be on thy lips and in thy heart; and in taking refuge with her in petition lose not sight of the example of her virtues. Following her thou canst not wander. Whilst thou prayest to her, thou canst not be without hope. As long as thou thinkest of her, thou wilt be on the right path. Thou canst not fail while she sustains thee; thou hast nothing to fear while she protects thee. If she favor thy voyage thou shalt reach the port of safety without weariness.[9]

PRAYER TO MARY : THE HAIL MARY

Hail Mary, full of Grace. The Lord is with Thee. Blessed art thou amongst women, and blessed is the fruit of thy womb, Jesus. Holy Mary, Mother of God, pray for us sinners now and at the hour of our death. Amen.[10]

The prerogatives of Mary are firmly established in the Catholic tradition from its beginning: The Virgin Birth, that Christ was born of a virgin, that Mary before and after the birth of Christ remained miraculously virgin; her role as Mediatrix of all Graces and Co-redemptrix of man and Queen of Heaven. Two major definitions have been made by solemn *ex cathedra* declaration (such declarations are exercises of Papal infallibility in declaring as absolute dogmas of faith certain truths which are contained within the deposit of faith).

MARY THE MOTHER OF GOD : ST. CYRIL OF ALEXANDRIA

. . . And since the holy Virgin brought forth corporally God made one with flesh according to nature, for this reason we also call her Mother of God, not as if the nature of the Word has the beginning of its existence from the flesh.[11]

THE IMMACULATE CONCEPTION : POPE PIUS IX

We declare, pronounce, and define that the doctrine which holds that the most blessed Virgin Mary, in the first instant of her conception, by a singular grace and privilege granted by almighty God, in view of the merits of Jesus Christ, the Saviour of the human race, was preserved free from all stain of original sin, is a doctrine revealed by God and therefore to be believed firmly and constantly by all the faithful.[12]

THE ASSUMPTION OF MARY : POPE PIUS XII

Wherefore, after We have unceasingly offered Our most fervent prayers to God, and have called upon the Spirit of Truth, for the glory of Almighty God who has lavished His special affection upon the Virgin Mary, for the honor of her Son, the immortal King of the Ages and Victor over sin and death, for the increase of the glory of that same august Mother, and for the joy and exultation of the entire Church; by the authority of our Lord Jesus Christ, of the blessed Apostles Peter and Paul, and by Our own authority, We pronounce, declare, and define it to be a divinely revealed dogma: that the Immaculate Mother of God, the ever Virgin Mary, having completed the course of her earthly life, was assumed body and soul into heavenly glory.[13]

JESUS CHRIST: THE WORD-BECOME-FLESH

At the "fiat" of Mary, Jesus Christ was conceived. This is the moment of Incarnation when the eternal Son of God, second Person of the Trinity, assumed the flesh of a human nature uniting it in His Person with His Divine Nature. Christ is, in every sense, God; in every sense He is man: this is the mystery of the Incarnation. As the Trinity is the mystery of the unity in three Persons, the Incarnation of Christ is the unity in one Person of a dual nature.

SALVATION IN CHRIST : ST. AUGUSTINE

Since we affirm that Christ is the Word of God, by whom all things were made, and is the Son because He is the Word, not a word uttered and completed in the part, but one abiding immutably with the immutable Father, Who is Himself immutable, and under whose rule the whole universe, spiritual and material, is ordered in the way best suited to different times and places; and that He has perfect wisdom and knowledge as to what should be done, and when and where everything should be done in the controlling and ordering of the universe—most certainly both before He gave being to the Hebrew nation, by which through sacraments fitting to the time He prefigured the manifestation of Himself in His advent, and during the time of the Israelitish Kingdom, and, after that, when He manifested Himself in mortal form to mortal men in the body which He received from the Virgin, and thenceforward even to our own day, in which He is fulfilling all that He predicted of old by the prophets, and from this time on to the end of the world, when He shall separate the holy from the wicked, and give to every man his due reward—in all these successive ages He is the same Son of God, co-eternal with the Father, and the immutable Wisdom, by whom universal nature was created, and by participation in whom every rational soul is blessed.

Therefore, from the beginning of the human race, whoever believed in Him and in any way knew Him, and led a pious and just life according to His commandments, was undoubtedly saved by Him, in whatever time and place He may have lived. For as we believe in Him both as dwelling with the Father and as having come in the flesh, so the men of old believed in Him both as dwelling with the Father and as destined to come in the flesh. And the nature of faith is not changed, nor is the salvation made different in our age, but in the fact that in consequence of the difference between the two epochs, that which was then foretold as future is now proclaimed as past. Moreover, we are not under necessity to suppose different things and different kinds of salvation to be signified, when the self-same thing is by different sacred acts and sacraments announced in the one case as fulfilled, in the other as to come. As to the manner and time, however, in which anything that pertains to the one salvation common to all believers and pious persons is brought to pass, let us ascribe wisdom to God, and for our part submit ourselves to His will. Wherefore the true religion, although formerly set forth and practised under other names and with other rites than it now has, and formerly more obscurely revealed and known to fewer persons but now more clearly and to many, is one and the same in both periods. . . . Thus the salvation provided by this religion, by which alone, as alone true, true salvation is truly promised, was never wanting to any one who was worthy of it, and he to whom it was wanting was unworthy of it.[14]

The Incarnation is a profound mystery, a "scandal to the Gentiles." But the Christian spirit does not shrink from mystery, for mystery is the more meaningful reality at the threshold of which reason grows faint. Yet mystery is the fulfillment of reason, without which nature would fall into absolute contradiction. The Christian rather rejoices in mystery, reveling in the triumphant paradoxes of revelation. In death is life, in not-having is having, in not-being is being: the mystery of the Incarnation tells man that if the man Christ be not God, then man himself cannot become the son of God.

This attitude is conveyed in the following selection from Gregory Nazianzen. One can sense a foreshadowing of the superb sense of paradox in a Chesterton and all those who find sublime wisdom in making themselves fools for Christ's sake.

THE MYSTERY OF THE INCARNATION : GREGORY OF NAZIANZEN
. . . He was born but He had been begotten. He was born of a woman—but she was a Virgin. The first is human, the second divine. In his human nature He had no Father, but also in his divine nature no mother. Both these belong to

Godhead. He dwelt in the womb—but He was recognized by the Prophet, himself still in the womb, leaping before the Word, for whose sake He came into being. He was wrapped in swaddling clothes (Luke 2:41) but He took off the swaddling bands of the Cross by rising again. He was laid in a manger—but He was glorified by angels and proclaimed by a Star and worshipped by Magi. He was driven into exile in Egypt—but He drove away Egyptian idols. He had no form or comeliness in the sight of the Jews but to David He is fairer than the children of men (Ps. 45:2). And on the mountain He was bright as the lightning (Matt. 17:2) and became more luminous than the sun, initiating us into the mystery of the future.

He was baptized as man—but He remitted sins as God (Matt. 3:13) not because He needed purificatory rites Himself, but that He might sanctify the element of water. He was tempted as man, but He conquered as God; yea, He bids us be of good cheer for He has overcome the world (John 16:33). He is hungry but He has fed thousands (John 6:10) for He is the Bread that giveth life and is of heaven. He thirsted, but cried "If any man thirst, let him come to me and drink" (John 7:37). Yea, He promised that fountains should flow from them that believe. He was wearied but He is the rest of them that are weary and heavy-laden (Matt. 11:28). He was heavy with sleep, but He walked lightly over the sea (Matt. 8:24). He rebuked the winds, He made Peter light as he began to sink (Matt. 14:25,30). He pays tribute but it is out of a fish (Matt. 17:24); yea, He is King of those who demanded it (John 19:19).

He is called a Samaritan and a demoniac (John 8:48), but he saved him that came down from Jerusalem and fell among thieves (Luke 10:30); the demons acknowledge him and He drives out demons and sinks in the sea legions of foul spirits (Luke 8:28-33) and sees the Prince of demons falling like lightning (Luke 10:18). He is stoned but is not taken. He prays, but He hears prayer. He weeps, but He causes tears to cease. He asks where Lazarus is laid, for He was man; but He raises Lazarus, for He was God (John 11:43). He is sold and very cheaply for it is only for thirty pieces of silver (Matt. 26:15) but He redeems the world

and that at a great price, for the price was His own blood
(1 Pet. 1:19). As a sheep He is led to the slaughter (Isa.
53:7) but He is the Shepherd of Israel and now of the whole
world also. As a Lamb He is silent, yet He is the Word and
is proclaimed by the Voice of one crying in the wilderness
(John 1:23). He is bruised and wounded, but He healeth
every disease and every infirmity (Isa. 53:23). He is lifted
up and nailed to the Tree but by the Tree of Life He re-
storeth us; yea, He saved even the Robber crucified with him
(Luke 23:43); yea, He wrapped the visible world in darkness.
He is given vinegar to drink mixed with gall. Who? He who
turned water into wine (John 2:1-11), who is the destroyer
of the bitter taste, who is Sweetness and altogether Desire
(Cant. 5:16). He lays down His life, but He has power to
take it again (John 10:18); the veil is rent for the mysterious
doors of Heaven are opened; the rocks are cleft, the dead
arise (Matt. 26:51). He dies, but He gives life and by his
life destroys death.[15]

The supreme condescension of God in the redemption
of man is exemplified in the nativity of the God-Man as
a helpless infant of humble parentage.

THE NATIVITY : ST. LUKE

And it came to pass that when they were there, her days
were accomplished that she should be delivered.

And she brought forth her firstborn son and wrapped him
in swaddling clothes and laid him in a manger: because there
was no room for them in the inn.

And there were in the same country shepherds watching
and keeping the night watches over their flock.

And behold an angel of the Lord stood by them and the
brightness of God shone round about them; and they feared
with a great fear.

And the angel said to them: Fear not; for, behold, I bring
you good tidings of great joy that shall be to all the people:

For, this day is born to you a Saviour, who is Christ the
Lord, in the city of David.

And this shall be a sign unto you. You shall find the infant
wrapped in swaddling clothes and laid in a manger.[16]

THE NATIVITY : ST. AUGUSTINE

He lies in the manger, but contains the world; He sucks at the breast, but feeds the Angels; He is wrapped in swaddling clothes, but vests us with immortality; He is suckled, but adored: He found no place in the inn, but makes for Himself a temple in the hearts of believers. For in order that weakness might become strong, strength became weak.[17]

THE FEAST OF THE NATIVITY : ST. BERNARD OF CLAIRVAUX

. . . *a child is born to us* who is at the same time the God of Majesty, submitting not only to mortal body, but even to the weak, helpless state of an infant. Oh, wondrous infancy whose weakness and silence are the strength and wisdom of God; this weakness which can effect in man the actions of God. The very weakness of the infant triumphs over the troubles of the world, attacks strong armies, imprisons cruel tyrants, and ends the servitude of men. The simplicity of this mute infant (or so he seemed to be) gives eloquence to the speech of infants endowing them with a language of angels and men, crowning them with tongues of fire; this innocent child is He who imparts all knowledge to men and angels as the God of knowledge, the Word, the Wisdom of God. What sweet and holy infancy, which has restored to man his innocence through which all ages may return to happy youth! may all men become like you, not in smallness of body, but in humility and meekness of heart. Children of Adam, so lofty in your own conceit, so grossly swollen with pride, "unless you become as little children, you shall not enter the Kingdom of Heaven" (Matt. 18:3). "I am the door of the sheepfold" (John 10:7), writes this child of himself; if men do not abase themselves from their pride, they can never pass through the low gate of humility. He "shall destroy the land and the head of many" and those who come to him, head high, will fall with broken skulls. How, then, O earth and high heaven, have you still pride, while almighty God is humble? Are you still so mighty in your own eyes when God has become an infant before you? He without whom nothing can be done, humbles Himself even to appearing as a newborn Babe while you pride yourselves without limit, when truly you are nothing. You deceive yourselves as the Apostle

told you (Gal. 6:3) for, even if you were of considerable
worth, it would be wise to act humbly. "The greater thou
art," wrote the wise man "the more humble thyself in all
things and thou shalt find grace before God" (Eccl. 3:20),
"who resists the proud and gives grace to the humble" (James
4:6) and who to give you good example, being above all other
beings, became the most humble of all. It was not enough to
make himself less than the angels by reason of his human
nature; he would even become less than man by reason of his
infancy and weakness. Let the pious heart behold this sight
and glory; let the wicked and proud behold and be confounded. Let them see infinite God became a baby, an ador-
able infant. O supreme miracle, redemption of the good,
glory of the humble, judgment of the wicked, downfall of the
proud. O tremendous sacrament! How holy and how terrible
is your name; how deep is your mercy; how profound your
judgments! Who has drunk at this fountain and not loved it?
Who has contemplated this depth and not been terrified? He
who has not feared is insane and unfortunate; He well may
fear the judgment if this sight does not arouse him to pity.
Our Lord prefers us to love him rather than to fear; he finds
more pleasant the gifts that are offered in filial love than those
seeking his favor with slavish fear. Therefore, the first time
that He appeared to men, He chose to be seen in the lovable
aspect of an infant, rather than as a terrible God, since in
coming to save men and not to condemn them, he preferred
to excite their love rather than fear.

Let us approach confidently his throne of grace, we who
would fear to approach his throne of glory.[18]

THE TEACHINGS OF CHRIST

In redeeming men, Christ also taught them how the
fruits of their redemption must be applied in working
out their individual salvations. Christ was a superb
teacher: the simplicity of His message is only surpassed
by its challenge. His message and His challenge are perfectly symbolized in His Cross: He teaches men the love
of God and fellow man and points to the ideal limit of

their love—the imitation of His own redemptive love on the Cross. Simple, concrete, challenging, His teaching is one: Love which will endure crucifixion.

THE CHALLENGE OF CHRIST : THE NEW TESTAMENT

Come all ye that labour and are heavily burdened and I will refresh you; for My yoke is sweet and My burden light.[19]

And you shall be betrayed by your parents and brethren and your kinsmen and friends: and some of you they will put to death.
And you shall be hated by all men for my name's sake.
But a hair of your head shall not perish.
In your patience you shall possess your souls.[20]

. . . If any man will follow me, let him deny himself and take up his cross and follow me.
For whosoever will save his life shall lose it: and whosoever shall lose his life for my sake and the gospel shall save it.
For what shall it profit a man if he gain the whole world and suffer the loss of his soul?
Or what shall a man give in exchange for his soul?
For he that shall be ashamed of me and my words, in this adulterous and sinful generation: The Son of man also will be ashamed of him, when he shall come in the glory of his Father with the holy angels.[21]

For three years Jesus Christ taught publicly. In all of His teaching he claims not to destroy, but to fulfill the teachings of the Old Testament. The omnipotent Creator is revealed to men as a Triune God; the God of wrath is a loving, forgiving Father. He teaches the day of judgment and eternal justice. But He shows the way to a sublime destiny.

In His moral teachings Christ specifically claimed to fulfill, by transforming, the Old Law. The Ten Commandments of Moses are unchanged, but they are restated in terms of love: the first three compass love of

God, the remaining seven the love of neighbor. Christian justice must be transfigured in Christian charity. All morality derives from love of God who is the end of man and love of neighbor who is made in the image of God. Thus, kindness, humility, good example, almsgiving are the marks of the true follower of Christ. So, too, Christ encourages chastity, obedience, and poverty of spirit.

The gospels are a marvel of simplicity comprehensible to Christ's audience of fishermen and shepherds, as "I am the good shepherd; the good shepherd lays down his life for his sheep." At the same time their profundity has challenged the greatest minds of all ages.

CHRIST AND THE OLD LAW

Do not think that I am come to destroy the law or the prophets. I am not come to destroy, but to fulfil.

For amen I say unto you, till heaven and earth pass, one jot or one tittle shall not pass of the law till all be fulfilled.

He therefore that shall break one of these least commandments and shall so teach men shall be called the least in the kingdom of heaven. But he that shall do and teach, he shall be called great in the kingdom of heaven.[22]

You have heard that it was said to them of old: Thou shalt not kill. And whosoever shall kill shall be in danger of the judgment.

But I say to you that whosoever is angry with his brother shall be in danger of the judgment. And whosoever shall say to his brother, Raca, shall be in danger of the council. And whosoever shall say, Thou fool, shall be in danger of hell fire.

If therefore thou offer thy gift at the altar, and there thou remember that thy brother hath any thing against thee;

Leave there thy offering before the altar and go first to be reconciled to thy brother: and then coming thou shalt offer thy gift.[23]

You have heard that it hath been said: An eye for an eye, and a tooth for a tooth.

But I say to you not to resist evil: but if one strike thee on thy right cheek, turn to him also the other:

And if a man will contend with thee in judgment and take away thy coat, let go thy cloak also unto him.

And whosoever will force thee one mile, go with him other two.[24]

You have heard that it hath been said: Thou shalt love thy neighbor and hate thy enemy.

But I say to you: Love your enemies: do good to them that hate you and pray for them that persecute and calumniate you.

That you may be the children of your Father who is in heaven, who maketh his sun to rise upon the good and bad and raineth upon the just and the unjust.

For if you love them that love you, what reward shall you have? Do not even the publicans this?

And if you salute your brethren only, what do you more? Do not also the heathens this?

Be you therefore perfect, as also your heavenly Father is perfect.[25]

THE BEATITUDES : SERMON ON THE MOUNT

He taught them, saying:

Blessed are the poor in spirit: for theirs is the kingdom of heaven.

Blessed are the meek; for they shall possess the land.

Blessed are they that mourn: for they shall be comforted.

Blessed are they that hunger and thirst after justice: for they shall have their fill.

Blessed are the merciful: for they shall obtain mercy.

Blessed are the clean of heart: for they shall see God.

Blessed are the peacemakers: for they shall be called the children of God.

Blessed are they that suffer persecution for justice' sake: for theirs is the kingdom of heaven.

Blessed are ye when they shall revile you and persecute you and speak all that is evil against you, untruly, for my sake:

Be glad and rejoice, for your reward is very great in heaven.

For so they persecuted the prophets that were before you.[26]

THE CLAIMS AND PROOFS OF CHRIST

Throughout his ministry Christ repeatedly claimed divinity for Himself. He claimed that He was the promised Messiah, the Son of God, and the Son of man. He claimed divine knowledge, divine powers, divine nature. He stated positively that His teaching was the Word of God and must be accepted by all. These claims were made not only to His apostles, but to the Jewish people, to His enemies including the Supreme Council of the Jews.

THE CLAIMS OF CHRIST TO DIVINITY

Again the high priest asked him and said to him: Art thou the Christ, the Son of the Blessed God?

And Jesus said to him: I am. And you shall see the Son of man sitting on the right hand of the power of God and coming with the clouds of heaven.[27]

The Jews therefore said: Now we know that thou hast a devil. Abraham is dead and the prophets; and thou sayest: If any man keep my word, he shall not taste death for ever.

Art thou greater than our father Abraham who is dead? And the prophets are dead. Whom dost thou make thyself?

Jesus answered: If I glorify myself, my glory is nothing. It is my father that glorifieth me, of whom you say that he is your God.

And you have not known him, but I know him. And if I shall say that I know him not, I shall be like to you, a liar. But I do know him and keep his word.

Abraham your father rejoiced that he might see my day; he saw it and was glad.

The Jews therefore said to him: thou art not yet fifty years old. And hast thou seen Abraham?

Jesus said to them: Amen, amen, I say to you, before Abraham was made, I am.

They took up stones therefore to cast at him. . . .[28]

Philip saith to him: Lord, shew us the Father; and it is enough for us.

Jesus saith to him: Have I been so long a time with you and have you not known me? Philip, he that seeth me seeth the Father also. How sayest thou, Shew us the Father?

Do you not believe that I am in the Father and the Father in me? The words that I speak to you, I speak not of myself. But the Father who abideth in me, he doth the works.[29]

In like manner also the chief priests, with the scribes and ancients, mocking said:

He saved others: himself he cannot save. If he be the king of Israel, let him now come down from the cross: and we will believe him.

He trusted in God: let him now deliver *him* if he will have him. For he said: I am the Son of God.[30]

Others have made such claims. But Christ offered proof of His claims. Primary among these proofs are His prophecies and His miracles: such are works which God alone can perform. And Christ made prophecy and performed miracles in His own name. He healed the sick, cured the lame, raised the dead to life. He forgave sins, using His visible power to heal bodies as witness to His invisible power to heal souls. The supreme test of His claim—the fact without which, St. Paul says, "our faith is in vain"—was His resurrection from the dead as He had prophesied.

PROOFS OF DIVINITY

And taking again the twelve, he began to tell them the things that should befall him.

Saying: Behold we go up to Jerusalem, and the Son of man shall be betrayed to the chief priests and to the scribes and ancients. And they shall condemn him to death and shall deliver him to the Gentiles.

And they shall mock him and spit on him and scourge him and kill him: and the third day he shall rise again.[31]

And whilst they were eating he said: Amen I say to you that one of you is about to betray me.

And they being very much troubled began every one to say: Is it I, Lord?

But he answering said: He that dippeth his hand with me in the dish, he shall betray me.

The Son of man indeed goeth, as it is written of him. But woe to that man by whom the Son of man shall be betrayed. It were better for him, if that man had not been born.

And Judas that betrayed him answering, said: Is it I, Rabbi? He saith to him: Thou hast said it.[32]

And when he drew near, seeing the city, he wept over it, saying:

If thou also hadst known, and that in this thy day, the things that are to thy peace: but now they are hidden from thy eyes.

For the days shall come upon thee: and thy enemies shall cast a trench about thee and compass thee round and straiten thee on every side.

And beat thee flat to the ground and thy children who are in thee. And they shall not leave in thee a stone upon a stone: because thou has not known the time of thy visitation.[33]

And behold they brought to him one sick of the palsy lying in a bed. And Jesus, seeing their faith, said to the man sick of the palsy: Be of good heart, son. Thy sins are forgiven thee.

And behold some of the scribes said within themselves: He blasphemeth.

And Jesus seeing their thoughts, said: Why do you think evil in your hearts?

Whether is easier, to say Thy sins are forgiven thee: or to say Arise, and walk?

But that you may know that the Son of man hath power on earth to forgive sins, (then said he to the man sick of the palsy): Arise, take up thy bed and go into thy house.

And he arose and went into his house.[34]

And he saith to them: How many loaves have you? Go and see. And when they knew, they said: Five, and two fishes.

And he commanded them that they should make them all sit down by companies upon the green grass.

And they sat down in ranks, by hundreds and by fifties.

And when he had taken the five loaves and the two fishes: looking up to heaven, he blessed and broke the loaves, and gave to his disciples to set before them. And the two fishes he divided among them all.

And they all did eat and had their fill.

And they took up the leavings, twelve full baskets of fragments and of the fishes.

And they that did eat were five thousand men.[35]

THE SACRIFICE OF CHRIST

After the three years of His ministry the time was come for Christ to offer His life as atonement to God for the sins of mankind. This was the purpose for which He had become incarnate. Now the Jews under the Old Law had always been accustomed to sacrifice. To indicate clearly that He had come to complete and fulfill the sacrifice of the Mosaic Law, Christ chose the occasion of the Feast of the Passover, the time of sacrifice of the Paschal Lamb.

Sacrifice is the offering of a victim by a priest to God and the destruction of the victim to acknowledge supremacy of the Godhead. In every sacrifice there must be a visible gift which is offered to God (oblation) and destroyed (immolation); the purpose of the gift must be religious and the gift must be acceptable and accepted by God.

In the Sacrifice of Christ, the Redeemer Himself is Priest and Victim. From the Offering of Himself as victim at the Last Supper on Thursday eve, Christ the Priest-

Victim passed to the culmination of His sacrifice in the immolation of the Cross.

THE LAST SUPPER : ST. MARK

And whilst they were eating, Jesus took bread; and blessing, broke and gave to them and said: Take ye. This is my body.

And having taken the chalice, giving thanks, he gave it to them. And they all drank of it.

And he said to them: This is my blood of the new testament, which shall be shed for many.

Amen I say to you that I will drink no more of the fruit of the vine until that day when I shall drink it new in the kingdom of God.[36]

The abasement of Christ on Calvary is the shining hour of Christendom for it is the supreme act of love by which the God-man redeemed man from God. The New Adam offered satisfaction not only for the sin of Adam but for all sins of all men. Since He is God, the merit of His sacrifice is infinite. The darkest hour is the brightest; the bitter wood and nails are sweet. It is thus that the Church sings on Good Friday:

Behold the wood of the Cross on which the Saviour of the world hath hung.
O faithful Cross, o Tree most noble of all! . . . .
Sweet the nails, sweet the wood
which sustained so sweet a burden.

And by that triumph of paradox, the disastrous fall of Adam is transfigured in the Holy Saturday liturgy into the *felix culpa:* O happy fault, that merited so great a Redeemer. Had Adam not sinned, there might have been no Incarnation.

PROPHECY OF THE PASSION : ISAIAS

And he shall grow up as a tender plant before him, and as a root out of a thirsty ground. There is no beauty in him, nor comeliness: and we have seen him, and there was no sightliness, that we should be desirous of him:

Despised, and the most abject of men, a man of sorrows and acquainted with infirmity: and his look was as it were hidden and despised. Whereupon we esteemed him not.

Surely he hath borne our infirmities and carried our sorrows: and we have thought him as it were a leper, and as one struck by God and afflicted.

But he was wounded for our iniquities: he was bruised for our sins. The chastisement of our peace was upon him: and by his bruises we are healed.

All we like sheep have gone astray, every one hath turned aside into his own way: and the Lord hath laid on him the iniquity of us all.

He was offered because it was his own will, and he opened not his mouth. He shall be led as a sheep to the slaughter and shall be dumb as a lamb before his shearer, and he shall not open his mouth.[37]

THE CRUCIFIXION : ST. MATTHEW

And they put on him his own garments and led him away to crucify him. . . .

And they came to the place that is called Golgotha, which is the place of Calvary. . . .

And after they had crucified him, they divided his garments, casting lots: that it might be fulfilled which was spoken by the prophet, saying: *They divided my garments among them and upon my vesture they cast lots.* . . .

And they put over his head his cause written: THIS IS JESUS THE KING OF THE JEWS. . . .

And they that passed by blasphemed him, wagging their heads.

And saying: Vah, thou that destroyest the temple of God and in three days dost rebuild it: save thy own self. If thou be the Son of God, come down from the cross. . . .

Now from the sixth hour, there was darkness over the whole earth, until the ninth hour.

And about the ninth hour, Jesus cried with a loud voice, saying: Eli, Eli, lamma sabacthani? That is, My God, My God, why hast thou forsaken me? . . .

And Jesus again crying with a loud voice, gave up the ghost.

And behold the veil of the temple was rent in two from the top even to the bottom: and the earth quaked and the rocks were rent.

And the graves were opened: and many bodies of the saints that had slept arose. . . .

Now the centurion and they that were with him watching Jesus, having seen the earthquake and the things that were done, were sore afraid, saying: Indeed this was the Son of God.[38]

THE CRUCIFIXION—REPROACHES SUNG ON GOOD FRIDAY

My people, what have I done to thee? or in what have I grieved thee? Answer me.

Because I brought thee out of the land of Egypt: thou hast prepared a cross for thy Saviour.

O holy God, O holy strong one, O holy immortal one, Have mercy on us.

Because I led thee through the desert forty years: and fed thee with manna, and brought thee into a land exceedingly good, thou hast prepared a cross for thy Saviour.

What more ought I to do for thee, that I have not done? I planted thee, indeed, my most beautiful vineyard: and thou hast become exceeding bitter to Me: for in My thirst thou gavest Me vinegar to drink: and with a spear thou hast pierced the side of thy Saviour.

For thy sake I scourged Egypt with its first-born: and thou hast scourged Me and delivered me up.

I brought thee out of Egypt having drowned Pharaoh in the Red Sea: and thou hast delivered Me to the chief priests.

I opened the sea before thee: and thou with a spear hast opened My side.

I went before thee in a pillar of a cloud: and thou hast brought me to the judgment hall of Pilate.

I fed thee with manna in the desert: and thou hast beaten Me with blows and scourges.

I gave thee the water of salvation from the rock to drink: and thou hast given Me gall and vinegar.

For thee I struck the kings of the Canaanites: and thou hast struck My head with a reed.

I gave thee a royal sceptre: and thou hast given to My head a crown of thorns.

I have exalted thee with great power: and thou hast hanged Me on the gibbet of the Cross.[39]

THE CRUCIFIXION : CYRIL OF JERUSALEM

Every deed of Christ is a boast of the Catholic Church, but her boast of boasts is the Cross, and knowing this, Paul says "But God forbid that I should glory, save in the cross of our Lord Jesus Christ" (Gal. 6:14). For wondrous indeed it was, that he who was blind from his birth should recover his sight in Siloam; but what is this compared with the blind of the whole world. It was a great thing and passing nature, for Lazarus to rise after four days; but this grace extended to him alone and what was it compared to the dead in sin throughout the world? Marvellous was it, that five loaves should issue forth into food for the five thousand; but what is that to those who are famishing in ignorance through all the world? It was marvellous that she should have been loosed who had been bound by Satan eighteen years. Yet what is this to all of us who are fast bound in chains of sin? Now the glory of the Cross has led into light those who were blind through ignorance, has loosed all who were held fast by sin and has ransomed the whole world of man. . . .

Let us not then be ashamed of the Cross of our Saviour but rather glory in it (1 Cor. 1:18) for to them that are saved, that is, to us, it is the power of God (1 Cor. 1:23). For it was not a mere man who died for us, as I said before, but the Son of God, God made man. . . .

Take therefore, first, as an unassailable foundation the Cross and build on it the rest of thy faith. Deny not the Crucified for if thou deny Him, thou hast many to arraign thee. The thirty pieces of silver bear witness; Gethsemane bears witness where the betrayal happened. The moon in the night bears witness and the darkened sun, for it endured not to look on the crime of the conspiracy. The fire remonstrates with thee, where Peter stood and warmed himself; if thou deny the Cross, the eternal fire awaits thee. Remember the swords that came against Him in Gethsemane that thou be not punished by the sword. The house of Caiphas will arraign thee, showing by its present desolation the power of Him who was once judged there. Even Herod shall rise against thee; and Pilate; as if saying "Why deniest thou Him who was slandered unto us by the Jews, Whom we knew to have done no wrong? For I Pilate then washed my hands." The false witnesses shall rise against thee and the soldiers who put on Him a purple robe and set on Him a crown of thorns and crucified Him on Calvary and cast lots for His coat. Simon the Cyrenean will cry out upon thee, who bore the Cross behind Jesus.

There will cry out upon thee, among the stars, the darkened Sun; among the things on earth, the Wine mingled with myrrh; among reeds, the Reed; among herbs, the Hyssop; among the things of the sea, the Sponge; among trees, the Wood of the Cross; the soldier who pierced His side with a spear; the women who then were present; the veil of the temple then rent asunder; the hall of Pilate, now laid waste by the power of Him who was then crucified; this Calvary rising on high and showing even to this day how because of Christ the rocks were riven; the sepulchre where He was laid; and the stone which was laid to the door which lies to this day by the tomb; the Angels who were present; the women who worshipped Him after His Resurrection; Peter and John who ran to the sepulchre; and Thomas who thrust his hand into His side and his fingers into the print of the nails. For it was for our sake that he so handled Him; for what thou who wert not there present, wouldst have sought, he being present, did seek for thee, by God's Providence.[40]

THE TRIUMPH OF CHRIST

The ultimate miracle, the resurrection of Jesus Christ from the dead, is recorded history. It is believed as historical fact that Christ, known to be dead and buried, on the third day by His own power rose from the dead. This triumphant event is, as well, a symbol of the future resurrection of man and of his immortality. It is the supreme proof of the divinity of Christ and is basic to all Catholic thought. Without this substantiation of His claim to divinity, all the other teaching of Christ would be invalidated, and His death on the cross would be meaningless.

THE RESURRECTION : ST. MATTHEW

And the angel answering, said to the women: Fear not you, for I know that you seek Jesus who was crucified.

He is not here. For he is risen, as he said. Come, and see the place where the Lord was laid.

And going quickly, tell ye his disciples that he is risen. And behold he will go before you into Galilee. There you shall see him. Lo, I have foretold it to you.

And they went out quickly from the sepulchre with fear and great joy, running to tell his disciples.

And behold, Jesus met them, saying: All hail. But they came up and took hold of his feet and adored him.

Then Jesus said to them: Fear not. Go, tell my brethren that they go into Galilee. There they shall see me.[41]

THE RESURRECTION : HYMN FROM THE BLESSING OF THE PASCHAL CANDLE ON HOLY SATURDAY

Let the angelic choirs of heaven now rejoice; let the divine mysteries be celebrated with joy; and let the trumpet of salvation resound for the victory of so great a King. Let the earth also rejoice, illumined with such resplendent rays; and enlightened with the brightness of the eternal King, let it feel that the darkness of the whole world is dispersed. Let also our mother the Church rejoice, adorned with the brightness of so great a light; and may this temple resound with the joyful voices of the people. Wherefore I beseech you, most dear brethren, who are here present in the wonderful brightness of this holy light, to invoke with me the mercy of almighty God. That He who has vouchsafed to number me without any merits of mine, among the Levites, would pour forth His brightness upon me, and enable me to celebrate the praise of this light. Through our Lord Jesus Christ His son, who with Him and the Holy Ghost liveth and reigneth one God, world without end. Amen.

It is truly meet and right to proclaim with affection of heart and mind and with the service of our voice, the invisible God, the Father almighty, and His only-begotten Son, our Lord Jesus Christ, who paid for us to His eternal Father the debt of Adam, and by His merciful blood cancelled the guilt incurred by original sin. For this is the Paschal solemnity, in which that true Lamb is slain, by whose blood the doorposts of the faithful are hallowed. This is the night in which Thou didst first cause our forefathers, the children of Israel, when brought out of Egypt, to pass through the Red Sea, with dry feet. This, therefore, is the night which purged away the darkness of sinners by the light of the pillar. This is the night which at this time throughout the world restores to grace and unites in sanctity those that believe in Christ, and are separated from the vices of the world and the darkness of sinners. This is the night in which, destroying the bonds of death, Christ arose victorious from the grave. For it would have profited us nothing to have been born, unless redemption had also been bestowed upon us. O wonderful condescension of Thy mercy toward us! O inestimable affection of charity; that Thou mightest redeem a slave, Thou didst deliver up Thy Son! O truly needful sin of Adam, which was blotted out by the death of Christ! O happy fault, that merited so great a redeemer! O truly blessed night, which alone deserved to know the time and hour in which Christ rose again from the grave! This is the night of which it is written: And the night shall be enlightened as the day: and the night is my light in my enjoyments. Therefore the holiness of this night drives away all wickedness, cleanses faults, and restores innocence to the fallen, and gladness to the sorrowful. It puts to flight hatred, brings peace and humbles pride.[42]

THE RESURRECTION : ST. JOHN VIANNEY, CURÉ D'ARS

. . . Jesus lives! What glad tidings for us; what joy and delight for us who are baptized in the name of Jesus who believe in the teaching of Jesus; for us, who may live in the blessed hope that we, too, may one day rise again to a better life. When the Man of Sorrows, His struggle and His sufferings ended, cried out to the world with a loud voice those mighty words "It is consummated," when He bowed His head and gave up the ghost, the sun was obscured; it did not wish to behold that dreadful spectacle; the earth was shaken mightily, its graves opened, and the dead arose. Today, however, one grave is open, and from it has risen a sun which will never be obscured, which will never set, a sun which creates new life. This new sun is the Crucified One, the Son of God, God Himself, blessed for all eternity. He it is in whom the words of the Apostle are fulfilled; for He humbled himself and was obedient even unto death on a cross, therefore has God exalted Him and given Him a name which is above all other names.

. . . The earth is jubilant with joy; heaven sends forth its messengers, the grave is empty, the Saviour is risen. Because He rose from the grave through His own almighty power, because He has built up again the temple of His body, He has proven the glory of His divinity and placed the seal of completeness upon the work of our redemption. If Christ had not risen, says the Apostle, our faith would be vain. On Good Friday, when the earth trembled and the rocks were split open, we struck our breasts with the centurion and said "Verily He was the Son of God." We may therefore cry out all the more joyfully beside the empty grave on Easter morning. He that is risen is the Son of God, He is the Messiah, He is the lamb of God and takes away the sins of the world. Is this not the day that the Lord has made? Should we not rejoice in Him and be glad? Let the chords of the organ peal forth in sweetest harmony, let the bells ring out, let the song of triumph resound. The Saviour is risen. Neither seal nor grave, rock nor stone could withstand Him. "You seek Jesus of Nazareth; He is risen; He is not here."[43]

CHAPTER FIVE

Pentecost

There shall be one fold and one shepherd.[1]

Jesus Christ claimed to be true God. His life and His sacrifice were the proof of His claim as they were the infinite means of human redemption. This is the foundation of all Catholic belief without which all faith is vain. If Christ claimed to be God, if He proved His claim, then the entire life and teaching of Christ are the revelation of God to man and His promises are the key to the destiny of man in history.

The Catholic Church is for its members the fulfillment of the promise of Christ. Christ became man not only to re-open for man the possibility of a supernatural destiny, but to teach him the way to realize this destiny and authoritatively to lead him towards this realization. For this purpose, Christ promised an abiding union with His followers in history, the continuing revelation through the Spirit in this union of the truth which can save men and the continuing visible presence of His authority for the governing of men. The revelation of God in Christ and the redemption of men through His merits would be realized in history through the continuing life of Christ in His Church.

The attitude of the Catholic to his Church can be understood only if one takes into account the firm conviction arising from faith in the divinity of Christ. This attitude is based on the promises of Christ and its security is as strong as the authority on which it claims to be based.

THE SCRIPTURAL FOUNDATIONS OF THE CHURCH

I am the vine: you the branches. He that abideth in me, and I in him, the same beareth much fruit: for without me you can do nothing.[2] . . . there shall be one fold and one Shepherd.[3]

And Jesus answering said to him: Blessed art thou, Simon Bar-Jona: because flesh and blood hath not revealed it to thee, but my Father who is in heaven. And I say to thee: That thou art Peter, and upon this rock I will build my church. And the gates of hell shall not prevail against it. And I will give to thee the keys of the kingdom of heaven. And whatsoever thou shalt bind upon earth, it shall be bound also in heaven: and whatsoever thou shalt loose on earth, it shall be loosed also in heaven.[4] All power is given to Me in heaven and in earth. Going therefore teach ye all nations: baptizing them in the name of the Father and of the Son and of the Holy Ghost.[5] He that heareth you heareth me, and he that despiseth you despiseth me; and he that despiseth me, despiseth him that sent me.[6]

And I will ask the Father: and he will give you another Paraclete, that he may abide with you for ever: The spirit of truth, whom the world cannot receive because it seeth him not, nor knoweth him. . . . I will not leave you orphans: I will come to you.[7] . . . he will teach you all things and bring all things to your mind, whatsoever I have said to you.[8] And there appeared to them parted tongues, as it were of fire: and it sat upon every one of them. And they were filled with the Holy Ghost: and they began to speak with divers tongues, according as the Holy Ghost gave them to speak.[9]

THE CATHOLIC CHURCH: THE MYSTICAL BODY OF CHRIST

The Catholic belief concerning the nature of the Church is most completely understood through the dogma of the Mystical Body. It is here that are summarized most of the distinctive elements of the Catholic Church: the reality of and need for an invisible and a visible Church; the meaning of grace; the function of authority and hierarchy; the unity and the unicity of the Church.

This body is called "mystical" in contradistinction to the Eucharistic Body of Christ which is received in Holy Communion and to the physical body of Christ which ascended into heaven. The head of the body is Jesus Christ as God-man; the members of the body are all the baptized except those who have cut themselves off from the life of the body by schism or apostasy; the vital principle of the body is the Holy Spirit, third Person of the Trinity, who informs the body through Grace. The inner life of the Church, the invisible aspect, is the life of grace; the visible aspect is the engagement of the physical members of the church in those activities by which the life of grace is communicated and furthered. The Church as Mystical Body of Christ, then, is the union of the many with each other and with Christ through the one life of grace.

The traditional interpretation of this doctrine will be exemplified in the selection from St. Paul which follows and from the contemporary statement of Pope Pius XII.

THE MYSTICAL BODY : ST. PAUL

For as the body is one and hath many members; and all the members of the body, whereas they are many, yet are one body: so also is Christ.

For in one Spirit were we all baptized into one body, whether Jews or Gentiles, whether bond or free: and in one Spirit we have all been made to drink.

For the body also is not one member, but many.

If the foot should say: Because I am not the hand, I am not of the body: Is it therefore not of the body?

And if an ear should say: Because I am not the eye, I am not of the body: Is it therefore not of the body?

If the whole body were the eye, where would be the hearing? If the whole were hearing, where would be the smelling?

But now God hath set the members, every one of them, in the body as it hath pleased him.

And if they all were one member, where would be the body?

But now there are many members indeed, yet one body. . . .

And if one member suffer any thing, all the members suffer with it; or if one member glory, all the members rejoice with it.[10]

THE MYSTICAL BODY : POPE PIUS XII

If we would define and describe this true Church of Jesus Christ—which is the One, Holy, Catholic, Apostolic Roman Church—we shall find nothing more noble, more sublime, or more divine than the expression "the mystical Body of Jesus Christ"—an expression which springs from and is, as it were, the fair flowering of the repeated teaching of the Sacred Scriptures and the holy Fathers.

That the Church is a body is frequently asserted in the Sacred Scriptures. . . . But it is not enough that the Body of the Church should be an unbroken unity; it must also be something definite and perceptible to the senses as Our predecessor of happy memory, Leo XIII, in his Encyclical *Satis Cognitum* asserts: "The Church is visible because she is a body." Hence they err in a matter of divine truth, who imagine the Church to be invisible, intangible, a something "pneumatological" as they say, by which many Christian communities, though they differ from each other in their profession of faith, are united by an invisible bond.

But a body calls also for a multiplicity of members, which are linked together in such a way as to help one another. And as in the body when one member suffers, all the other members share its pain, and the healthy members come to the assistance of the ailing, so in the Church the individual members do not live for themselves alone, but also help their fellows, and all work in mutual collaboration for the common comfort and for the more perfect building up of the whole Body. . . .

Nor must one imagine that the Body of the Church, just because it bears the name of Christ, is made up during the days of its earthly pilgrimage only of members conspicuous for their holiness, or that it consists only of those whom God has predestined to eternal happiness. It is owing to the Saviour's infinite mercy that place is allowed in His mystical Body here below for those whom, of old, He did not exclude from the banquet. For not every sin, however grave it may be, is such as of its own nature to sever a man from the Body of the Church, as does schism or heresy or apostasy. Men may lose charity and divine grace through sin, thus becoming incapable of supernatural merit, and yet not be deprived of all life if they hold fast to faith and Christian hope, and if, illumined from above, they are spurred on by interior promptings of the Holy Spirit to salutary fear and are moved to prayer and penance for their sins. . . .

But if our Saviour, by His death, became, in the full and complete sense of the word, the Head of the Church, it was likewise through His blood that the Church was enriched with the fullest communication of the Holy Spirit, through which, from the time when the Son of man was lifted up and glorified on the Cross by His sufferings, she is divinely illumined. For then, as Augustine notes, with the rending of the veil of the temple it happened that the dew of the Paraclete's gifts, which heretofore had descended only on the fleece, that is on the people of Israel, fell copiously and abundantly (while the fleece remained dry and deserted) on the whole earth, that is on the Catholic Church, which is confined by no boundaries of race or territory. Just as at the first moment of the Incarnation the Son of the Eternal Father adorned with the fullness of the Holy Spirit the human nature which was substantially united to Him, that it might be a fitting instrument of the Divinity in the sanguinary work of the Redemption, so at the hour of His precious death He willed that His Church should be enriched with the abundant gifts of the Paraclete in order that in dispensing the divine fruits of the Redemption she might be, for the Incarnate Word, a powerful instrument that would never fail. For both the juridical mission of the Church, and the power to teach, govern and administer the Sacraments, derive their supernatural efficacy and force for the building up of the Body of Christ from the fact that Jesus Christ, hanging on the Cross, opened up to His Church the fountain of those divine gifts, which prevent her from ever teaching false doctrine and enable her to rule them for the salvation of their souls through divinely enlightened pastors and to bestow on them an abundance of heavenly graces. . . .

It is the will of Jesus Christ that the whole body of the Church, no less than the individual members, should resemble Him. And we see this realized when, following in the footsteps of her Founder, the Church teaches, governs, and offers the divine Sacrifice. When she embraces the evangelical counsels she reflects the Redeemer's poverty, obedience, and virginal purity. Adorned with institutes of many different kinds as with so many precious jewels, she represents Christ deep in prayer on the mountain, or preaching to the people, or healing the sick and wounded and bringing sinners back to the path of virtue—in a word, doing good to all. What wonder then, if, while on this earth she, like Christ, suffer persecutions, insults and sorrows. . . .

And now, Venerable Brethren, We come to that part of Our explanation in which We desire to make clear why the Body of Christ, which is the Church, should be called mystical. This name, which is used by many early writers, has the sanction of numerous Pontifical documents. There are several reasons why it should be used; for by it we may distinguish the Body of the Church, which is a Society whose Head and Ruler is Christ, from His physical Body, which, born of the Virgin Mother of God, now sits at the right hand of the Father and is hidden under the Eucharistic veils; and, that which is of greater importance in view of modern errors, this name enables us to distinguish it from any other body, whether in the physical or the moral order.

In a natural body the principle of unity unites the parts in such a manner that each lacks its own individual subsistence; on the contrary, in the mystical Body the mutual union, though intrinsic, links the members by a bond which leaves to each the complete enjoyment of his own personality. Moreover, if we examine the relations existing between the several members and the whole body, in every physical, living body, all the different members are ultimately destined to the good of the whole alone; while if we look to its ultimate usefulness, every moral association of men is in the end directed to the advancement of all in general and of each single member in particular; for they are persons. And thus—to return to Our theme—as the Son of the Eternal Father came down from heaven for the salvation of us all, He likewise established the body of the Church and enriched it with the divine Spirit to ensure that immortal souls should attain eternal happiness according to the words of the Apostle: "All things are yours; and you are Christ's; and Christ is God's." For the Church exists both for the good of the faithful and for the glory of God and of Jesus Christ whom He sent.

But if we compare a mystical body with a moral body, it is to be noted that the difference between them is not slight; rather it is very considerable and very important. In the moral body the principle of union is nothing else than the common end, and the common co-operation of all under the authority of Society for the attainment of that end; whereas in the mystical Body of which We are speaking, this collaboration is supplemented by another internal principle, which exists effectively in the whole and in each of its parts, and whose excellence is such that of itself it is vastly superior to whatever bonds of union may be found in a physical or moral body. As We said above, this is something not of the natural but of the supernatural order; rather it is something in itself infinite, uncreated: the Spirit of God, who, as the Angelic Doctor says, "numerically one and the same, fills and unifies the whole Church."

Hence, this word in its correct significance gives us to understand that the Church, a perfect society of its kind, is not made up of merely moral and juridical elements and principles. It is far superior to all other human societies; it surpasses them as grace surpasses nature, as things immortal are above all those that perish. Such human societies, and in the first place civil Society, are by no means to be despised or belittled; but the Church in its entirety is not found within this natural order, any more than the whole of man is encompassed within the organism of our mortal body. Although the juridical principles, on which the Church rests and is established, derive from the divine constitution given to it by Christ and contribute to the attaining of its supernatural end, never-theless that which lifts the Society of Christians far above the whole natural order is the Spirit of our Redeemer who pene-trates and fills every part of the Church's being and is active within it until the end of time as the source of every grace and every gift and every miraculous power. Just as our com-posite mortal body, although it is a marvellous work of the Creator, falls far short of the eminent dignity of our soul, so the social structure of the Christian community, though it proclaims the wisdom of the divine Architect, still remains something inferior when compared to the spiritual gifts which give it beauty and life, and to the divine source whence they flow. . . .

This communication of the Spirit of Christ is the channel through which all the gifts, powers, and extraordinary graces found superabundantly in the Head as in their source flow into all the members of the Church, and are perfected daily in them according to the place they hold in the mystical Body of Jesus Christ. Thus the Church becomes, as it were, the filling out and the complement of the Redeemer, while Christ in a sense attains through the Church a fullness in all things. Here-in we find the reason why, according to the opinion of Augus-tine already referred to, the mystical Head, which is Christ, and the Church, which here below as another Christ shows forth His person, constitute one new man, in whom heaven and earth are joined together in perpetuating the saving work of the Cross: Christ We mean, the Head and the Body, the whole Christ.[11]

The living body has a dual aspect: the principle of life which in itself is invisible and functionally undiversified; the physical, visible structure through which life is diver-sified and expressed. So, too, the Mystical Body reveals an organic and an organizational aspect, an eternal and a temporal, a spiritual and a physical nature. The Church as the Mystical Body fulfills its spiritual life and its his-torical calling through human, visible modes of operation.

The insistence on this dual aspect of the Body distinguishes Catholicism from many other religious groups. The Church is not merely an invisible fellowship in Christ; it is not merely an external, physical institution: it is both. It is a living body, living by the invisible life of Grace, visible by the physical structures and institutions through which it expresses itself. The Church is organic.

This important distinction is made by Pope Leo XIII in the following selection.

THE TWOFOLD NATURE OF THE CHURCH : POPE LEO XIII

. . . It is obvious that nothing can be communicated amongst men save by means of external things which the senses can perceive. For this reason the Son of God assumed human nature—"who being in the form of God, thought it not robbery to be equal with God but emptied Himself taking the form of a servant, being made in the likeness of a man" (Phil. 2:6-7) and thus living on earth He taught His doctrine and gave His laws, conversing with men.

And since it is necessary that His divine mission should be perpetuated to the end of time, He took to Himself disciples, trained by Himself and made them partakers of His own authority. And when He had invoked upon them from heaven the Spirit of Truth He bade them go through the whole world and faithfully preach to all nations what He had taught and what He had commanded, so that by the profession of His doctrine and the observance of His laws, the human race might attain to holiness and never-ending happiness in heaven. In this wise and on this principle, the church was begotten. . . . The apostles received a mission to teach by visible and audible signs and they discharged their mission only by words and acts which certainly appealed to the senses.

Jesus Christ commissioned His apostles and their successors to the end of time to teach and rule the nations. He ordered the nations to obey their authority and accept their teaching. But this correspondence of rights and duties in the Christian commonwealth not only could not have been made permanent, but could not even have been initiated, except through the senses, which are of all things the messengers and interpreters.

For this reason the Church is so often called in holy writ *a body* and even the body of Christ (1 Cor. 12:27). Now you are the body of Christ—and precisely because it is a body is the Church visible; and because it is the body of Christ it is living and energizing, because by the infusion of His power Christ guards and sustains it, just as the vine gives nourishment and renders fruitful the branches united to it. And as in animals the vital principle is unseen and invisible and is evidenced by the movements and actions of the members, so the principle of supernatural life in the Church is clearly shown in that which was done by it.

From this it follows that those who arbitrarily conjure up and picture to themselves a hidden and invisible Church are in grievous and pernicious error, as also are those who regard the Church as a human institution which claims a certain obedience in discipline and external duties, but which is without the perennial communication of the gifts of divine grace and without all that which testifies by constant and undoubted signs to the existence of that life which is drawn from God. It is assuredly as impossible that the Church of Jesus Christ can be the one or the other as that man should be a body alone or a soul alone. The connection and union of both elements is as absolutely necessary to the true Church as the intimate union of the soul and body is to human nature. The Church is not something dead; it is the body of Christ endowed with supernatural life. As Christ, the Head and exemplar, is not wholly in His visible human nature nor wholly in the invisible divine nature, but is one, from and in both natures, visible and invisible; so the mystical body of Christ is the true Church only because its visible parts draw life and power from the supernatural gifts and other things whence spring their very essence and nature. But since the Church is *such* by divine and will and constitution, *such* it must remain uniformly to the end of time. . . . The union, consequently of visible and invisible elements, because it harmonized with the natural order and by God's will belongs to the very essence of the Church, must necessarily remain so long as the Church itself shall endure. . . .

Wherefore, Christ instituted in the Church a *living, author-itative and permanent magisterium* which by His own power He strengthened, by the Spirit of Truth He taught and by miracles confirmed. He willed and ordered, under gravest penalties, that its teachings should be received as if they were His own. As often, therefore, as it is declared on the author-ity of this teaching that this or that is contained in the deposit of divine revelation, it must be believed by every one as true. If it could in any way be false, an evident contradiction fol-lows for then God himself would be the author of error in man.[12]

THE SUPERNATURAL UNITY OF THE CHURCH: THE LIFE OF GRACE

The Church is in the fullest sense an organism: it lives by the interior, spiritual unity of grace which is visibly expressed through the human form of the institu-tional Church.

It is customary to distinguish among the Church Tri-umphant (the faithful in Heaven), the Church Militant (the members on earth), and the Church Suffering (the souls in Purgatory). The three groups, in their unity, constitute what is called "the Communion of Saints." In this unity is explained the practice of prayer to those in heaven for intercession and prayer and sacrifice for the souls in purgatory.

The unity of the Communion of Saints is the unity of a shared life. It admits of hierarchy only in the sense of degrees of sanctity: the value of a person is found only in the degree of his faith and union with Christ in Grace. In the life of Grace the earthly dignitary may be the inferior of the most humble soul: what counts only is the spirit.

The life-principle of the Church is grace, that gift of God which confers a new life on souls, a sharing in the life of God Himself. The Church distinguishes between two types of grace, habitual and actual. Habitual or sanctifying grace is a supernatural quality inherent in the soul which makes the soul partake of the divine nature and divine life in a real manner. The presence of sanctifying grace in the soul makes the soul pure and pleasing to God: such a soul is the spiritual temple of God. This presence of grace places the soul in the supernatural order. Now, just as in the natural order the created agent is incapable of acting without the concurrence of God, so too in the supernatural order a concurrence is needed for each act; such a supernatural concurrence is Actual grace. Actual grace is customarily defined as a supernatural, transient help given to enlighten the mind and strengthen the will in the performance of supernatural acts. Without grace, no act is supernatural or meritorious: with grace, every act can be meritorious.

All merit is primarily of Christ, since His redemption won infinite merit for us. There is no implication of inadequacy in His redemptive act when we speak of human merit. But since man is a creature of free will, his own acts are subject to judgment, consequently to reward or punishment. It is reasonable that when an act is humanly virtuous, God would reward it in proportion to its excellence. If man does good works in honor of God, then aided by divine grace, they are indeed meritorious. Man does not merit eternal life because of his human choices; it is grace within the soul which gives worth to his acts.

Sell what you possess and give alms. Make to yourselves bags which grow not old, a treasure in heaven which faileth not. . . .[13]

Every man shall receive his own reward, according to his own labour.[14]

GRACE : THE COUNCIL OF TRENT

Eternal life is proposed to those who do good and hope in God, both AS A GRACE mercifully promised to the children of God through Jesus Christ, and AS A REWARD to be faithfully rendered to their good works and merits, in virtue of the promise of God Himself (2 Tim. 4:7) . . . For since Jesus Christ Himself constantly communicated His virtue to those who are justified, as the Head to the members and as the Vine to the branches, which virtue always preceded, accompanied and followed their good works, and without which they could be nowise agreeable to God and meritorious; we must believe that nothing more is wanting to the justified, nor is there any reason why they should not be considered as having fully satisfied the divine Law, as far as the condition of this life admits, by such works as are done in God, and truly merited the attainment of eternal life in due time, if they die in the state of grace.[15]

The growth into the unity of the Church is a growth in grace. The Catholic Church teaches that the two principal means of obtaining grace are prayer and the reception of the sacraments. The sacraments *produce* grace in the soul, those special graces for which each was instituted. Prayer *obtains* grace of various kinds other than those given only by the sacraments.

PRAYER

In Christ, through Christ and with Christ man renders to God infinite homage, obtains grace, asks assistance and propitiates for sin: this is prayer, the uniting of mind and heart with God. Christ urged all men to pray and gave them the great example in the "Our Father." Likewise, in numerous lessons He taught the way of prayer— humility and confidence. He taught that the Father is never deaf to the true needs of His children.

PRAYER : ST. JOHN CHRYSOSTOM

"Ask and ye shall find . . . " (Matt. 7:6). So after all He adds also to the pinnacle of all facility, devising as no ordinary relief to our toils, the assistance derived from persevering prayers. Thus, we are not ourselves, saith He, to strive alone, but also to invoke help from above; and it will surely come and be present with us and will aid us in our struggles and make all easy. Therefore He commanded us to ask and pledged himself to the giving. . . . and if thou dost not receive straightway, do not even thus despair. For to this end He said "Knock" to signify that even if He should not straightway open the door, we are to continue there.

And if thou doubt my affirmation, at any rate believe His example. "For what man is there among you, of whom if his son shall ask bread, will he reach him a stone?" (Matt. 7:9), and if thou continue asking, though thou receive not at once, thou surely wilt receive. For to this end was the door shut, that He may induce thee to knock: to this end He doth not straightway assent, that thou mayest ask. Continue then to do these things and thou wilt surely receive. For that thou mightest not say "What if I ask and not receive?" He hath blocked thy approach with that similitude, again framing arguments, and by those human things urging us to be confident on these matters, implying by them that we must not only ask, but ask what we ought.

"For which of you is there, a father, of whom if his son shall ask bread, will he reach him a stone?" So that if thou receive not, thy asking a stone is the cause of thy non-receiving. For though thou be a son, this suffices not for thy receiving, that being a son, thou ask what is not profitable.

Do thou, therefore, ask nothing worldly, but all things spiritual and thou wilt surely receive. Two things now, you see, should be in him that prays; as asking earnestly and doing what he ought; since ye, too, saith He, though ye be fathers, wait for your sons to ask; and if they ask anything inexpedient, ye refuse the gifts; just as, if it be expedient, ye consent and bestow it.[16]

THE MEANING OF PRAYER : ST. AUGUSTINE

. . . Now this is the temple, that is, men themselves, wherein God is prayed to, and hears. For whosoever except he be the temple of God, prays to God, is not heard unto that peace of the heavenly Jerusalem, although he is heard for certain temporal things, which God has given to the heathen also. For the devils themselves were heard when they asked that they might enter the swine (Matt. viii, 31 *sq*.). To be heard unto eternal life is another thing, nor is it granted save to him who prays in the temple of God. Now he prays in the temple of God who prays in the peace of the Church, in the unity of Christ's body; which body of Christ consists of the many in the whole world who believe. And therefore he who prays in the temple is heard. For he prays in spirit and in truth who prays in the peace of the Church, not in that temple wherein was the figure.[17]

THE SACRAMENTS

The seven sacraments of the Church are the second principal source or means of Grace. A sacrament is an outward or sensible sign instituted by Christ which signifies and imparts a particular grace to the soul. Three elements constitute the sacrament. The sensible sign is composed of the matter (water, oil, bread, wine, etc.) and the form (the words pronounced by the minister in applying the matter). This outward sign makes known the particular inward grace which is being produced in the soul. Finally, the sacrament was instituted by Christ who alone can determine the channels by which Grace enters the soul. The Church itself cannot institute sacraments.

Christ granted to His Church the power to administer the sacraments; consequently, the Church has the power to prescribe ceremonies and prayers to be used in their administration. These ceremonies are directed to the proper preparation of the recipient, the increase of his devotion, and the proper dignity of the sacrament.

The Council of Trent declared that there are seven, and only seven, sacraments instituted by Christ: Baptism, Confirmation, Holy Eucharist, Penance, Extreme Unction, Holy Orders and Matrimony. In the case of four of these, Baptism, Holy Eucharist, Penance, Holy Orders, we know when Christ instituted them. Confirmation and Extreme Unction were clearly administered by the Apostles, while Holy Scripture indicates the sacramental character of Matrimony.

The effect of the sacraments is to impart grace *ex opere operato* (by the deed done), that is in virtue of the sacramental act itself if no obstacle is placed in the way. All that is required for a valid sacrament is that the soul be properly disposed to receive it: the effect is not *ex opere operantis*, that is, the activity of the sacrament does not depend on the acts of the recipient or the worthiness of the minister. Each sacrament produces a twofold grace: sanctifying grace and a special actual grace which is called sacramental grace. The special or sacramental grace of each sacrament is suggested by the matter and form of the sacrament itself.

Baptism is the sacrament in which the soul is cleansed from original sin, becomes a child of God and an heir of heaven. The baptized person, who has borne the stain of the sin of Adam, receives spiritual regeneration through the merits of Jesus Christ, admission to the mystical life of the Church, and a right to heaven that no power but his own free will can take from him. Baptism infuses into the soul the theological virtues of faith, hope, and charity and the four cardinal virtues (those on which all other depend): justice, prudence, temperance, and fortitude.

The visible sign of Baptism is the pouring of water accompanied by the words of the priest, "N., I baptize thee in the name of the Father and of the Son and of the Holy Ghost." Water is the primordial material: we read in Genesis that God proceeded in His creation by breathing His spirit on the water. In this sacrament the spirit of God again moves over the water to form the new man.

Christ insisted on the necessity of baptism for salvation; so the church has always baptized infants as well as adult converts. Many who gave their lives for Christ in the early centuries had not come to the baptismal font, but theirs was a baptism of blood. Also, the person who dies in perfect love and contrition is considered to have baptism of desire, that is, he would be baptized if he were aware of the necessity.

Amen, amen, I say to thee, unless a man be born again, he cannot see the kingdom of God.

Nicodemus saith to him: How can a man be born when he is old? Can he enter a second time into his mother's womb and be born again?

Jesus answered: Amen, amen, I say to thee, unless a man be born again of water and the Holy Ghost, he cannot enter into the kingdom of God.[18]

Confirmation is the sacrament in which the soul receives the Holy Ghost to make him a perfect Christian and a soldier of Christ. It is the spiritual coming-of-age, a strengthening of the gifts of Baptism, so that one who is confirmed becomes a militant Christian, ready to bear witness to Christ even to martyrdom. It is the individual Pentecost. The bishop, who is the ordinary minister of Confirmation, places his hand on the head of the recipient and signs his forehead with chrism in the form of the cross. The sign of Christ is now borne on his forehead to testify his willingness to take up the cross. The bishop also gives the recipient a slight blow on the cheek to symbolize the sufferings that the follower of Christ may encounter.

But when the Paraclete cometh, whom I will send you from the Father, the Spirit of truth, who proceedeth from the Father, he shall give testimony of me.[19]

Now, when the apostles, who were in Jerusalem, had heard that Samaria had received the word of God, they sent unto them Peter and John.

Who, when they were come, prayed for them that they might receive the Holy Ghost.

For he was not as yet come upon any of them: but they were only baptized in the name of the Lord Jesus.

Then they laid their hands upon them: and they received the Holy Ghost.[20]

In *Holy Eucharist* is seen most clearly the role of the sacraments as the way of salvation. For this is the sacrament in which is received the Body and Blood of Jesus Christ in the form of bread and wine. It is the Sacrament of Love, the Christian agape in which Christ and his followers are most intimately united.

The Eucharist is the nourishment of the soul, the sustenance of spirit. When it is received at the time of death, it is called Viaticum, the preparation for the journey.

The Catholic Church teaches absolutely that the Eucharist involves an actual transubstantiation: that the bread and wine are actually changed into the Body and Blood of Christ, that only the accidents of bread and wine remain after the act of consecration. At the Lateran Council of 1215 the name of "transubstantiation" was applied to this change of substance without change of accidents. The accidentals of bread and wine—their color, taste, etc.—symbolize the nourishment of spirit through the reception of the sacrament. But in faith the Catholic accepts that the sacrament does more than symbolize, it *is* the Body and Blood of Christ.

In the early years of the Church the congregation communicated under both species, although the sick and imprisoned sometimes received wine only while the persecuted frequently carried the Sacred Bread to their homes in reverence and there communicated under one species. The danger of spilling the Sacred Wine, the fear of plague, the difficulty of caring for a larger quantity of wine, all caused the rule of communion under one species to be established in the Roman rite. This is a disciplinary rule only, having no intrinsic relation to the reception of the sacrament since Christ is believed wholly present, Body and Blood, Soul and Divinity, in every particle and drop of the consecrated substances. In certain non-Roman rites the communion under both species is still practiced.

I am the bread of life.
Your fathers did eat manna in the desert: and are dead.
This is the bread which cometh down from heaven: that if any man eat of it, he may not die.
I am the living bread which came down from heaven.
If any man eat of this bread, he shall live for ever: and the bread that I will give is my flesh, for the life of the world.
The Jews therefore strove among themselves, saying: How can this man give us his flesh to eat?
Then Jesus said to them: Amen, amen, I say unto you: except you eat the flesh of the Son of man and drink his blood, you shall not have life in you.
He that eateth my flesh and drinketh my blood hath everlasting life: and I will raise him up in the last day.
For my flesh is meat indeed: and my blood is drink indeed.
He that eateth my flesh and drinketh my blood abideth in me: and I in him.

As the living Father hath sent me and I live by the Father: so he that eateth me, the same also shall live by me.[21]

Penance is the sacrament in which sins committed after Baptism are forgiven if the penitent is sorry for them, confesses them sincerely and is willing to make satisfaction for them. The outward sign of the sacrament is the statement of the priest: "I absolve thee from thy sins in the name of the Father and of the Son and of the Holy Ghost."

Penance is an inward disposition as well as the name of a sacrament. Unless the sinner be truly contrite—and this includes the intention not to commit the sin again—he cannot be forgiven. The words of absolution are ineffectual to an unrepentant soul; and if the priest has evidence that the spirit of penance is lacking, he withholds absolution.

Except in emergency oral confession is required for forgiveness of sin. Christ gave to his apostles and their successors the power to forgive sins; consequently, the Church has ordained that sin must be confessed to Her priests in order that they be forgiven. Christ gave also the power to retain forgiveness: consequently, the matter confessed is submitted to the judgment of a qualified confessor.

It is required that the penitent confess all mortal sins in confession. He is encouraged as well to include his venial sins. In order that absolution be given it is further required that the priest learn all qualifying conditions or circumstances of the sin. Such confession is a great source of spiritual comfort as well as guidance to the penitent, especially since to the actual confession are frequently added the words of counsel and comfort of the priest.

The sacrament of Penance produces the sacramental effect of forgiving all sins confessed and of remitting the eternal punishment due them. The soul is restored to sanctifying grace if it has fallen. The confession of venial sins increases grace in the soul and strengthens it against future temptation.

At the conclusion of the confession the priest assigns a penance to the penitent which he is to perform in satisfaction for his sins.

I will give to thee the keys of the Kingdom of heaven. And whatsoever thou shalt bind upon earth, it shall be bound also in heaven: and whatsoever thou shalt loose on earth it shall be loosed also in heaven.[22]

Receive ye the Holy Ghost. Whose sins you shall forgive, they are forgiven them: and whose sins you shall retain, they are retained.[23]

THE RITE OF THE SACRAMENT OF PENANCE

The penitent enters the confessional; the priest opens a window behind a curtain or grill.

Penitent: Bless me, Father, for I have sinned.

Priest: The Lord be in thy heart and on thy lips so that thou mayest worthily confess thy sins.

Penitent: It is (how long) since my last confession. I confess that: (here are mentioned the sins, their number and circumstances altering their seriousness). For these and all the sins of my past life, I am heartily sorry, beg pardon of God, and of you, Father.

Priest: (Here the priest gives advice and imposes the penance).

Penitent: Oh my God I am heartily sorry for having offended thee and I detest all my sins because I dread the loss of heaven and the pains of hell. But most of all because they have offended thee, my God, who art all good and deserving of all my love. I firmly resolve with the help of thy grace to confess my sins, do penance and amend my life. Amen.

Priest: (while penitent is saying Act of Contrition) May Almighty God have mercy upon thee, and forgive thee thy sins, and bring thee to life everlasting. Amen. May the Almighty and merciful God grant thee pardon, absolution and remission of thy sins. Amen. May our Lord Jesus Christ absolve thee; and I, by His authority, absolve thee from every bond of excommunication and interdict, inasmuch as in my power lieth and thou standest in need of.

Finally, I absolve thee from thy sins in the name of the Father and of the Son and of the Holy Ghost. Amen.

May the Passion of our Lord Jesus Christ, the merits of the Blessed Virgin Mary and of all the saints, whatsoever thou shalt have done of good and borne of evil, be unto thee for remission of sins, increase of grace, and reward of life everlasting. Amen.

Go in peace.[24]

Extreme Unction, more properly called "the anointing of the sick," is administered to those in danger of death from sickness or accident. Its outward sign is the anointing of the organs of sense, accompanied by the words: "By this holy unction and His most tender mercy, may the Lord pardon thee whatever sin thou hast committed by thy sight, by thy hearing, etc."

Extreme Unction heals the soul by its remission of all sin for which the person is truly contrite if he is no longer able to confess them; it confers sanctifying grace; it prepares the soul for death by destroying fear of death, remitting temporal punishment of sin; it gives the soul fortitude for the temptations of the hour of death.

EXTREME UNCTION : ST. JOHN CHRYSOSTOM

Our parents beget us unto the present life; but priests beget us in the life to come. And the former cannot ward off even the death of the body from their children; but the latter have often saved the sick soul and one about to perish; in some making the punishment lighter, and preventing others entirely from falling; and this not by doctrine and admonition only, but also by the help of their prayers. For not only when they regenerate us, but they have power to forgive sins committed afterward, for he [James] says, "Is any man sick among you? Let him call in the priests of the church and let them pray over him, anointing him with oil in the name of the Lord. And the prayer of faith shall save the sick man. And the Lord shall raise him up; and if he be in sins, they shall be forgiven him" (James 5:14-15).[25]

Holy Orders is the sacrament which gives to its recipients a share in the priesthood of Christ with the power and the grace to discharge their duties validly and worthily. The word "order" indicates the organization it gives to the church. All baptized persons share in the priesthood of believers; but those validly ordained serve as personal representatives of Christ. Through them the worship of man ascends to God; through them the blessings of God descend to man. Christ is the perfect priest, and it is only in His name that priests have power.

The efficacy of the priestly administration of the sacraments does not depend on their dispositions. The priest is an instrument, rather, in Christ's work of imparting Grace to men. If a priest has valid orders, that is, orders handed down in an unbroken line from the apostles, his Masses and sacramental acts are effective *ex opere operato*. The outward sign of the sacrament of orders is, therefore, the imposition of hands by a bishop to indicate the passing on of the apostolic powers.

The principal powers of the priesthood are those given by Christ to his apostles, the first priests: to offer Mass, to forgive sins, to administer the sacraments and to preach the Gospel.

The priests of the early Church were often married, but before many years it was decided that bishops should be unmarried so that they might better serve the interests of the Church. Rules regarding the celibacy of the priesthood became more widespread and by the Lateran Council of 1123 celibacy became the rule of the Roman Rite.

CHRIST THE HIGH PRIEST :
JOHN HENRY CARDINAL NEWMAN

. . . Christ is the only Ruler and Priest in his Church dispensing gifts; and has appointed none to supersede Him, because He is departed only for a brief season. Aaron took the place of Christ, and had a priesthood of his own; but Christ's priests have no priesthood but His. They are merely his shadows and organs, they are His outward signs; and what they do, He does; when they baptize, He is baptizing; when they bless, He is blessing. He is in all the acts of the Church and one of its acts is not more truly His act than another, for all are His. Thus we are, in all times of the Gospel, brought close to His cross.[26]

Matrimony is the sacrament by which the Christian man and woman bind themselves together forever as husband and wife and receive the graces necessary to discharge the duties of their state faithfully. The ministers of this sacrament are the parties to the marriage, while the priest is the witness to the contract. The general Catholic principles on the unity and permanence as well as the purpose of marriage will be outlined in a later section.

The sacramental grace of marriage is the aid to the married persons in conjugal fidelity and reverence for the marriage vows. It strengthens them as well in the proper upbringing of their children within a Christian family.

From the beginning of the creation, God made them male and female.

For this cause, a man shall leave his father and mother and shall cleave to his wife.

And they two shall be in one flesh. Therefore now they are not two, but one flesh.

What therefore God hath joined together, let no man put asunder.[27]

Let women be subject to their husbands, as to the Lord:
Because the husband is the head of the wife, as Christ is the head of the church. He is the saviour of his body.
Therefore as the church is subject to Christ: so also let the wives be to their husbands in all things.
Husbands, love your wives, as Christ also loved the church and delivered himself up for it:
That he might sanctify it, cleansing it by the laver of water in the word of life:
That he might present it to himself, a glorious church, not having spot or wrinkle or any such thing; but that it should be holy and without blemish.
So also ought men to love their wives as their own bodies. He that loveth his wife loveth himself.
For no man ever hated his own flesh, but nourisheth and cherisheth it, as also Christ doth the church:
Because we are members of his body, of his flesh and of his bones. . . .
This is a great sacrament: but I speak in Christ and in the church.[28]

The Sacramentals

Sacramentals are holy objects or actions that the Church has set apart for use as a help toward salvation. They may inspire devotion or their use may serve as an act of homage to God.

The crucifix, holy pictures and statues act upon the senses of man, bringing to his mind thoughts of God or his saints. Of themselves the sacramentals have no power, and only bring grace in virtue of the prayers of the Church.

The use of sacramentals is salutary but is not binding upon the Catholic. Unlike the sacraments instituted by Christ, these devotional objects have been chosen by the Church for their beneficial effects. The blessing given them remains unless they are sold, as this is never permitted.

The Sacrifice of the Church: The Mass

The ultimate prayer and the central act of Catholic worship is the Sacrifice of the Mass. Every day throughout the world the Sacrifice of Christ is renewed in the Mass, the sacrifice of the Cross offered in an unbloody manner. The same Victim is offered, the same High Priest makes the offering. The Mass both represents the Sacrifice of the Cross and offers the same sacrifice. It is the same death of Christ which is offered and represented. The Sacrifice of the Mass is then for Catholics the same as the Sacrifice of the Cross: the Victim is the same, the Priest is the same; only the manner is different.

SACRIFICE : ST. AUGUSTINE

A true sacrifice is every work which brings about that we cleave to God in holy association; is related, that is to say, to that end by which we may be truly blessed . . . whence in so far as man himself, consecrated by God's name and dedicated to God, dies to the world that he may live for God, he is a sacrifice. . . . It follows truly that the whole body of the redeemed, that is the congregation and society of the saints, be offered to God by that great Priest, for He offered himself as an oblation for us, that we might be members of so great a head in the form of a servant. . . . This is the Christian sacrifice that "we, being many, are one body in Christ" (Rom. xii, 5). This the Church celebrates in the Sacrament of the altar, so well known to the faithful, wherein is shown that in that oblation the Church is offered.[29]

THE MASS : COUNCIL OF TRENT

Our Lord and God, although He was about, *by means of His death,* to offer Himself once to God the Father on the altar of the cross, that on it He might operate *an eternal redemption*; yet, because by death His priesthood was not to be extinct, He, at the last supper, the same night on which He was betrayed, that He might, as the nature of man requires, leave to His spouse, the Church, a visible sacrifice, by which the Bloody sacrifice once to be completed on the cross, might be represented; and its memory might continue to the end of the world, and its salutary virtue might be applied to the remission of the sins which we daily commit, declaring Himself constituted *a priest forever according to the order of Melchisedech*, He offered to His Father His body and blood, under the species of bread and wine; and under the symbol of these things, He delivered His body and blood to the Apostles; whom He then appointed priests of the New Testament; and to them and their successors in the priesthood, He gave a command to offer, by these words: Do this for a commemoration of me (Luke 22:19). So the Catholic Church has always understood and taught. And this is indeed that clean oblation, which cannot be defiled by any unworthiness or malice of those that offer it; which the Lord foretold by Malachias was to be offered in every place, to His name, which would be great among the Gentiles. And because in this divine Sacrament, which is performed in the Mass, the same Christ is contained and is immolated in an unbloody manner, who, on the altar of the Cross, offered Himself once in a bloody manner, the holy synod teaches, that this sacrifice is truly propitiatory; and that by it is effected, that if with a sincere heart and a right faith, with fear and reverence, we come, contrite and penitent, unto God, we obtain mercy and *find grace in seasonable aid*. . . . For it is one and the same victim; the same Christ now offering Himself by the ministry of priests, who then offered Himself on the cross; the manner alone of offering being different. By this offering then, the fruits of that bloody offering most plentifully are received; so far is it from truth, that by this oblation, that bloody one is in any way derogated from. Wherefore not merely is it rightly offered, agreeably to the tradition of the Apostles, for the sins, pains, and satisfactions and the other necessities of the faithful who are living, but also for those who have died in Christ, and who are not as yet fully purified.

And although the Church has been at times accustomed to celebrate certain Masses in honour and memory of the Saints, not therefore does she teach that sacrifice is offered up to them, but unto God alone, who crowned them; whence neither does the priest say "I offer sacrifice to thee, Peter, or Paul," but giving thanks to God for their victories, he implores their patronage, that they may vouchsafe to intercede for us in heaven, whose memory we celebrate on earth.[30]

CHRIST THE HIGH PRIEST : ST. CYPRIAN

In the deed of the priest Melchisedech we see a type of the Sacrament of the Lord's sacrifice. For thus it is written in the writings of God: "Melchisedech the king of Salem, bringing forth bread and wine, for he was the priest of the most high God" (Gen. 14:18). That Melchisedech was a type of Christ, the Holy God himself doth testify, in the Psalms, where the first Person of the Holy Trinity, even the Father, is set before us as saying unto the second Person: "Before the day star have I begotten thee. . . . Thou art a priest forever according to the order of Melchisedech" (Ps. 109:3-4). And verily that sameness of order cometh of this sacrifice, and proceedeth from this, that Melchisedech was the priest of the Most High God; that he offered bread and wine; and that he blessed Abraham. . . .

In Genesis, therefore, in order that the priest Melchisedech might in due order pronounce the blessing upon Abraham, there was first offered a typical sacrifice, consisting of bread and wine. This was the offering which Our Lord Jesus Christ completed and fulfilled, when He offered up bread and a cup of wine. This fulfillment by Him who came to fulfill (Matt. 5:17) utterly satisfied the truth of the image which had gone before.[31]

The purpose of the Mass is fourfold: to glorify God, to expiate sin, to express sorrow for wrongdoing and to petition for spiritual and temporal needs.

The Church as Mystical Body offers the Mass. While there is no concelebration with the priest by the laity, all participate actively—"Orate, fratres"—and the priest offers the sacrifice as one speaking for the people.

The prayers of the Mass consist of the Common, the unchanging part of the ritual, and the Proper, which changes with the liturgical season or feast day. In the Proper of the Saints, special commemorations are made on feast days of the saint of the day. It is in the Proper of the season, however, that the great cycle is found which is called the liturgical year. This liturgical year is divided into the Christmas and the Easter cycles. For each of these feasts the cycle is divided into a period of preparation, of celebration and fulfillment.

The liturgy of the Mass developed over the first several centuries, but the essentials remained unchanged. At the first Mass on Holy Thursday, Christ the High Priest took bread, gave thanks to the Father, said the words of Eucharistic Institution, broke the Bread and gave It to the Apostles. So was founded the basic structure of the Mass as practiced in the Church. By the fifth century the Roman rite was well established and there have been no changes in the Canon (the central part of the Mass) since the days of Gregory the Great (540–604). Until the eleventh century Masses were usually Solemn High Masses, sung by a celebrant assisted by a Deacon and Subdeacon with responses sung by the choir. The growth of the population made necessary the celebration of Low Mass (one priest with altar boys reciting the responses) and High Mass (one priest with responding choir). All three forms are used today according to the solemnity of the occasion and the resources of the parish.

As an example of the liturgy the complete text is given here for the Mass which is said on the Feast of the Holy Trinity.

THE MASS ON THE FEAST OF THE HOLY TRINITY

The Prayers at the Foot of the Altar

Priest: In the name of the Father, and of the Son, and of the Holy Ghost. Amen.
Priest: I will go in unto the altar of God.

Response: Unto God, who giveth joy to my youth.

Priest: Judge me, O God, and distinguish my cause against an ungodly nation: O deliver me from the unjust and deceitful man.

Response: For Thou, O God, art my strength: why hast Thou cast me from Thee, and why go I sorrowful while the enemy afflicteth me?

Priest: O send out Thy light and Thy truth: they have led me and brought me unto Thy holy hill, even unto Thy tabernacles.

Response: Then will I go unto the altar of God, unto God, who giveth joy to my youth.

Priest: I will praise thee upon the harp, O God, my God: why art thou cast down, O my soul? and why art thou disquiet within me?

Response: Hope thou in God: for yet will I praise Him, who is the health of my countenance, and my God.

Priest: Glory be to the Father, and to the Son, and to the Holy Ghost.

Response: As it was in the beginning, is now, and ever shall be, world without end. Amen.

Priest: I will go in unto the altar of God.

Response: Unto God, who giveth joy to my youth.

Priest: Our help is in the name of the Lord.

Response: Who hath made heaven and earth.

Priest: I confess to almighty God, to Blessed Mary ever Virgin, to blessed Michael the archangel, to blessed John the Baptist, to the holy apostles Peter and Paul, to all the saints, and to you, brethren, that I have sinned exceedingly in thought, word, and deed; through my fault, through my fault, through my most grievous fault. Therefore I beseech blessed Mary ever Virgin, blessed Michael the archangel, blessed John the Baptist, the holy apostles Peter and Paul, all the saints, and you brethren, to pray to the Lord our God for me.

Response: May almighty God have mercy upon you, forgive you your sins, and bring you to life everlasting.

Priest: Amen.

Response: I confess etc.

Priest: May the almighty and merciful Lord grant us pardon, absolution, and remission of our sins.

Repsonse: Amen.
Priest: Thou wilt turn, O God, and bring us to life.
Response: And Thy people shall rejoice in Thee.
Priest: Show us, O Lord, Thy mercy.
Repsonse: And grant us Thy salvation.
Priest: O Lord, hear my prayer.
Response: And let my cry come unto Thee.
Priest: The Lord be with you.
Response: And with thy spirit.
Priest: Let us pray. Take away from us our iniquities, we beseech Thee, O Lord, that with pure minds we may worthily enter into the holy of holies. Through Christ our Lord. Amen.

We beseech Thee, O Lord, by the merits of Thy saints, whose relics are here, and of all the saints, that Thou wouldst vouchsafe to forgive me all my sins. Amen.

The Introit

Tob. 12:6—Blessed be the Holy Trinity, and undivided unity: we will give glory to Him, because He hath shown His mercy to us. O Lord, our Lord, how wonderful is Thy name in all the earth. Glory be to the Father and to the Son and to the Holy Ghost. As it was in the beginning, is now and ever shall be, world without end. Amen. Blessed be the Holy Trinity, and undivided unity: we will give glory to Him, because He hath shown His mercy to us.

The Kyrie

Priest: Lord, have mercy on us.
Response: Lord, have mercy on us.
Priest: Lord, have mercy.
Response: Christ, have mercy on us.
Priest: Christ, have mercy on us.
Response: Christ, have mercy on us.
Priest: Lord, have mercy on us.
Response: Lord, have mercy on us.
Priest: Lord, have mercy on us.

The Gloria

Priest: Glory to God in the highest. And on earth peace to men of good will. We praise thee. We bless thee. We adore thee. We glorify thee. We give thanks to Thee for Thy great glory. O Lord God, heavenly King, God the Father almighty. O Lord, the only-begotten Son, Jesus Christ. O Lord God, Lamb of God, Son of the Father. Thou who takest away the sins of the world, have mercy upon us. Thou who takest away the sins of the world, receive our prayer. Thou who sittest at the right hand of the Father, have mercy upon us. For Thou only art holy. Thou only art the Lord. Thou only, O Jesus Christ, art most high. With the Holy Ghost, in the glory of the God the Father. Amen.

The Collect

Priest: The Lord be with you.
Response: And with thy spirit.
Priest: Almighty and everlasting God, who hast given to Thy servants grace, in the confession of the true faith to acknowledge the glory of the eternal Trinity, and in the power of Thy majesty to worship the Unity; grant that by steadfastness in the same faith we may evermore be defended from all adversities. Through our Lord.

The Epistle

Rom. 11:33-36—Lesson from the Epistle of blessed Paul the Apostle to the Romans. O the depth of the riches of the wisdom and of the knowledge of God! How incomprehensible are His judgments and how unsearchable His ways! For who hath known the mind of the Lord? Or who hath been His counselor? Or who hath first given to Him, and recompense shall be made him? For of Him, and by Him, and in Him, are all things: to Him be glory for ever. Amen.
Response: Thanks be to God.

The Gradual

Priest: Dan. 3:55-56—Blessed art Thou, O Lord, that beholdest the depths and sittest upon the Cherubim. Blessed art Thou, O Lord, in the firmament of heaven, and worthy of praise for ever. Alleluia, Alleluia. Blessed art Thou, O Lord the God of our Fathers, and worthy to be praised for ever. Alleluia.

The Gospel

Priest: Cleanse my heart and my lips, O almighty God, who didst cleanse the lips of the prophet Isaias with a burning coal: vouchsafe through Thy gracious mercy so to cleanse me that I may worthily proclaim Thy holy Gospel. Through Christ our Lord. Amen.

Priest: May the Lord be in my heart and on my lips, that I may meetly and fitly announce His Gospel.

Priest: The Lord be with you.

Response: And with thy spirit.

Priest: The beginning of the Holy Gospel according to St. Matthew.

Response: Glory be to Thee, O Lord.

Priest: Matt. 28:18-20—At that time Jesus said to His disciples: All power is given to Me in heaven and on earth. Going therefore, teach ye all nations, baptizing them in the name of the Father and of the Son and of the Holy Ghost, teaching them whatsoever I have commanded you; and behold I am with you all days, even to the consummation of the world.

Response: Praise be to Thee, O Christ.

Priest: By the words of the Gospel may our sins be blotted out.

The Creed

(The priest recites the Nicene Creed.)

The Offertory

Priest: The Lord be with you.

Response: And with thy spirit.

Priest: Let us pray.

Priest: Tob. 12:6—Blessed be God the Father, and the only-begotten Son of God, and also the Holy Spirit; because He hath shown His mercy to us.

Receive, O holy Father, almighty and eternal God, this spotless host, which I, Thy unworthy servant, offer unto Thee, my living and true God, for mine own countless sins, offenses, and negligences, and for all here present; as also for all faithful Christians living and dead, that it may avail both for my own and their salvation unto life eternal. Amen.

O God who in a wonderful manner didst create and ennoble human nature, and still more wonderfully hast renewed it; grant that by the mystery of this water and wine, we may be made partakers of His divinity, who vouchsafed to become partaker of our humanity, Jesus Christ Thy Son, our Lord: who liveth and reigneth with Thee in the unity of the Holy Ghost, one God, world without end. Amen.

We offer unto Thee, O Lord, the chalice of salvation, beseeching Thy clemency, that it may ascend in the sight of Thy divine majesty with a sweet savor, for our own salvation and for that of the whole world. Amen.

In the spirit of humility and with a contrite heart receive us, O Lord, and grant that the sacrifice which we offer this day in Thy sight, may be pleasing unto Thee, O Lord God.

Come, O Sanctifier, almighty and eternal God, and bless this sacrifice prepared for Thy holy name.

The Washing of the Hands

Ps. 25:6-12—I will wash my hands among the innocent: and will encompass Thy altar, O Lord.

That I may hear the voice of Thy praise, and tell of all Thy wondrous works.

I have loved, O Lord, the beauty of Thy house and the place where Thy glory dwelleth.

Take not away my soul, O God, with the wicked, nor my life with men of blood.

In whose hands are iniquities; their right hand is filled with gifts.

But as for me, I have walked in my innocence: redeem me and have mercy on me.

My foot hath stood in the direct way: in the churches I will bless thee, O Lord.

Glory be to the Father and to the Son and to the Holy Ghost:

As it was in the beginning, is now, and ever shall be, world without end. Amen.

Receive, O Holy Trinity, this oblation which we make to Thee in remembrance of the Passion, Resurrection and Ascension of our Lord Jesus Christ, and in honor of Blessed Mary ever Virgin, of blessed John the Baptist, the holy apostles Peter and Paul, of the martyrs whose relics are here, and of all the saints that it may avail to their honor and our salvation: and, that they may vouchsafe to intercede for us in heaven, whose memory we now keep on earth. Through the same Christ our Lord. Amen.

The Orate Fratres and Secret Prayers

Priest: Brethren, pray that my sacrifice and yours may be acceptable to God the Father almighty.

Response: May the Lord receive the sacrifice at thy hands, to the praise and glory of His name, to our own benefit, and to that of all His holy Church.

Priest: Amen.

Priest: Sanctify, we beseech thee, O Lord our God, by the invocation of Thy holy name, the victim of this oblation, and by its means make us an eternal oblation to Thee. Through our Lord, Jesus Christ, who liveth and reigneth with thee in the unity of the Holy Ghost, one God, world without end.

Response: Amen.

The Preface to the Canon

Priest: The Lord be with you.

Response: And with thy spirit.

Priest: Lift up your hearts.

Response: We lift them up unto the Lord.

Priest: Let us give thanks to the Lord our God.

Response: It is meet and right.

Priest: It is truly meet and just, right and availing unto salvation, that we should at all times and in all places give thanks unto Thee, O holy Lord, Father almighty and everlasting God. Who with Thine only-begotten Son and the Holy Ghost art one God, one Lord; not in the oneness of a single person, but in the Trinity of one substance. For that which we believe from Thy revelation concerning Thy glory, that same we believe also of Thy Son, and of the Holy Ghost, without difference or separation. So that in confessing the true and everlasting Godhead, we shall adore distinction in persons, oneness in being, and equality in majesty. Which the angels and archangels, the cherubim also and the seraphim do praise, nor cease to cry out as with one voice:

Holy, holy, holy, Lord God of hosts. Heaven and earth are full of Thy glory. Hosanna in the highest.

Blessed is He that cometh in the name of the Lord. Hosanna in the highest.

The Canon of the Mass

Priest: We therefore humbly pray and beseech thee, O most merciful Father, through Jesus Christ thy Son, our Lord, that Thou wouldst vouchsafe to receive and bless these gifts, these offerings, these holy and unblemished sacrifices.

The Reading of the Diptychs: the Living

Which in the first place, we offer up to Thee for Thy holy Catholic Church that it may please Thee to grant her peace, to protect, unite and govern her throughout the world, together with Thy servant John our Pope, N. our Bishop, and all true believers and professors of the Catholic and Apostolic faith.

Be mindful O Lord, of Thy servants and handmaids N. and N. and of all here present, whose faith and devotion are known to Thee, for whom we offer, or who offer up to Thee this sacrifice of praise for themselves and all those dear to them, for the redemption of their souls, the hope of their safety and salvation: who now pay their vows to Thee, the eternal, living and true God.

In communion with, and venerating the memory in the first place of the glorious ever Virgin Mary Mother of our God and Lord Jesus Christ: also of Thy blessed Apostles and Martyrs, Peter and Paul, Andrew, James, John, Thomas, James, Philip, Bartholomew, Matthew, Simon and Thaddeus; Linus, Cletus, Clement, Sixtus, Cornelius; Cyprian, Laurence, Chrysogonus, John and Paul, Cosmas and Damian; and of all Thy saints; by whose merits and prayers grant that we may be defended in all things by the help of Thy protection. Through the same Christ our Lord. Amen.

This oblation, therefore, of our service and that of Thy whole family, we beseech Thee, O Lord, graciously to accept, and to order our days in Thy peace and bid us to be delivered from eternal damnation and numbered among the flock of Thy elect. Through Christ our Lord. Amen.

Which oblation do Thou, O God, vouchsafe in all things to bless, approve, ratify, make worthy and acceptable: that it may become for us the Body and Blood of Thy most beloved Son our Lord Jesus Christ.

The Transubstantiation and Major Elevation

Who, the day before He suffered took bread into His holy and venerable hands, and with His eyes lifted up to heaven, unto Thee, God, His almighty Father, giving thanks to Thee, He blessed, broke and gave it to His disciples, saying: Take and eat ye all of this, FOR THIS IS MY BODY.

In like manner, after He had supped, taking also this excellent chalice into His holy and venerable hands, and giving thanks to Thee, He blessed and gave it to His disciples, saying: Take and drink ye all of this, FOR THIS IS THE CHALICE OF MY BLOOD, OF THE NEW AND ETERNAL TESTAMENT: THE MYSTERY OF FAITH: WHICH SHALL BE SHED FOR YOU AND FOR MANY UNTO THE REMISSION OF SINS.

As often as ye shall do these things, ye shall do them in remembrance of me.

Wherefore, O Lord, we Thy servants, and likewise Thy holy people, calling to mind the blessed Passion of the same Christ Thy Son our Lord, and also His Resurrection from hell and also His glorious Ascension into heaven, offer unto Thy most excellent Majesty, of Thy gifts and presents, a pure Victim, a holy Victim, a spotless Victim, the holy Bread of eternal life, and the Chalice of everlasting salvation.

Upon which vouchsafe to look with a propitious and serene countenance, and to accept them as Thou wert pleased to accept the gifts of Thy just servant Abel, and the sacrifice of our Patriarch Abraham, and that which Thy high priest Melchisedech offered to Thee, a holy sacrifice, a spotless Victim.

We most humbly beseech Thee, almighty God, command these things to be carried up by the hands of Thy holy angel to Thine altar on high, in the sight of Thy divine majesty, that as many of us who, by participation at this altar, shall receive the most sacred Body and Blood of Thy Son may be filled with every heavenly blessing and grace. Through the same Christ our Lord. Amen.

The Reading of the Diptychs: the Dead

Be mindful also, O Lord, of Thy servants and handmaids N. and N. who are gone before us with the sign of faith and repose in the sleep of peace. To these, O Lord, and to all that rest in Christ, grant, we beseech Thee, a place of refreshment, light and peace. Through the same Christ our Lord. Amen.

And to us sinners also, Thy servants, hoping in the multitude of thy mercies, vouchsafe to grant some part and fellowship with Thy holy apostles and martyrs: with John, Stephen, Matthias, Barnabas, Ignatius, Alexander, Marcellinus, Peter, Felicitas, Perpetua, Agatha, Lucy, Agnes, Cecilia, Anastasia, and with all Thy saints, into whose company admit us, we beseech Thee, not considering our merits but pardoning our offenses. Through Christ our Lord.

Through whom, O Lord, Thou dost always create, sanctify, quicken, bless, and bestow upon us all these Thy gifts.

Through Him, and with Him, and in Him, be unto Thee, O God the Father almighty, in the unity of the Holy Ghost, all honor and glory, world without end. Amen.

The Communion of the Mass

Priest: Let us pray.
Priest: Taught by Thy saving precepts and guided by the divine institution, we make bold to say:

Our Father, who art in heaven, hallowed be Thy name; Thy kingdom come; Thy will be done on earth as it is in heaven. Give us this day our daily bread; and forgive us our trespasses, as we forgive those who trespass against us. And lead us not into temptation.

Response: But deliver us from evil.
Priest: Amen.
Priest: Deliver us, we beseech Thee, O Lord, from all evils, past, present, and to come, and by the intercession of the blessed and glorious ever Virgin Mary, Mother of God, together with Thy blessed Apostles Peter and Paul and Andrew, and all the saints, mercifully grant peace in our days: that through the bounteous help of Thy mercy we may be always free from sin and secure from all disturbance. Through the

same Jesus Christ, Thy Son our Lord, who liveth and reigneth with Thee in the unity of the Holy Ghost, one God, world without end.

Response: Amen.

Priest: The peace of the Lord be always with you.

Response: And with thy spirit.

Priest: May this mingling and consecration of the Body and Blood of our Lord Jesus Christ be to us who receive it effectual to life everlasting. Amen.

Priest: Lamb of God, who takest away the sins of the world, have mercy on us.

Lamb of God, who takest away the sins of the world, have mercy on us.

Lamb of God, who takest away the sins of the world, grant us peace.

O Lord Jesus Christ, who saidst to Thy Apostles, Peace I leave with you, My peace I give unto you; look not upon my sins but upon the faith of Thy Church; and vouchsafe to grant her peace and unity according to Thy will; O God who livest and reignest world without end. Amen.

O Lord Jesus Christ, Son of the living God, who according to the will of the Father, through the co-operation of the Holy Ghost, hast by Thy death given life to the world, deliver me by this Thy most Holy Body and Blood from all my transgressions and from all evils; make me always adhere to Thy commandments and never suffer me to be separated from Thee; who with the same God the Father and the Holy Ghost livest and reignest God, for ever and ever. Amen.

Let not the partaking of Thy Body, O Lord Jesus Christ, which I, though unworthy, presume to receive, turn to my judgment and condemnation: but through Thy goodness may it be a safeguard and a healing remedy both of soul and body; who livest and reignest with God the Father in the unity of the Holy Ghost, God, world without end. Amen.

I will take the bread of heaven, and call on the name of the Lord.

Lord, I am not worthy that Thou shouldst enter under my roof; say but the word and my soul shall be healed.

May the Body of our Lord Jesus Christ preserve my soul to life everlasting. Amen.

What shall I render to the Lord for all the things that He hath rendered to me? I will take the chalice of salvation, and I will call upon the name of the Lord.

Praising, I will call upon the Lord, and I shall be saved from my enemies.

May the Blood of our Lord Jesus Christ preserve my soul to life everlasting. Amen.

Grant, O Lord, that what we have taken with our mouth, we may receive with a pure mind; and that from a temporal gift it may become for us an eternal remedy.

May Thy Body, O Lord, which I have received, and Thy Blood which I have drunk, cleave to my inmost parts, and grant that no stain of sin may remain in me, whom these pure and holy sacraments have refreshed. Who livest and reignest world without end. Amen.

Priest: Tob. 12:6—We bless the God of heaven, and before all living we will praise Him; because He has shown His mercy to us.

Priest: The Lord be with you.

Response: And with thy spirit.

Priest: May the reception of this sacrament, O Lord our God, and the confession of the holy and eternal Trinity and of its undivided unity, profit us to the salvation of body and soul. Through our Lord.

Response: Amen.

Priest: The Lord be with you.

Response: And with thy spirit.

Priest: Go, you are dismissed.

Response: Thanks be to God.

Priest: May the homage of my bounden duty be pleasing to Thee, O holy Trinity; and grant that the sacrifice which I, though unworthy, have offered in the sight of Thy majesty may be acceptable to Thee, and through Thy mercy be a propitiation for me and for all those for whom I have offered it. Through Christ our Lord. Amen.

Priest: May almighty God bless you, The Father, the Son and the Holy Ghost.

Response: Amen.

Priest: The Lord be with you.

Response: And with thy spirit.

Priest: The beginning of the holy Gospel according to Saint John.
Response: Glory be to thee, O Lord.
Priest: (The Gospel according to John 1:1-14).
Response: Thanks be to God.[32]

THE CHURCH AS INSTITUTION

The Church as an organism has, as we have indicated, a double aspect: the supernatural unity in Grace of all who share in the Divine Life and the human mode in which this life is expressed on earth. As an institution, the Church is the human form of this inner life of the Mystical Body. It is a legal institution, a social structure which is clearly hierarchical and functionalized. Its visible head is the Pope, successor to Saint Peter as Vicar of Christ. The Pope is not the successor of Christ, but His Vicar; Christ remains the head of the Church through all time, the Pope serving as His visible representative.

The nature of the Church viewed as organization is social; its purpose is to promote the common good of its membership. It is not a society separated from the Communion of Saints, but it is the temporal embodiment or expression of that unity among those living on earth. When, however, the Church has fulfilled its mission on earth, its human mode will cease to exist with the end of time; its inner life will continue unchanged in the Kingdom of God.

THE VISIBILITY OF THE CHURCH : ST. CHROMATUS

"A city seated upon a hill cannot be hid." By this city is meant here the church, concerning which the divine Scripture in many places gives testimony and of which David especially speaks, saying "Glorious things are said of thee, oh city of God" (Ps. 86) and again, "the stream of the river meets the city of God" (Ps. 45) and again "As we have heard, as we have seen, in the city of the Lord of hosts, in the city of our God: God hath founded it for ever" (Ps. 47). As a city, therefore, placed upon a hill, he points out the church, upon the faith of our Lord and Saviour placed in heavenly glory— a church which, visible to the whole world, has been made glorious and he subjoins "Neither do men light a candle and put it under a bushel, but upon a candlestick, that it may shine to all that are in the house" (Matt. 5:15). Wherefore this light of the law and of faith is not to be hidden from us, but is to be always placed in the church, as it were in a candlestick, for the salvation of many, that both we may enjoy the light of its truth and all believers may be enlightened.[33]

UNITY OF THE CHURCH : ST. JOHN CHRYSOSTOM

"For as the body is one and hath many members; and all the members of the body, whereas they are many yet are one body" (1 Cor. 12:12). Seest thou the accurate comprehension? He points out the one and the many. He said not "being many are of that one body," but that "the one body itself is many and those so many members are this one thing." If, therefore, one is many and many are one, where is the difference? And, having clearly demonstrated it from the common judgment of all, he added, so also is Christ. And he might have said, "So also is the church" for this came next in order. For what he means is this "So also is the body of Christ which is the church." For as both body and head are one man, so he declared the church and Christ to be one. Therefore did he put Christ instead of the church, designating in this way His body. "As then" he says "our body is one thing, although it be composed of many, so also in the church we all are one thing. Yea, for though the church be composed of many members, yet these many form one body."[34]

THE CATHOLICITY OF THE CHURCH : CYRIL OF JERUSALEM

It (the one, holy, Catholic church) is called Catholic because it extends over all the world, from one end of the earth to the other, and because it teaches universally and completely all the doctrines which ought to come to men's knowledge, concerning things both visible and invisible, heavenly and earthly; and because it brings into subjection to godliness the whole race of mankind, governors and governed, learned and unlearned, and because it universally treats and heals the whole class of sins, which are committed by soul or body and possesses in itself every form of virtue which is named, both in deeds and words, and in every kind of spiritual gifts.[35]

The Hierarchical Structure of the Church

The structure of the church is hierarchical. At its apex is the Papacy. Taking Simon Bar-Jona to be the first leader of His church on earth, Christ altered his name to Peter—the Rock—to show the firm base on which His Church would stand. Not Peter a man, but Peter the Rock, was promised the lasting wisdom of the Holy Ghost, the fullness of truth till the consummation of the world. No claim of personal sanctity is made for all the men who have occupied Peter's Chair at Rome; the Chair will remain, by Christ's own words, till the end of time.

This had been established in the command to Peter to "feed my sheep," not only those of the first century till the death of Peter, but through all time, there would be a visible shepherd. Peter immediately assumed leadership of the Apostles, and the references to "Peter and others" are many. After the defection of Judas, it was Peter who called for an election to replace him. His leadership throughout his life was never questioned.

While church problems were local, the jurisdiction of the Papacy was not frequently required; but as an instance, in the year 96 A.D. while the Apostle John was still living, it was Pope Clement of Rome who wrote to the Corinthians enjoining them to listen to their ecclesiastical superiors. And by the time of Pope Victor I (189–198) his settlement of the Easter controversy was assumed by the church membership. Especially through the writings of the Fathers of the Church in the early centuries is stressed the continuity of the Papacy from the time of Christ in the See of Peter at Rome.

When the Holy Ghost descended on the Apostles at Pentecost, the Church was born. The Spirit of Truth, to teach all truth, came to abide eternally in the church. Thus it could teach only truth. This is the meaning of infallibility, that the Holy Ghost speaking through the Vicar of Christ, could not teach error. Thus, from Pentecost onward, the Pope has been infallible in matters of faith and morals, made in solemn pronouncement (*ex cathedra*). The definition of this dogma was proclaimed in comparatively recent times in answer to a need felt on the part of the bishops throughout the world, but the infallibility came with the Holy Ghost to remain "till the consummation of the world."

INFALLIBILITY OF THE POPE : VATICAN COUNCIL

Faithfully adhering to the tradition received from the beginning of the Christian faith . . . we teach and define that it is a dogma divinely revealed that the Roman Pontiff, when he speaks *ex cathedra*, that is, when in discharge of the office of pastor and teacher of all Christians, by virtue of his supreme Apostolic authority, he defines a doctrine, regarding faith and morals to be held by the universal church, by the divine assistance promised him in the Blessed Peter, is possessed of that infallibility with which the Divine Redeemer willed that His Church should be endowed for defining doctrine regarding faith and morals; and that, therefore, such definitions of the Roman Pontiffs are irreformable of themselves and not from the consent of the church.[36]

THE PAPACY : POPE LEO I

. . . He has delegated the care of His sheep to shepherds, yet He has not abandoned the guardianship of the flock. And with His overruling and eternal protection we have received the support of the Apostles' aid also, which assistance does not cease from its operation; and the strength of the foundation, on which the whole superstructure is reared, is not troubled by the weight of the temple that rests upon it. For the solidity of that faith which was praised in the chief of the Apostles is perpetuated; and as that remains which Peter believed in Christ, so that remains which Christ instituted in Peter. . . .

The dispensation of truth, therefore, abides and the blessed Peter persevering in the strength of the Rock, which He has received, has not abandoned the helm of the church, which he undertook. For he was ordained before the rest in such a way that from his being called the Rock, from his being pronounced foundation, from his being constituted the Doorkeeper of the kingdom of heaven, from his being set as umpire to judge and loose, whose judgments shall retain their validity in heaven, from all these mystical titles we might know the nature of his association with Christ. And still today he fully and effectually performs what is entrusted to him and carries out every part of his duty and charge in Him and with Him through Whom he has been glorified. And so if anything is done rightly and rightly decreed by us, if anything is won from the mercy of God by our supplications, it is of his work and merits whose power lives and whose authority prevails in his see. For throughout the church Peter daily says "Thou art the Christ, the Son of the living God."[37]

THE HIERARCHY : GREGORY OF NAZIANZEN

Order has settled, even in the churches, that some be sheep and others shepherds; some the ruled, and others the rulers; that this be as it were the head, this the foot, this the hand, this the eye, and this as some other member of the human body, for the perfect harmony and benefit of the whole, as well of the highest as of the lowest. And as, in our bodies, the members are not severed from each other, but the whole is one body composed of different members . . . so it is with us who are the common body of Christ. For we are all one body in Christ, being individual members of Christ and of each other; for one indeed rules and is seated in honor, another is guided and governed, and the employment of both is not the same—unless to rule and be ruled be the same thing

—yet do they both belong one unto one Church, being built up and joined together by the same Spirit.[38]

The Three Functions of the Church:

As an institution, the Church has three functions commissioned to her by Christ: to enlighten the minds of men by teaching, to govern them by law, and to assist in the sanctification of their souls.

The function of the Church in sanctifying its members is fulfilled in all those activities by which She assists in bringing to fulness the life of grace in her members. Chief among these activities is the administration of the Sacraments as outlined above.

The Apostles were likewise commissioned to teach. "Going, therefore, teach ye all nations" (Matt. 28:20). Where a duty is given, the corresponding right is likewise given: thus, The Church has not only the duty but the right to teach and interpret the revelation of Christ. It is this conviction which governs the Catholic attitude toward "individual interpretation." It is for the Church alone to interpret the truth of Christ; the deposit of faith is entrusted to Her for interpretation and for dissemination.

Finally, the Church is a governing power. As in all social structure authority must be invested in a governing agent, so in the realization of the teaching and sanctifying functions of the Church, She must be invested with the authority to demand that She be heeded.

The Church as a complete society requires, therefore, that legislative and punitive powers be vested in those who are entrusted with the care of the community of the Church. These powers are vested in the ecclesiastical hierarchy: in addition to the power of orders held by priests to sanctify the faithful, power of jurisdiction is granted to holders of ecclesiastical orders to govern the faithful for the attainment of their salvation. The power of jurisdiction presupposes the power of orders.

The governance of the Church is twofold: it is legislative and juridical. Legislations of the Church regulate the conduct of the Church under earthly conditions; its laws and decisions are temporal. Among the best-known of these legislations are the Six Commandments of the Church by which She seeks to keep men in vital touch with the inner life of the Church.

The six chief commandments of the Church are these:

1. To assist at Mass on Sundays and holydays of obligation.
2. To fast and abstain on the days appointed.
3. To confess one's sins at least once a year.
4. To receive Holy Communion during the Easter time.
5. To contribute to the support of the Church.
6. To observe the laws of the Church concerning marriage.

The juridical governance of the Church is fulfilled by a system of courts whose function is to decide in matters of moral interpretation and to apply penalties where called for. The ultimate penalty which the Church applies is that of excommunication. A ruling of excommunication declares a person cut off from the life of the Church, from the reception of the sacraments and, as much as possible, from contact with the body of the Church. Likewise, those dying under sentence of excommunication are denied ecclesiastical burial. The causes of excommunication are numerous. A contemporary example will be found in the act of excommunication following upon the imprisonment of Archbishop Stepinac in Yugoslavia.

EXCOMMUNICATION : SACRED CONGREGATION
OF THE COUNCIL

The judicial action by which His Eminence, Aloysius Stepinac, Archbishop of Zagreb, was arbitrarily thrown into prison and unjustly condemned by a civil magistrate of Yugoslavia, has deeply shocked the whole Catholic world and civil society itself.

The church protects her sacred Pastors and safeguards their dignity and liberty, chiefly by three Canons of the Code of Canon Law, threatening with excommunication to be incurred *ipso facto* those persons:

1. Who summon a Bishop, especially their own, before a lay tribunal (2341)
2. Who lay violent hands upon the person of an Archbishop or Bishop (2343)
3. Who directly or indirectly impede the exercise of ecclesiastical jurisdiction or power, and for this purpose have recourse to any lay authority (2334)

All these excommunications are reserved to the Holy See simply or specially according to the case.

Therefore, the Sacred Congregation of the Council which is in charge of the discipline of the Catholic clergy and people, since it is known that the aforementioned crimes had no attending circumstances which diminish their imputability but that they were attended by circumstances which increase it, especially the singular dignity of the Most Excellent Archbishop whom they injured, does by these presents declare that all persons who participated physically or morally in the perpetration of the aforesaid crimes, or who were necessary cooperators in them, incurred the above mentioned excommunications, and will remain affected by them until they obtain absolution from the Holy See.

Given at Rome, the 14th of October, 1946.[39]

The Necessity of the Church for Salvation

The Fourth Lateran Council in 1215 stated that outside the Church there is no salvation. Before the papacy of Pius XII there was considerable misunderstanding of this doctrine. As clarified in the following decree (1949), the doctrine means that it is through the Church that salvation comes and must come. To be saved, one must belong to the Church in some way, either as a member through the sacrament of Baptism, or by a desire, explicit or implicit, to be united to or related to the Church.

Nulla Salus : SUPREME SACRED CONGREGATION OF THE HOLY OFFICE

Now, among those things which the Church has always preached and will never cease to preach is contained also that infallible statement by which we are taught that there is no salvation outside the church.

However, this dogma must be understood in the sense in which the church herself understands it. . . .

Now, in the first place, the Church teaches that in the matter there is question of a most strict command of Jesus Christ. For He explicitly enjoined on His apostles to teach all nations to observe all things whatsoever He had commanded (Matt. 28:19-20).

Now, among the commandments of Christ, that one holds not the least place by which we are commanded to be incorporated by baptism into the Mystical Body of Christ, which is the Church; and to remain united to Christ and to His Vicar, through whom He himself in a visible manner governs the Church on earth.

Therefore, no one will be saved who, knowing the Church to have been divinely established by Christ, nevertheless, refuses to submit to the Church or withholds obedience from the Roman Pontiff, the Vicar of Christ on earth.

Not only did the Saviour command that all nations should enter the Church, but He also decreed the Church to be a means of salvation without which no one can enter the kingdom of eternal glory.

In His infinite mercy God has willed that the effects, necessary for one to be saved, of those helps to salvation which are directed toward man's final end, not by intrinsic necessity, but only by divine institution, can also be obtained in certain circumstances when those helps are used only in desire and longing. Thus we see clearly stated in the Sacred Council of Trent, both in reference to the sacrament of regeneration and in reference to the sacrament of penance.

The same in its own degree must be asserted of the church, in as far as she is the general help to salvation. Therefore, that one may obtain eternal salvation, it is not always required that he be incorporated into the Church actually as a member, but it is necessary that at least he be united to her by desire and longing.

However, this desire need not always be explicit, as it is with catechumens; but when a person is involved in invincible ignorance God accepts also an implicit desire, so called because it is included in that good disposition of soul whereby a person wishes his soul to be conformed to the will of God.[40]

The Mission of the Church

By definition as the Mystical Body and by commandment of Christ, the potential membership of the church is all men. Since Christ repeatedly stated that he came to save *all,* the Church has an obligation to seek out souls, to bring to them the Gospel of salvation. This is done in numerous ways. The example of the faithful is a fruitful source of converts to the Church: it is legendary that no soul comes to heaven alone, that it must have aided in the salvation of others to attain its own sanctity. The martyrs are particularly credited with winning so many that "the blood of martyrs" is said to be "the seed of Christians."

A particular pride of the Catholic Church is her missionaries, the dedicated men and women who sacrifice home, comfort, the society of loved ones, to endure hardship and risk death carrying the message of Christ to all lands and people.

Their meaning lies in the doctrine of the Mystical Body. Christ wished his disciples to go into the world and preach the Gospel to every creature (Mark 16: 15). There were at that time about one hundred and twenty members of His Church, none a distinguished leader in any field. Their human potential was sharply limited, but as members of a body permeated by the Holy Spirit, all things were possible to them. The Church grew in such striking fashion that its very being testified to its origin. Its missionaries were motivated by love of the Christ they preached, love of their fellow-men made in the image of God, appreciation of the gift of faith they had received, an awareness of the need of men for the Church, a personal response to the challenge of Christ to take up His cross and follow Him.

But missionary work is not limited to the frontier or jungle. Each member of the Mystical Body is a potential missionary. The patron saint of the great mission society for training native clergy—Society of St. Peter the Apostle—is a Carmelite nun who had never been outside France and who died at the age of twenty-four promising to "spend heaven doing good upon earth." The charity of Christ compels the support of missionaries and prayers for their success. "The harvest indeed is great but the labourers are few. Pray ye the Lord of the harvest, that he send forth labourers into his harvest" (Matt. 9: 37-38).

CHAPTER SIX

Faith

This is the victory which overcometh the world, our faith.[1]

The experience of "being a Catholic" begins in the commitment of Faith. Until there is understanding of precisely what constitutes faith for the Catholic, what its presuppositions are, and what commitments its entails, there can be no comprehension of the attitudes of the Catholic or of his unique relationship to the Church of which he is a living member in faith. To the word of God—the revelation of God in nature, in Christ, and in the Church—the Catholic response is one integral act. By faith the believer accepts the revelation of God wherever this be found; faith places him in a relationship of openness to the Truth, an attentiveness in trust which opens the vast reaches to which Catholic experience may attain.

THE NECESSITY FOR FAITH : THE SCRIPTURES

And he said to them: Go ye into the whole world and preach the gospel to every creature.

He that believeth and is baptized shall be saved: but he that believeth not shall be condemned.[2]

Then he said to Thomas: Put in thy finger hither and see my hands. And bring hither thy hand and put it into my side. And be not faithless, but believing.

Thomas answered and said to him: My Lord and my God.

Jesus saith to him: Because thou hast seen me, Thomas, thou hast believed: blessed are they that have not seen and have believed.[3]

For I am not ashamed of the gospel. For it is the power of God unto salvation to every one that believeth: to the Jew first and to the Greek.

For the justice of God is revealed therein, from faith unto faith, as it is written: *The just man liveth by faith.*[4]

For this is the charity of God: That we keep his commandments. And his commandments are not heavy.

For whatsoever is born of God overcometh the world. And this is the victory which overcometh the world: Our faith.

Who is he that overcometh the world, but he that believeth that Jesus is the Son of God?[5]

JUSTIFICATION BY FAITH : COUNCIL OF TRENT

And so men are disposed to justice itself (i.e. the state of Grace) when urged and aided by divine Grace and conceiving faith by hearing they are freely moved towards God, believing those things to be true which have been revealed and promised. . . . For when the apostle says that man is justified by faith, and so by God's free gift, the words are to be understood in that sense which the constant consent of the Catholic Church has held and set forth, namely, that we are said to be justified by faith on this account because faith is the beginning of man's salvation, the foundation and root of all justification, without which it is impossible to please God and to join the company of His children.[6]

VISION THE REWARD OF FAITH : ST. AUGUSTINE

On account of those good things which God will only bestow upon the good, and because of those ills which will only be inflicted on the evil; since both will only be made manifest at the last end, God wishes us to believe in Him. For where is the reward of faith, where indeed the very name of faith, if thou now wishest to see, that thou mayest hold it? Thou shouldst not therefore see in order that thou mayest believe, but believe in order that thou mayest see: believe so long as thou dost not see, lest thou blush with shame when thou dost see. Let us therefore believe while the time of faith lasts, until the time of seeing comes. . . . We walk by faith, so long as we believe that which we do not see, but sight will be ours, when we see Him face to face, as He really is.[7]

A right faith is the beginning of a good life, and to this also eternal life is due. Now it is faith to believe that which you do not yet see; and the reward of this faith is to see that which you believe. In the time of faith, therefore, as in a seeding time, let us not weaken. To the very end let us not weaken, but let us persevere until we gather that which we have sown.[8]

In common usage, in philosophical and theological tradition, and in the Scriptures, faith has many shades of meaning. The language is filled with such expressions as "have faith in me," "in all good faith," "keep faith with," "take it on faith." In all such uses there is an element of trust, adherence, and loyalty which motivates an acceptance of some responsibility. Faith must contain an element of response or surrender from the motive of a recognized value in another person which is proposed as guarantee. In this sense, religious faith is a response to God which is based on trust in God. In its broadest sense, religious faith is a total response of the human person to God. This wider concept of faith is readily identified with the interpretation of faith in the Protestant tradition. In the Catholic tradition the relationship of total response is by no means absent; it is, however, a composite relationship of which faith, hope and charity are distinguishable dimensions. For Catholicism, faith is strictly a personal response to God as Revealer, an assent to truth as revealed based on trust in the Revealer. It is formally an intellectual act; but it is rooted in the total person and is ultimately motivated by the human will. To distinguish faith from the total personal relationship is not, for Catholicism, to isolate it.

Faith is, then, for the Catholic a free intellectual assent to propositions revealed by God as true, the assent motivated by the absolute reliability of the Divine witnessing authority. "I believe this is true, not because I see it by reason or direct experience, but because God tells me it is so; and God is an absolutely reliable authority who can neither deceive nor be deceived."

At first this does sound like a rather coldly rational human act; it appears to be a far cry from the total self-surrender which faith was for Protestant reformers. A closer inspection of the act of faith and a realization that it takes place within the total context of a personal life, that it overcomes all of the influences which would pull a person from commitment to God: these should make it evident that faith is a precise point or phase in a tremendous about-face of man and that the submission of the mind to whatever God says can in no way be a bloodless act.

FAITH : ST. PAUL

Now, faith is the substance of things to be hoped for, the evidence of things that appear not.

For by this the ancients obtained a testimony.

By faith we understand that the world was framed by the word of God: that from invisible things visible things might be made. . . .

But without faith it is impossible to please God. For he that cometh to God must believe that he is: and is a rewarder to them that seek Him.[9]

FAITH : THE VATICAN COUNCIL

Man being wholly dependent upon God, as upon His creator and Lord, and created reason being absolutely subject to uncreated truth, we are bound to yield to God, by faith in His revelation, the full obedience of our will and intelligence. And the Catholic Church teaches that this faith, which is the beginning of man's salvation, is a supernatural virtue, whereby, inspired and assisted by the grace of God, we believe that the things He has revealed are true; not because the intrinsic truth of things is plainly perceived by the natural light of reason but because of the authority of God Himself, who reveals them and who can neither deceive nor be deceived.

For faith, as the Apostle testifies, is the substance of things to be hoped for, the evidence of things that appear not.

Nevertheless, in order that the obedience of our faith might be in harmony with reason, God willed that to the interior help of the Holy Spirit, there should be joined exterior proofs of His revelation, to wit, divine facts, and especially miracles and prophecies, which, as they manifestly display the omnipotence and infinite knowledge of God, are most certain proofs of His divine revelation adapted to the intelligence of all men. Wherefore, both Moses and the prophets and most especially Christ our Lord showed forth many and most evident miracles and prophecies.

But though the assent of faith is by no means a blind action of the mind, still no man can assent to the Gospel teaching, as is necessary to obtain salvation, without the illumination and inspiration of the Holy Spirit who gives to all men sweetness in assenting to and believing the truth. Wherefore faith itself, even when it does not work by charity (Gal. 5:6), is in itself a gift of God and the act of faith is a work appertaining to salvation, by which man yields voluntary obedience to God himself, by assenting to and cooperating with His grace, which he is able to resist. Further, all those things are to be believed with divine and Catholic faith which are contained in the Word of God, written or handed down, and which the Church, either by a solemn judgment or by her ordinary and universal teaching (magisterium), proposes for belief as having been divinely revealed.

And since without faith it is impossible to please God and to attain to the fellowship of His children, therefore without faith no one has ever attained justification; nor will anyone obtain eternal life unless he shall have persevered in faith unto the end (Matt. 10:22). And that we may be able to satisfy the obligation of embracing the true faith and of constantly persevering in it, God has instituted the church through His only-begotten Son and has bestowed on it manifest marks of that institution, that it may be recognized by all men as the guardian and teacher of the revealed Word; for to the Catholic Church alone belong all those many and admirable tokens which have been divinely established for the evident credibility of the Christian faith. Nay, more, the Church itself, by reason of its marvellous extension, its eminent holiness and its inexhaustible fruitfulness in every good things, its Catholic unity and its invincible stability, is a great and perpetual motive of credibility and an irrefutable witness of its own divine mission.[10]

THE MOTIVE OF FAITH

Faith, as we have said, is the assent to whatever God reveals as true simply because God has revealed it. It is based, therefore, on the motive of the absolute reliability of the revealing witness: as with all assent on authority, faith is as good as its authority. The act of faith, then, can in no way violate the human intelligence if the authority of God is established. To do this, both the existence of the authority and His trustworthiness must be established along with the fact that He has spoken, or revealed a truth.

The motive of faith is established in what the theologians call the "preambles to faith" or the "motives of credibility." These are statements of fact which demand assent before anything can be accepted as truth on the basis of divine authority. If these statements are accepted intellectually, the intelligence is in possession of all that is *rationally* required for the assent of faith. Since, as we shall see, faith for the Catholic is exercised within the experience of the Church, the motives of credibility contain the justification as well for the Church's role in faith. We may briefly summarize the motives of credibility:

There exists a God who is personal, all-knowing, all good and truthful. Jesus Christ claimed to be God. Jesus Christ proved His Divinity. Jesus Christ founded one Church. Jesus Christ transmitted His teachings to His Church and guaranteed the Church against error. Man has an intellectual duty of believing what Christ's Church teaches as a truth revealed by God.

These are statements which establish both the existence and the authority, as well as the locus, of the Revealer. They are statements which a Catholic does not accept on the authority of his Church alone; if he did, he would be engaged in the fallacy of the "vicious circle." They are rational convictions upon which man establishes the motive for his faith, the authority of God and the authority of His Church.

To establish an authority one must establish two properties of the witness: knowledge—a likelihood that the witness would have knowledge in the field of which he speaks; and veracity—the moral character of the witness must be such that he is unlikely to deceive his listeners. The theologians say a witness must be *sciens* and *verax;* the traditional Act of Faith says that God can neither deceive nor be deceived. In establishing the motives of credibility, therefore, the human mind establishes God as an absolute authority and this becomes the motive for faith: I believe *because* God says so. Once the motives are established, the believer no longer measures the veracity of the authority by the rational plausibility of His statements; rather he measures the plausibility of the statements by the trust he has in the veracity of the revealing witness. Faith is not, therefore, intellectual suicide.

THE DIVINE AUTHORITY : ST. AUGUSTINE

We are guided in a twofold way, by authority and by reason. In time, authority has the prior place; in matter, reason. . . . Thus it follows that to those desiring to learn the great and hidden good it is authority which opens the door. And whoever enters by it and, leaving doubt behind, follows the precepts for a truly good life, and has been made receptive to teaching by them, will at length learn how pre-eminently possessed of reason those things are which he pursued before he saw their reason, and what that reason itself is, which, now that he is made steadfast and equal to his task in the cradle of authority, he now follows and comprehends, and he learns what that intelligence is in which are all things, or rather what He is who is all things, and what beyond and above all things is their prime cause. But to this knowledge few attain in this life; and beyond it even after this life no one can progress.

Now the authority . . . which is true, firm, supreme is that which is called divine. . . . That authority is to be called divine which not only transcends all human capability, but, taking on the actual form of man, shows man to what depth It has condescended for man's sake; and enjoins him not to be bound by the senses, through which those miracles are seen, but to ascend from them to the intellect, at the same time demonstrating how great the things are of which it is here capable, why it does them, and how little store it sets on them. For its office is to teach its power by works, its clemency by humility, and its nature by the commandments it gives. And all these things by the holy rites in which we are initiated, are bestowed on us the more secretly and enduringly. And in these the life of good men is cleansed, not by vague disputations, but by the authority of the holy mysteries.[11]

THE RULE OF FAITH

If faith is the assent to something as true from the motive of divine authority, one may ask how he is to discover precisely what God has revealed. To assent to a truth on faith, one must be certain that God has revealed *this* truth. What we are looking for, then, is the "rule of faith," that guide which will define exactly the content of divine Revelation. For Catholics this rule of faith is found in the Catholic Church.

God, we have seen, reveals Himself in nature, in Christ, and in the Church which is the Body of Christ.

The voice of the Church is for Catholics the teaching and guiding voice of God. Consequently, the immediate and primary locus of encounter with divine Revelation is, for Catholics, in the Church teaching and guiding its members. Commitment to God in faith is commitment to the Church, for the Church is Christ present through His Spirit.

The rationale of this commitment is clear: God is the supreme authority worthy of intellectual trust; Christ *is* God and, therefore, the subject of trust; Christ founded a Church, promised the presence of the Spirit in the Church and assured its infallibility; the episcopate, with the Pope at its head, is the embodiment of the authority transmitted by Christ to His teaching Church. The Church is, therefore, the legitimate and necessary teaching body for redemption, sanctification and doctrine: it is the immediate locus of divine Revelation and it is the rule of faith.

It follows from this that all other sources of religious truth assume a secondary, instrumental role within the immediate reality of the Church. The Scriptures themselves, the inspired word of God, are interpreted through the teaching voice of the Church: Christ's presence in the Church is more immediate than in the Scriptures which, by their very nature, demand an interpreter. Not only Scripture, but tradition, liturgy, all sources of truth, are instrumental to the teaching function of the Church. The Church as Christ present has primacy; it is even the responsibility and the right of the Church to weigh the validity of new revelation, public or private. Mystical experience must conform to the voice of the Church; non-conformity would constitute proof of its own invalidity.

It cannot be sufficiently emphasized that this follows

from all the prior statements concerning Catholic belief
in the foundation and nature of the Church: if the
Church is no more than a fellowship of men, it can by
no means constitute a rule of faith; if, however, it is the
Mystical Body of Christ, it constitutes not only the possible, but the only rule of faith. The divine infallibility
becomes readily and with relentless logic the infallibility
of the Church which is the body of Christ, the God-man,
present among men. Faith in the infallibility of God is
readily transformed into faith based on the infallibility
of God's Church.

The Catholic, then, submits to the Church as the rule
of faith. Whereas others *construct* religious truth from
experience and interpret tradition without appeal to
authority, the Catholic *receives* the body of doctrine.

The place of the Church as the authority on which
doctrines of faith are accepted leads often to the charge
of "mediation" between Christ and the soul. It is supposed that Catholicism has wandered far from the *Deus
et anima* of St. Augustine and that the Church abrogates
to itself as a finite institution the salvific powers which
God alone possesses. The reply can only be found in the
understanding of the nature of the Church as outlined
previously. The Church of the Catholics is neither a
purely man-made institution nor is it divorced from the
reality of Christ: it is the body of Christ present. When
Christ works in the spirit of man, He works through
His Church as through His body. In this sense, there is
"no salvation outside the Church."

One must distinguish two areas, that of worship and
that of intellectual conviction. In the area of worship,
there is no mediation between Christ and the soul:
Christ is directly operative through His Spirit in the
human soul; the soul of man is immediately in relation-

ship with God in prayer. Grace can come from God alone. In doctrine, however, the Church does mediate between Christ and the soul: the Church teaches and commands directly in her own voice, but only insofar as Christ imparts His authority. In a word, the Catholic goes to God by way of, or rather in the Church, but only because the Church is the Body of Christ in Whom alone truth and sanctification may be found. It is for this reason that the Church constitutes the rule of faith, that by which man may know precisely what constitutes the actual revelation of God. "Rome has spoken," Augustine wrote. "The matter is finished."

How does the Church function as the rule of faith? Concretely, the Church determines and defines what is contained in the deposit of faith and in tradition. She does not innovate, does not assert "new" revelations; She makes explicit what is contained in the body of divine revelation, the deposit of faith. Once a truth is explicated from the deposit of faith, however "new" it might appear, it is defined as a revealed truth, an implicit content in the act of faith by which a Catholic adheres to the Church.

The deposit of faith is the body of truth taught by Christ to the apostles and taught and confirmed by the Pentecostal Spirit. The whole of revelation was committed to the Apostles in this way: Catholicism admits of no new revelation after the Apostolic Age. These truths which the Apostles learned were delivered to the whole Church, both verbally and in the written Scriptures. The inspiration of the Scriptures is constituted by the infallible guidance of the divine Spirit in the bringing into form the faith of the Apostolic Church. It is, therefore, these teachings of the Apostles, both written and oral, which constitute the deposit of faith.

The passing on of the deposit of faith by authorized

teachers constitutes the tradition of the Church. Tradition, again, does not innovate truth; it receives and passes
on truth and at most makes explicit the actual, but implicit content of the deposit of faith.

Catholic theologians maintain that as a source of
truth, tradition is superior to Scripture. Scripture is, after
all, incomplete; it not only requires interpretation, but
it required tradition in order that it might be recognized
and established. Further, Scripture is not a textbook; in
a sense, it is a dead word which must be brought to life
in the living voice of tradition.

The Church, therefore, acts as the rule of faith in
making explicit what is contained in the deposit of faith
and in the tradition of the Church. For faith, the living
Church is the only living Voice of God speaking to man.

THE UNITY OF TRADITION : IRENAEUS

The Church, though scattered through the world to the ends
of the earth, has received from the apostles and their disciples
the faith in one God the Father Almighty, who made the
heaven and the earth and the seas and all that in them is; and
in one Christ Jesus, the son of God, who became flesh for
our salvation; and in the Holy Ghost. . . . The Church, having received this preaching and this faith, as before said,
though scattered throughout the whole world, zealously pre-
serves it as one household . . . and unanimously preaches
and teaches the same, and hands it down as by one mouth;
for although there are many different dialects in the world,
the power of the tradition is one and the same. And in no
other manner have either the churches established in Germany
believed and handed down, nor those in Spain, nor among
the Celts, nor in the East, nor in Egypt, nor in Libya, nor
those established in the middle of the world. But as the sun,
God's creature, is one and the same in all the world, so, too,
the preaching of the truth shines everywhere and enlightens
all men who wish to come to the knowledge of the truth. And
neither will he who is very mighty in language among those

who preside over the churches say other than this (for the disciple is not above his Master), nor will he who is weak in word impair the tradition. For as the faith is one and the same, neither he who is very able to speak on it adds thereto, nor does he who is less mighty diminish therefrom.[12]

THE ARTICLES OF FAITH

The Articles of Faith constitute the explicit subject matter of faith, which has in the long tradition of the Church been summarized in the various Creeds. As we have seen, the general subject matter of faith is divine Revelation, whatever God has revealed. A truth may be contained in this revelation explicitly or implicitly so that an implicitly contained truth may not come into public awareness until some later period in the history of the Church. When, however, the Catholic Church defines a dogma *de fide*, when She says that every Catholic must believe a particular truth, She must find that truth explicitly or implicitly contained in Revelation; she must find it in Scripture and tradition, in the teachings of the Fathers or in the records of the beliefs of the universal Church. These beliefs as they become defined constitute articles of faith for members of the Church.

One may distinguish, too, in the faith of the member of the Church, between his implicit faith in *whatever* God reveals and his explicit faith in a particular article of faith as it has become defined by the Church. Faith in its essential nature must embrace in assent the total implicit content of the deposit of faith; reservation here would constitute reservation towards the absolute authority of God.

The explicit articles of faith are expressed in the Creeds of the Church, two of which follow.

THE APOSTLES' CREED

I believe in God the Father Almighty, Maker of heaven and earth, and in Jesus Christ, His only Son, our Lord, Who was conceived by the Holy Ghost, born of the Virgin Mary, suffered under Pontius Pilate, was crucified, died, and was buried: He descended into hell: the third day He rose again from the dead. He ascended into heaven. And sitteth on the right hand of God the Father Almighty: from thence He shall come to judge the quick and the dead.

I believe in the Holy Ghost, the holy Catholic Church: the Communion of saints, the forgiveness of sins: the resurrection of the body, and the life everlasting.[13]

THE NICENE CREED

I believe in one God, the Father almighty, maker of heaven and earth, and of all things visible and invisible. And in one Lord Jesus Christ, the only-begotten Son of God. Born of the Father before all ages. God of God, light of light, true God of true God. Begotten not made; being of one substance with the Father; by whom all things were made. Who for us men, and for our salvation, came down from heaven. AND WAS INCARNATE BY THE HOLY GHOST OF THE VIRGIN MARY: AND WAS MADE MAN. He was crucified also for us, suffered under Pontius Pilate, and was buried. And the third day He rose again according to the Scriptures. And ascended into heaven. He sitteth at the right hand of the Father. And He shall come again with glory to judge both the living and the dead; of whose kingdom there shall be no end. And I believe in the Holy Ghost, the Lord and giver of life: Who proceedeth from the Father and the Son. Who together with the Father and the Son is adored and glorified. Who spake by the Prophets. And in one, holy, catholic and apostolic Church. I confess one baptism for the remission of sins. And I look for the resurrection of the dead. And the life of the world to come. Amen.[14]

THE ACT OF FAITH

Faith is, as we have seen, a free intellectual assent to whatever God reveals as true. At times such an act of assent is depicted as though it were a coolly logical, rational act similar to the deductive process in mathematics. Actually, the act of faith is an existential act, it rises from the concrete context of a man's life and is deeply influenced by his circumstances and his temperament. There is a difference between the assent a child gives to facts about the Civil War and the assent which a man gives to divine Revelation. The differences may be summarized briefly in pointing out the psychological structure of the act of faith as a *free* act and its supernatural structure insofar as it is influenced by divine Grace.

The commitment of faith releases a new dynamism of the human spirit, a thirst for deeper comprehension of the realities which faith reveals. The truths of faith are, by definition, beyond man's comprehension; man can but "see in a glass darkly." Yet the revelation of the Trinity, for example, releases movement of hope and charity towards God as well as a desire of the intelligence to fuller intimacy with the truth of the Trinity, a "face-to-face" encounter which in faith is the promise of the hereafter. Faith incites the understanding to stretch to its limits to penetrate the mysteries which faith indicates; understanding, limited as it is, renews and strengthens faith; and thus the dynamic relation of faith and understanding proceeds towards ultimate fruition.

FAITH IS A GIFT OF GOD :
JOHN HENRY CARDINAL NEWMAN

What thanks ought we to render to Almighty God, that He has made us what we are. It is a matter of grace. There are, to be sure, many cogent arguments to lead one to join the Catholic Church, but they do not force the will. We may know them and not be moved to act on them. We may be convinced without being persuaded. The two things are quite distinct from each other—seeing you ought to believe and believing; reason, if left to herself, will bring you to the conclusion that you have sufficient grounds for belief, but belief is the gift of grace. You are then what you are, not from any excellence or merit of your own, but by the grace of God who has chosen you to believe. You might have been as the barbarians of Africa or the freethinkers of Europe, with grace sufficient to condemn you, because it had not furthered your salvation. You might have had strong inspirations of grace and have resisted them and then additional grace might not have been given to overcome your resistance. God gives not the same measure of grace to all.[15]

FREEDOM AND GRACE IN FAITH : ST. AUGUSTINE

For what is believing but consenting to the truth of what is said? And this consent is certainly voluntary. . . . [But] the very will by which we believe is attributed to a gift of God, because it arises out of the free will which we received at our creation, . . . but also because God acts upon us by the suasion of our perceptions, so that we may will and believe, either externally, . . . or internally where no man can control what shall enter his mind, although it appertains to his own will whether to consent or to dissent. . . . It surely follows that it is God who both works in man the will to believe and in all things prevents us with His mercy. To yield our consent, however, to God's summons is . . . the function of our own will. . . . For the soul cannot receive and possess these gifts . . . except by yielding its consent. And thus whatever it possesses, and whatever it receives, is from God; and yet the act of receiving and possessing belongs, of course, to the receiver and possessor.[16]

FAITH AND THEOLOGY :
JOHN HENRY CARDINAL NEWMAN

. . . why has not the Catholic Church limited her *credenda* to propositions such as those in her Creed, concrete and practical, easy of apprehension, and of a character to win assent? such as "Christ is God"; "This is My Body"; "Baptism gives life to the soul"; "The Saints intercede for us"; "Death, judgment, heaven, hell, the four last things"; "There are seven gifts of the Holy Ghost," "three theological virtues," "seven capital sins," and the like, as they are found in her catechisms. On the contrary, she makes it imperative on every

one, priest and layman, to profess as revealed truth all the
canons of the Councils, and innumerable decisions of Popes,
propositions so various, so notional, that but few can know
them, and fewer can understand them. What sense, for instance, can a child or a peasant, nay, or any ordinary Catholic, put upon the Tridentine Canons, even in translation? . . .
Or again, consider the very anathematism annexed by the
Nicene Council to its Creed, the language of which is so obscure, that even theologians differ about its meaning. It runs
as follows:—"Those who say that once the Son was not, and
before He was begotten He was not, and that He was made
out of that which was not, or who pretend that He was of
other hypostasis or substance, or that the Son of God is
created, mutable, or alterable, the Holy Catholic and Apostolic Church anathematizes." These doctrinal enunciations
are *de fide*; peasants are bound to believe them as well as
controversialists, and to believe them as truly as they believe
that our Lord is God. How then are the Catholic *credenda*
easy and within reach of all men?

I begin my answer to this objection by recurring to what
has already been said concerning the relation of theology with
its notional propositions to religious and devotional assent.
Devotion is excited doubtless by the plain, categorical truths
of revelation, such as the articles of the Creed; on these it
depends; with these it is satisfied. It accepts them one by one;
it is careless about intellectual consistency; it draws from each
of them the spiritual nourishment which it was intended to
supply. Far different, certainly, is the nature and duty of the
intellect. It is ever active, inquisitive, penetrating; it examines
doctrine and doctrine; it compares, contrasts, and forms them
into a science; that science is theology. Now theological science, being thus the exercise of the intellect upon the *credenda*
of revelation, is, though not directly devotional, at once natural, excellent, and necessary. It is natural, because the intellect is one of our highest faculties; excellent, because it is
our duty to use our faculties to the full; necessary, because
unless we apply our intellect to revealed truth rightly, others
will exercise their minds upon it wrongly. Accordingly, the
Catholic intellect makes a survey and a catalogue of the doctrines contained in the *depositum* of revelation, as committed

to the Church's keeping; it locates, adjusts, defines them each, and brings them together into a whole. Moreover, it takes particular aspects or portions of them; it analyzes them, whether into first principles really such, or into hypotheses of an illustrative character. It forms generalizations, and gives names to them. All these deductions are true, if rightly deduced, because they are deduced from what is true; and therefore in one sense they are a portion of the *depositum* of faith or *credenda*, while in another sense they are additions to it: however, additions or not, they have, I readily grant, the characteristic disadvantage of being abstract and notional statements.

Nor is this all: the disavowal of error is far more fruitful in additions than the enforcement of truth. There is another set of deductions, inevitable also, and also part or not part of the revealed *credenda*, according as we please to view them. If a proposition is true, its contradictory is false. If then a man believes that Christ is God, he believes also, and that necessarily, that to say He is not God is false, and that those who so say are in error. Here then again the prospect opens upon us of a countless multitude of propositions, which in their first elements are close upon devotional truth—of groups of propositions, and those groups divergent, independent, ever springing into life with an inexhaustible fecundity, according to the ever-germinating forms of heresy, of which they are the antagonists. These too have their place in theological science.

Such is theology in contrast to religion; and as follows from the circumstances of its formation, though some of its statements easily find equivalents in the language of devotion, the greater number of them are more or less unintelligible to the ordinary Catholic, as law-books to the private citizen. And especially those portions of theology which are the indirect creation, not of orthodox, but of heretical thought, such as the repudiations of error contained in the Canons of Councils, of which specimens have been given above, will ever be foreign, strange, and hard to the pious but controversial mind; for what have good Christians to do, in the ordinary course of things, with the subtle hallucinations of the intellect? This is manifest from the nature of the case; but then the question recurs, why should the refutations of heresy be our objects of faith? if no mind, theological or not, can believe what it cannot understand, in what sense can the Canons of Councils and other ecclesiastical determinations be included in those *credenda* which the Church presents to every Catholic as if apprehensible, and to which every Catholic gives his firm interior assent?

In solving this difficulty I wish it first observed, that, if it is the duty of the Church to act as "the pillar and ground of the Truth," she is manifestly obliged from time to time, and to the end of time, to denounce opinions incompatible with that truth, whenever able and subtle minds in her communion venture to publish such opinions.

But it is not the necessary result of unity of profession, nor is it the fact, that the Church imposes dogmatic statements on the interior assent of those who cannot apprehend them. The difficulty is removed by the dogma of the Church's infallibility, and of the consequent duty of "implicit faith" in her word. The "One Holy Catholic and Apostolic Church" is an article of the Creed, and an article, which, inclusive of her infallibility, all men, high and low, can easily master and accept with a real and operative assent. It stands in the place of all abtruse propositions in a Catholic's mind, for to believe in her word is virtually to believe in them all. Even what he cannot understand, at least he can believe to be true; and he believes it to be true because he believes in the Church.

The *rationale* of this provision for unlearned devotion is as follows:—It stands to reason that all of us, learned and unlearned, are bound to believe the whole revealed doctrine in all its parts and in all that it implies according as portion after portion is brought home to our consciousness as belonging to it; and it also stands to reason, that a doctrine, so deep and so various, as the revealed *depositum* of faith, cannot be brought home to us and made our own all at once. No mind, however large, however penetrating, can directly and fully by one act understand any one truth, however simple. What can be more intelligible than that "Alexander conquered Asia," or that "Veracity is a duty"? but what a multitude of propositions is included under either of these theses! still, if we profess either, we profess all that it includes. Thus, as regards the Catholic Creed, if we really believe that our Lord is God, we believe all that is meant by such a belief; or, else, we are not in earnest, when we profess to believe the proposition. In the act of believing it at all, we forthwith commit ourselves by anticipation to believe truths which at present we do not believe, because they have never come before us; —we limit henceforth the range of our private judgment in prospect by the conditions whatever they are, of that dogma. Thus the Arians said that they believed in our Lord's divinity, but when they were pressed to confess His eternity, they denied it: thereby showing in fact that they never had believed in His divinity at all. In other words, a man who really believes in our Lord's proper divinity, believes *implicitè* in His eternity.

And so, in like manner, of the whole *depositum* of faith, or the revealed word:—If we believe in the revelation, we believe in what is revealed, in all that is revealed, however it may be brought home to us, by reasoning or in any other way. He who believes that Christ is the Truth, and that the Evangelists are truthful, believes all that He has said through them, though he has only read St. Matthew and has not read St. John. He who believes in the *depositum* of Revelation, believes in all the doctrines of the *depositum*; and since he cannot know them all at once, he knows some doctrines, and does not know others; he may know only the Creed, nay, perhaps only the chief portions of the Creed; but whether he knows little or much, he has the intention of believing all that there is to believe whenever and as soon as it is brought home to him, if he believes in Revelation at all. All that he knows now as revealed, and all that he shall know, and all that there is to know, he embraces it all in his intention by one act of faith; otherwise, it is but an accident that he believes this or that, not because it is a revelation. This virtual, interpretative, or prospective belief is called a believing *implicitè;* and it follows from this, that, granting that the Canons of Councils and the other ecclesiastical documents and confessions, to which I have referred, are really involved in the *depositum* or revealed word, every Catholic, in accepting the *depositum*, does *implicitè* accept those dogmatic decisions.

I say, "granting these various propositions are virtually contained in the revealed word," for this is the only question left; and that it is to be answered in the affirmative, is clear at once to the Catholic, from the fact that the Church declares that they really belong to it. To her is committed the care and the interpretation of the revelation. The word of the Church is the word of the revelation. That the Church is the infallible oracle of truth is the fundamental dogma of the Catholic religion; and "I believe what the Church proposes to be believed" is an act of real assent, including all particular assents, notional and real; and, while it is possible for un-learned as well as learned, it is imperative on learned as well as unlearned. And thus it is, that by believing the word of the Church *implicitè*, that is, by believing all that that word does or shall declare itself to contain, every Catholic, according to his intellectual capacity, supplements the shortcomings of his knowledge without blunting his real assent to what is elementary, and takes upon himself from the first the whole truth of revelation, progressing from one apprehension of it to another according to his opportunities of doing so.[17]

THE ACTS OF FAITH, HOPE AND LOVE

O my God, I firmly believe that Thou art one God in three divine Persons, Father, Son and Holy Ghost. I believe that Thy divine Son became man and died for our sins, and that He will come to judge the living and the dead. I believe these and all the truths which the holy Catholic Church teaches, because Thou hast revealed them Who canst neither deceive nor be deceived.

O my God, relying on Thy infinite goodness and promises, I hope to obtain the pardon of my sins, the help of Thy grace, and life everlasting through the merits of Jesus Christ, my Lord and Redeemer.

O my God, I love thee above all things with my whole heart and soul, because Thou art all good and worthy of all love. I love my neighbor as myself for the love of Thee. I forgive all who have injured me and ask pardon of all whom I have injured.[18]

CHAPTER SEVEN

The Transformation in Christ

I live, now not I; but Christ liveth in me.[1]

In faith the total wealth of Catholic experience is opened to a man when through Baptism he is reborn supernaturally and begins to share in the life of grace, the divine life communicated to man. This renascence in faith begins a transformation of the integral person in his values, his life and his destiny.

THE WAY OF SALVATION : SERMON ON THE MOUNT

Enter ye in at the narrow gate: for wide is the gate and broad is the way that leadeth to destruction: and many there are who go in thereat.

How narrow is the gate and strait is the way that leadeth to life: and few there are that find it![2]

Lay not up to yourselves treasures on earth: where the rust and moth consume, and where thieves break through and steal.

But lay up to yourselves treasures in heaven: where neither the rust nor moth doth consume, and where thieves do not break through nor steal.

For where thy treasure is, there is thy heart also.[3]

THE VOCATION:

"A new Commandment I give unto you"

Grace restores to man the power to love fully, and it is in the growth towards perfect love that the ideal of the Christian is found. To love God and other men in God is the vocation whose fulfillment brings nature and supernature to perfect fruition. In this love all other goods find meaning.

God is the creator upon whom all existence depends totally. He is the good from whom all goods must flow gratuitously. He is the Life of all living, the Truth of all truth. So nature itself and man, even if he had not a supernatural vocation, would find their good in God. All nature desires God, all nature praises God. As the natural perfection of man would have been to know, love, serve and glorify God, even more has he been called in his supernatural vocation to a deeper intimacy of love. He is called to love God with the same love, and through the same power and life, by which God loves Himself.

The commandment to love is the highest counsel of Christ's legacy, and, as we shall see, it is in Christ Himself that the supreme example of such love is found. This love is the total personal adherence to the good of another and total dedication to the preservation and increase of this good. Love of the total person is the motive force of human life: it is adherence to another with ultimate willingness to sacrifice the self for another.

The love of God, as Christ exemplified it, is expressed in the fulfillment of the divine image in man. Love is the Incarnation renewed in each person, the will to bring God into being in creation, to realize or express God from love of God. As the being of Christ was the incarnation of the Divine in human nature, so his total being was Love incarnate.

Such love is a commandment; yet it is a gift. Love is both a will and a passion. As will, it is the deliberate adherence to the will and the good of another; it is expressed in all the acts which dispose one for love and the acts of devotion and dedication which express and establish the relation of love. As passion, love is a spontaneous, gratuitous inclination towards another person and his good; as passion, love is a gift. The will and the passion are dynamically related: it is from the passion that the will derives its motivation, and from the will that the passion receives its expression. As will or as passion, love of God is a gift of God Himself, His greatest gift. Man is empowered and called by grace to the freedom and the power to love.

THE COMMANDMENT TO LOVE : ST. JOHN

As the Father hath loved me, I also have loved you. Abide in my love.

If you keep my commandments, you shall abide in my love: as I also have kept my Father's commandments and do abide in his love. . . .

This is my commandment, that you love one another, as I have loved you.

Greater love than this no man hath, that a man lay down his life for his friends.

You are my friends, if you do the things I command you.[4]

CHARITY : ST. PAUL

If I speak with the tongues of men and of angels and have not charity, I am become as sounding brass or a tinkling cymbal.

And if I should have prophecy and should know all mysteries and all knowledge, and if I should have all faith, so that I could remove mountains, and have not charity, I am nothing.

And if I should distribute all my goods to feed the poor, and if I should deliver my body to be burned, and have not charity, it profiteth me nothing.

Charity is patient, is kind: charity envieth not, dealeth not perversely, is not puffed up.

Is not ambitious, seeketh not her own, is not provoked to anger, thinketh no evil:

Rejoiceth not in iniquity, but rejoiceth with the truth:

Beareth all things, believeth all things, hopeth all things, endureth all things.

Charity never falleth away: whether prophecies shall be made void or tongues shall cease or knowledge shall be destroyed.

For we know in part, and we prophesy in part.

But when that which is perfect is come, that which is in part shall be done away.

When I was a child, I spoke as a child. I understood as a child, I thought as a child. But, when I became a man, I put away the things of a child.

We see now through a glass in a dark manner: but then face to face. Now I know in part: but then I shall know even as I am known.

And now there remain faith, hope and charity, these three: but the greatest of these is charity.[5]

CHARITY AND CHRISTIAN LIFE : ST. AUGUSTINE

In order that we might receive that love whereby we should love, we were ourselves loved, while as yet we had it not. . . . For we would not have wherewithal to love Him, unless we received it from Him by His first loving us.[6]

The love of a created thing to be enjoyed without the love of God is not from God. The love of God (however) by which we attain to God, is not, except it be from God the Father through Jesus Christ with the Holy Ghost. Through this love of the Creator, every one can make a good use even of created things.[7]

Love, and do what thou wilt; whether thou hold thy peace, of love hold thy peace; whether thou cry out, of love cry out; whether thou correct, of love correct; whether thou spare, through love do thou spare; let the root of love be within, of this root can nothing spring but what is good.[8]

LOVE OF NEIGHBOR : ST. FRANCIS DE SALES

God, who created man in His own image, commands us to love all men with a love similar to the love which should influence hearts for his divine Majesty. "Thou shalt love thy God" (Matt. 22:37-39).

Why do we love God? St. Bernard replies: "The motive for which we love God is God Himself" (*De Diligendo Deo*); thereby he insinuates that we love God because He is the sovereign and infinite goodness. But why do we love ourselves with a love of charity. Because we are the image and likeness of God. The dignity of resembling the Almighty is common to all men; we should then love them all as ourselves, as living images of the Deity. It is on this title that we belong to God; it is this which forms the strict alliance we have contracted with him and that bond of dependence by which we have become the children of God who assumes the tender name of parent. It is as images of God that we are capable of being united to His divine essence, of enjoying His sovereign goodness and of being happy with the bliss of God himself. It is in this quality that grace is communicated to us, that our soul is closely united with that of God and that according to the expression of St. Leo, we participate in some degree in the divine nature. The acts of love of God and our neighbor both proceed from the same charity. One end of the ladder seen by Jacob touched the heavens and the other rested on the earth, as if to enable the angels to descend and man to ascend. Thus the same love extends to God and our neighbor; by it we are elevated to union with the Divinity and descend to man, to live in union with him; yet by this love we always consider our neighbor as created to the image of God and thereby communicate with the goodness of God, participating in His graces and destined to enjoy His glory.

Whence it follows that to love our neighbor with a love of charity is to love God in man or man in God and consequently, to love God alone for His own sake and creatures for the love of God.

When we behold in our neighbor the lively image of God, should we not love him tenderly and wish him every blessing; not for his own sake, as I suppose that we are yet ignorant of his personal qualities; but for the love of God, who has created him to His own image, and consequently rendered him capable of participating in the effects of his goodness, both in the order of grace and of glory; for the love of that God whose hands have formed his being, to Whom he belongs, by Whom he subsists, in Whom he lives, for Whom he has been created and Whom he particularly resembles.

Therefore, the love of God not only frequently commands love of our neighbor, but produces and diffuses it in the heart, as its image and likeness. For as man is the image of God, so the perfect and holy love of our neighbor is the image of the love which inflames the heart of man for God.[9]

LOVE OF NEIGHBOR : ST. AUGUSTINE

Such is the unity of the body that if one member suffer, all the members suffer (1 Cor. xii, 26). Thou art in trouble to-day, I too; another is in trouble to-morrow, I too; after this generation other descendants, who succeed your descendants, are in trouble, I am in trouble; down to the end of the world, whoever are in trouble in My body, I am in trouble.[10]

As with any ideal, there are degrees of realization of the love of God. These degrees of love, as they have been described by the Christian writers, constitute the stages in the Christian way towards perfection.

The primary division is that between self-interested and altruistic love: the love of God based on the need for the favor of God for self-fulfillment, on the one hand, and the love of God because of God's intrinsic goodness, on the other. These degrees of love are reflected in the Catholic distinction between imperfect contrition (sorrow for sin because it brings damnation) and perfect contrition (sorrow for sin because it offends a good God). The first is love based on a healthy fear of the consequences of violation of the will of God; the other is the love beyond self-concern, the response of pure charity (agape). The dynamic of love is the transformation of eros (self-interested love) into agape, the other-directed love. This development is not a continuous one, the difference is qualitative: agape is born with the reflection of the divine image in man.

A further distinction is made among degrees of love

which correspond to the three stages of the spiritual life which shall be described in a later section: *amor concupiscentiae,* the love of self-interest; *amor amicitiæ,* the love of friendship and of sharing; *amor benevolentiae,* the love of union and identity. The three are dynamically related one to the other: the attainment of the love of union cannot exclude the continuing presence of the motives of the first degree of love. In the highest moment of mystical union with God, fear of God is present, but in a transfigured manner.

The higher degrees of love are the ideal toward which man is called; they constitute the perfection of his being. All will not achieve the ultimate degree of love, perhaps: "Many are called, but few are chosen." The Catholic Church wisely decrees that imperfect contrition (*amor concupiscentiae*) expressed within the authority of her confessional is sufficient for salvation. She does not cease, however, to hold up to all Catholics the example of all who have most perfectly approached the example of Christ in perfect love.

THE EXEMPLAR:

"Take up your cross, and come follow me"

The Christian response to the commandment of love is a response to the call of Christ to follow Him; it is realized in the imitation of Christ. The perfection of man can only be found in the imitation of the most perfect man, the God-Man. Christ is the head of regenerated humanity: He is not only the meritorious cause of human perfection, but the supreme exemplary cause.

God incarnate, at once divine and human in nature, Christ realized perfectly the union of love between God and man. And as God became incarnate in Christ, the commandment to love summons men to incarnate God in each human life: to unite the finite will to the divine, to become an instrument of divine expression, to become other "sons of God." Christ is the model; to become "other Christs," to "put on Christ Jesus," the ideal.

The Christian life becomes a growth, then, in the Christlikeness of the person. It is the continuing and deepening response to the call of Christ, the "restoration of all things in Christ." In Christ it finds the perfect model, one who can be imitated, one who attracts and one who has power to bring about that which He commands. The virtues of Christ are the measure of a man's perfection, the sacrifice of Christ the measure of man's love. The measure of Christ sets a new scale of values which is a scandal to the world: a man's worth is measured only by the extent to which he is willing to "leave all things" and "Come, follow Me."

THE IMITATION OF CHRIST : ST. AUGUSTINE

How are we to imitate the ways of Christ? Are we to imitate Him in the glorious power which He had as God in the flesh? . . . Is it to govern with Him heaven and earth and all that is therein, that He calls men? . . . He does not say that to thee. Thou shalt not be my disciple unless thou hast walked upon the sea (Matt. xiv, 25), or raised one who was four days dead (John xi, 38 *sqq.*), or opened the eyes of one blind from birth (*id.* ix, 1 *sqq.*). Nor this either. . . . What then doth He say? "Learn of me, because I am meek and humble of heart" (Matt. xi, 29). That which He became for thy sake is what thou shouldst attend to in Him, and that thou mayest imitate Him. . . . To what doth He exhort thee? To imitate Him in those works which He could not have done had He not been made man. For how could He endure sufferings, unless He had become man? How could He otherwise have died, been crucified, been humbled? Thus then do thou, when thou sufferest the troubles of this world. . . . Be strong, be long-suffering, thou shalt abide under the protection of the Most High.[11]

Love is, for man, impossible without sacrifice, if only because of the tendencies of fallen nature which remain. To maintain spiritual integrity is often a struggle and must entail the willingness and the actuality of sacrifice. The Cross of Christ, the symbol of redemption for the Christian, is, too, the call to loving sacrifice. Sacrifice which might be bitter is transfigured in the Cross, becoming an immolation which is a supreme act of love. In sacrifice the old man is stripped away; in the Cross the Christian is identified with the sacrifice and the love of the New Man who is Christ.

THE CROSS OF CHRIST : ST. AUGUSTINE

"And they that are Jesus Christ's have crucified their flesh, with the passions and concupiscences" (Gal. v, 24). On this cross, indeed, throughout the whole of this life which is spent in the midst of trials and temptations, the Christian must continually hang. For there is no time in this life to draw out the nails, of which it is said in the psalm, "Pierce thou my flesh with the nails of thy fear" (Ps. cxviii, 120); the flesh is the carnal concupiscences; the nails are the commandments of justice; with the latter the fear of the Lord pierces the former, and it crucifies us as an acceptable sacrifice to Him. Therefore in like manner the Apostle says, "I beseech you therefore, brethren, by the mercy of God, that you present your bodies a living sacrifice, holy, pleasing unto God" (Rom. xii, 1). This cross, therefore, in which the servant of God not only is not confounded but even glories in the words, "God forbid that I should glory, save in the cross of our Lord Jesus Christ: by whom the world is crucified to me, and I to the world" (Gal. vi, 14), this cross, I say, is not merely for forty days but for the whole of this life. . . . In this wise ever live, O Christian: if thou does not wish thy steps to sink in the slime of the earth, descend not from this cross.[12]

THE CROSS OF CHRIST THE MEANING OF THE WORLD :
JOHN HENRY CARDINAL NEWMAN

A great number of men live and die without reflecting at all upon the state of things in which they find themselves. They take things as they come, and follow their inclinations as far as they have the opportunity. They are guided mainly by pleasure and pain, not by reason, principle or conscience; and they do not attempt to interpret the world to determine what it means, or to reduce what they feel and see to system. But when persons, either from thoughtfulness of mind, or from intellectual activity, begin to contemplate the visible state of things into which they are born, then forthwith they find it a maze and a perplexity. It is a riddle which they cannot solve. It seems full of contradictions and without a drift. Why it is, and what it is to issue on, and why it is what it is, and how we come to be introduced into it, and what is our destiny, are all mysteries.

In this difficulty, some have formed one philosophy of life and some another. Men have thought they had found the key, by means of which they could read what is so obscure. Ten thousand things come before us one after another in the course of life, and what are we to think of them? what colour are we to give them? Are we to look at things in a gay and mirthful way? Are we to make light of life altogether, or to treat the whole subject seriously? Are we to make greatest things of little consequence, or least things of great consequence? Are we to keep in mind what is past and gone, or are we to look to the future, or are we to be absorbed in what is present? How are we to look at things? This is the question which all persons of observation ask themselves and answer each in his own way. They wish to think by rule; by something within them, which may harmonize and adjust what is without them. Such is the need felt by reflective minds. Now, let us ask, what *is* the real key, what is the Christian interpretation of this world? What is given us by revelation to estimate and measure this world by? The event of this season [Season of Lent]—the Crucifixion of the Son of God.

It is the death of the eternal word of God made flesh, which is our great lesson how to think and how to speak of this world. His Cross has put its due value upon everything which we see, upon all fortunes, all advantages, all ranks, all dignities, all pleasures; upon the lust of the flesh, and the lust of the eyes, and the pride of life. It has set a price on the excitements, the rivalries, the hopes, the fears, the desires, the efforts, the triumphs of mortal man. It has given a meaning to the various, shifting course, the trials, temptations, the suffering of this earthly state. It has brought together and made consistent all that seemed discordant and aimless. It has taught us how to live, how to use the world, what to expect, what to desire, what to hope. It is the tone into which all the strains of this world's music are ultimately to be resolved.

Look around and see what the world presents of high and low. Go to the court of princes. See the treasure and skill of all nations brought to honour a child of man. Observe the prostration of the many before the few. Consider the form and ceremonial, the pomp, the state, the circumstance and the vainglory. Do you wish to know the worth of it all? Look at the Cross of Christ.

Go to the political world and see nation jealous of nation, trade rival trade, armies and fleets matched against each other. Survey the ranks of the community, its parties and their contests, the strivings of the ambitious, the intrigue of the crafty. What is the end of all this turmoil? The grave. What is the measure? The Cross.

Go, again, to the world of intellect and science; consider the wonderful discoveries which the human mind is making; the variety of arts to which its discoveries give rise, the all but miracles by which it shows its power; and next, the pride and confidence of reason, and the absolute devotion of thought to transitory objects, which is the consequence. Would you form a right judgment of all this; look at the Cross.

Again, look at misery, look at poverty and destitution, look at oppression and captivity; go where food is scanty and lodging unhealthy. Consider pain and suffering, diseases long or violent, all that is frightful and revolting. Would you know how to rate all these? gaze upon the Cross.

Thus in the Cross and Him who hung upon it, all things meet; all things subserve it, all things need it, it is their centre and interpretation. For He was lifted up on it, that He might draw all men and all things up to Him. . . . It may be granted, then, that the doctrine of the Cross is not on the surface of the world. The surface of things is bright only and the Cross is sorrowful. It is a hidden doctrine; it lies under a veil; it at first sight startles us and we are tempted to revolt from it. Like St. Peter we cry out, "Be it far from thee, Lord; this shall not be unto thee" (Matt. 16:22). And yet it is a true devotion; for truth is not on the surface of things, but in the depths.

And as the doctrine of the Cross, though it be the true interpretation of this world, is not prominently manifested in it, upon its surface, but is concealed; so again, when received into the faithful heart, there it abides as a living principle, but deep and hidden from observation. Religious men, in the words of Holy Scripture, live by the faith (Gal. 2:20), but they do not tell this to all men; they leave others to find it out as they may. Our Lord's own command to His disciples was, that when they fast, they should "anoint the head and wash the face" (Matt. 6:17); thus they are bound not to make a display but ever to be content to look outwardly different from what they are inwardly. They are to carry a cheerful countenance with them, and to control and regulate their feelings that those feelings, by not being expended on the surface, may retire deep into their hearts and there live. And thus "Jesus Christ and He crucified" is, as the Apostle tells us, "a hidden wisdom"; hidden in the world, which seems at first sight to speak a far other doctrine—and hidden in the faithful soul, which to persons at a distance, or to chance beholders, seem to be living but an ordinary life, while really it is in secret holding communion with Him who was "manifested in the flesh," "crucified through weakness," "justified in the Spirit," and "received up into glory."

This being the case, the great and awful doctrine of the Cross of Christ, which we now commemorate, may fitly be called the *heart* of religion. The sacred doctrine of Christ's atoning sacrifice is the vital principle on which the Christian lives, and without which Christianity is not. Without it no other doctrine is held profitably; to believe in Christ's divinity or in His manhood, or in the Holy Trinity, or in a judgment to come, or in the resurrection of the dead, is an untrue belief, not Christian faith, unless we receive also the doctrine of Christian sacrifice. On the other hand it presupposes the reception of other high truths of the gospel besides; it involves the belief in Christ's true divinity, in His true incarnation and in man's sinful state by nature; and it prepares the way to belief in the sacred Eucharistic feast, in which He who was once crucified is ever given to our souls and bodies, verily, in His Body and in His Blood.

It must not be supposed, because the doctrine of the Cross makes us sad, that the Gospel is a sad religion. The Psalmist says "they that sow in tears shall reap in joy" and Our Lord says "Blessed are they that mourn." Let no one go away with the impression that the Gospel takes a gloomy view of the world and of life. It hinders us indeed from taking a superficial view and finding a transient joy in what we see, but it forbids immediate enjoyment only to grant enjoyment in truth and fulness after. It forbids us to *begin* with enjoyment. It only says "If you begin with pleasure, you will end with pain." It bids us begin with the Cross of Christ, and in that Cross we shall at first find sorrow but in a while peace and comfort will rise out of that sorrow. The Cross will lead us to mourning, repentance, humiliation, prayer and fasting; we shall sorrow for our sins, we shall sorrow with Christ's sufferings; but all this sorrow will only issue, nay, will be undergone in a happiness far greater than the enjoyment which the world gives . . .

And thus, all that is bright and beautiful, even on the surface of the world, though it has no substance, it may not suitably be enjoyed for its own sake, yet is a figure and promise of that true joy which issues out of the Atonement. It is a promise beforehand of what is to be; it is a shadow, raising hope because the substance is to follow, but not to be rashly taken instead of the substance. And it is God's usual mode of dealing with us, in mercy to send the shadow before the substance, that we may take comfort in what is to be, before it comes.

And so, too, as regards the world with all its enjoyment yet disappointment. Let us not trust it, let us not give our hearts to it; let us not begin with it. Let us begin with faith;

let us begin with Christ; let us begin with His cross and the humiliation to which it leads. Let us first be drawn to Him who is lifted up, that so He may, with Himself, freely give us all things. Let us "seek first the Kingdom of God and His righteousness" and then all those things of the world will be added to us. They alone are truly able to enjoy this world, who begin with the world unseen. They alone are truly able to enjoy this world who have first abstained from it. They alone can truly feast, who have first fasted; they alone are able to use the world who have learned not to abuse it; they alone inherit it, who take it as a shadow of the world to come and who for that world to come relinquish it.[13]

THE INTERIOR LIFE

To "put on Christ" in attitudes, intention, and modes of action is the aim of the interior life. In spatial metaphors, it consists in a *conversion,* a wheeling about in re-collection of the spirit towards the innermost source of its life; a *commitment,* the acceptance of God in faith, hope, and love; and a *metanoia,* "putting on the mind of Christ," the identification with the divine plan in which faith aspires to vision, hope to fulfillment, love towards complete assimilation.

HUMILITY : ST. PAUL

For let this mind be in you, which was also in Christ Jesus:
Who being in the form of God, thought it not robbery to be equal with God:
But emptied himself, taking the form of a servant, being made in the likeness of men, and in habit found as a man.
He humbled himself, becoming obedient unto death, even to the death of the cross.[14]

Ascetical theologians have described in great detail the stages of the interior life. One of the most traditional is the distinction of three ways: the purgative, the illuminative, and the unitive. These are stages in the deepening relation to God which, broadly considered, correspond to the three degrees of love previously mentioned: the purgative way aims at evoking the fullness of the love of concupiscence; the illuminative way calls forth the affections of the love of friendship; the unitive way is the call to the highest challenge of the love of benevolence.

In the purgative way, the Christian labors to purify the soul and to rekindle the primary awareness of radical dependence, fear, and trust. Here the aim is a transformation of the person such that he will conform to what Ignatius of Loyola called The Principle and Foundation of the Christian life, the radical dependence and Christian indifference necessary for a single-mindedness in pursuit of perfection. The minimum fruits of this way are the conditions for salvation according to Catholic belief. Consequently, during this stage the person is attentive to the facts of creation, creatureliness, sin and damnation, temptation against the primary responsibilities towards God. He concentrates on prayer to achieve the power to atone for sinfulness, penance in his struggle against sinfulness, and mortification as a safeguard against future sin and temptation. It is often said that the test of the purgative way is the ability to make a "good confession." It must be indicated, however, that the principles of the purgative way contain implicitly the possibilities of the furthest reaches in the progress of the soul.

PRINCIPLE AND FOUNDATION : ST. IGNATIUS LOYOLA

Man was created for a certain end. This end is to praise, to reverence, and to serve the Lord God, and by this means to arrive at eternal salvation.

All the other beings and objects which surround us on the earth were created for the benefit of man, and to be useful to him, as means to his final end; hence his obligation to use, or abstain from the use of, these creatures according as they bring him nearer that end or tend to separate him from it.

Hence we must above all endeavor to establish in ourselves a complete indifference toward all created things, though the use of them may not be otherwise forbidden; not giving, as far as depends on us, any preference to health over sickness, riches over poverty, honour over humiliation, a long life over a short. But we must desire and choose definitively in every thing what will lead us to the end of our creation.[15]

RULES FOR THE DISCERNMENT OF SPIRITS : ST. IGNATIUS LOYOLA

The soul is moved by diverse spirits, which it is important to discern, in order to follow the good and repel the bad. . . .

Let us suppose a soul that falls easily into mortal sin and goes from fall to fall; to plunge deeper into crime and fill up the measure of iniquity, the infernal enemy ordinarily employs the charms of voluptuousness and all the baits of the senses, which he incessantly places before the eyes. On the contrary, to turn him from sin, the good spirit never ceases to prick his conscience with the sting of remorse and the counsels of reason.

But if this soul should set itself to use every effort in order to purify itself from its sins and to advance every day more and more in the service of God, the evil spirit, to stop and embarrass it, throws in its way every kind of scruple, disquiet, specious pretext, and subject of trouble and agitation. The good spirit, on the other hand, as soon as we begin to amend, encourages, fortifies, consoles, softens even to tears, enlightens the understanding, spreads peace in the heart, smooths all difficulties and obstacles, so that every day more freely, more joyously, and more rapidly, we advance in virtue by the practice of good works.

True spiritual consolation may be known by the following signs. A certain interior impulse raises the soul toward the Creator, makes it love Him with an ardent love and no longer permits it to love any creature but for Him; sometimes gentle tears cause this love, tears which flow from repentance of past faults, or the sight of the sorrows of Jesus Christ, or any other motive that enlightened religion inspires; finally, all that increases faith, hope, charity, all that fills the soul with holy joy, makes it more attached to meditation on heavenly things and more careful of salvation; all that leads it to find repose and peace in the Lord—all this is true and spiritual consolation.

On the contrary, all that darkens the soul, that troubles it, that inclines it to inferior and terrestrial objects, that disquiets it and agitates it, that would lead it to despair of salvation, that weakens hope and banishes charity, that renders the soul sad, tepid, languid, distrustful even of the clemency of its Creator and its Redeemer—this is what may be called spiritual desolation. *Desolation* and *consolation* are two opposite terms; so the thoughts and affections arising from each are diametrically opposed.

During times of desolation, the bad spirit makes us feel his influence. By following his inspirations we cannot arrive at any good or useful decision; we must, therefore, beware at such times of reconsidering or making any innovation whatsoever in what relates to our resolutions or choice of a state in life; but we must persevere in what we have decided on in the day or hour of consolation and consequently under the influence of the good spirit.

And yet, without changing anything that was before laid down and defined, man, when a prey to desolation, would do well to employ means, or to multiply them, in order to dissipate it,—such as prayer offered with more importunity, examination, awaking and arousing the conscience, some penance as a punishment for faults known or unknown.

Under the pressure of desolation the following are the thoughts which should sustain us; Divine grace remains to us although it may have ceased to be sensible; although the first order of our charity is no longer felt, we still have all that is requisite for doing good and working out our salvation. What, then, does the Lord expect of us? He would see, whether if furnished with the ordinary assistance of nature and grace, we can resist the enemy. Oh, without doubt we can.

The unquiet spirit, which agitates and torments us, has a direct antagonist and adversary in the spirit of patience. To preserve patience and calm will, then, be of wonderful assistance to us against it. Finally, we must call hope to our aid; and if we know how to employ the above means against desolation, we may say to ourselves, consolation will not be long in coming.

Desolation most frequently arises from one or another of three causes: (1) Perhaps we have deserved from want of diligence and fervour in our spiritual exercises to be deprived of Divine consolation. (2) Perhaps God is trying us, and He wishes to see what we are and how we employ ourselves for His service and glory, even though He does not bestow on us every day the rewards of His spirit in gifts and sensible graces. (3) Or perhaps it is a lesson He is giving us: He wishes to prove to us by experience that to procure fervour of devotion, ardent love, abundant tears, or to preserve ourselves in these spiritual joys, is beyond our natural strength and is a gratuitous gift of His Divine bounty. All this cannot be claimed by us as our own right, unless we are possessed by a pride and self-love very dangerous to our salvation.

When consolation abounds in the heart, we must consider the conduct to be observed in time of trial; and to sustain the shock, we must provide in good time a supply of courage and vigorous resolution.

We must also humble ourselves, deprecate ourselves, foresee as much as possible how weak, how cowardly, we shall be under the stroke of desolation if Divine grace do not come quickly to our aid; while the tempted man must, on the contrary, persuade himself that with the aid of God, he is all-powerful and that he will easily overcome all his enemies, provided he establish his confidence in the Divine strength and is courageous.

Satan, with his weak but obstinate character, may be compared when he attacks us, to a woman daring to contend with her husband. Let her husband oppose her firmly, she soon lays aside her warlike mood, and quickly leaves the field to him; on the contrary, let her see in him any timidity or inclination to fly or give way, she becomes insolent, cruel as a fury. So when Satan sees the soldier of Jesus Christ, the heart imperturbable, his head erect, repulsing every attack without floundering, he immediately loses courage; but if he perceive him trembling at the first shock and ready to ask quarter, he immediately attacks him with a rage, a fury, a ferocity which is unexampled among wild beasts enraged against their prey; obstinate in his infernal malice, he only seeks and breathes our ruin.

We may also compare him in some of his artifices to a libertine seeking to lead astray a young girl, the child of good parents, or the wife of an honest man. What he recommends to the object of his passion is, above all things, secrecy;— secrecy as to his proposals; secrecy as to his interviews; if he does not obtain this secrecy, if the daughter does not observe it to her parents, the wife toward the husband, all is lost for him; his projects are ruined. So the grand artifice of the great calumniator is to induce the soul he wishes to gain to keep secret his suggestions; and when they are discovered to a confessor or an enlightened director, his rage and torment are at their height, because his snare is discovered and his efforts rendered useless.

Finally, in his tactics our enemy imitates a general of an army besieging a citadel who first studies the ground and the state of the fortifications; so as to concentrate his attack on the weakest part. To make a like study, our enemy makes as it were the round of our soul; he examines which are the theological and moral virtues that serve as its ramparts, or in which it is wanting and against the point we have left without guard and defence, he turns all his batteries and says "It is here I will try the assault."[16]

The illuminative way finds the soul moving towards an awareness of the meaning of Christ, His call, and His challenge. It aims at making Christ the center of one's life in a spirit of charity which goes beyond self-interest. Here begins what is called the affective life in Christ, the deepening of interest in and attachment to Christ, and the growth in the theological and moral virtues which are essential to the imitation of Christ. The activities of the soul at this stage consist in more affective types of prayer, concentrating more on the life of Christ, and a deepening of the sacramental and liturgical life.

The spirit moves with the mysteries of Christ toward the ultimate challenge embodied in the call of Christ: the willingness to give oneself over entirely into the hands of God.

The unitive way opens before the soul which accepts the total implications of the call of Christ. After purification and affective practices, the spirit moves towards ultimate union with God and total transfiguration. The prayer becomes more contemplative, the soul is open to mystical experience. The Catholic Church recognizes such mystical experiences and higher modes of prayer as an integral part of Her experience and as the divine gesture towards the loving soul. They are free gifts of God which the Church encourages her members to welcome as such and for which she encourages preparation. It is important to emphasize at this point that Catholic mysticism is activity *within* the Church. However alone the mystic be with God, neither the mystic nor the Church will accept that such experiences are "outside" the Church and her discipline. Joan of Arc must submit her visions to the Church. The stubbornness of refusal on the part of a mystic in submitting to the Church would be clear indication that the experience does not come from God. So, too, in the furthest reaches of the spirit the basic disciplines of the purgative and the illuminative way are present. The mystic or contemplative is ever subject to the discipline and the responsibilities of the full Christian life of action.

PRAYER FOR THE THREE DEGREES OF HUMILITY :
ST. IGNATIUS LOYOLA

This exercise is called, in the first place, the three Degrees, because it contains the three degrees of Christian perfection which consist (1) in the firm resolution to avoid mortal sin, even at the risk of life; (2) in the firm resolution to avoid deliberate venial sin at any price; and (3) in the voluntary choice of whatever is most perfect for the service of God; in the second place it is so called because these three degrees suppose the abasement and, as it were, the annihilation of the old man in us.

First Point: The first degree of humility consists in perfect submission to the law of God, so that we should be ready to refuse the empire of the whole world, or even to sacrifice our lives, rather than willingly transgress any precept which obliges us under pain of mortal sin.

This first degree is absolutely necessary for eternal salvation, and is, as it were, the fruit of our exercises of the first week. To establish ourselves firmly in it, we may well recall what faith teaches us: (1) of the infinite malice of mortal sin, and the terrible vengeance with which God pursues it in time and in eternity; (2) of the supreme dominion of God and His right to the obedience of every creature; (3) of the certainty and nearness of death, which will leave the sinner without resource in the hands of the living God; (4) the rewards which await in eternity the faithful observers of God's law; (5) the sacrifices of the saints and Mary, who renounced everything—fortune, pleasures, liberty, life itself—in order to escape mortal sin: "They were stoned, they were cut asunder, they were tempted, they were put to death by the sword" (Heb. 11:37).

Second Point: The second degree is more perfect; it consists in the indifference of the soul toward riches or poverty, honour or shame, health or sickness, provided the glory of God and salvation are equally secured on both sides; further, that no consideration of interest or temporal disgrace, not even the consequence of immediate death, should be capable of drawing us into deliberate venial sin.

This second degree is the consequence of the exercise on the "End of creatures." In that exercise we saw that according to the order of creation, creatures are only the means given to man to lead him to his true end. Reason tells us that, in the choice of means, man should only consider what brings him nearer or takes him farther from this end. Hence it follows that man should be indifferent to poverty or riches, honour or shame; and that to commit venial sin in order to escape shame or poverty is to sin against this indifference, is to reverse the order, and convert the means into the end itself.

To arrive at this second degree, we may meditate (1) on the malice of venial sin, the greatest of evils after mortal sin; (2) the hatred with which God pursues it and the torments with which He punishes it in the other life; (3) its effects with regard to the soul, in which it weakens charity and disposes to mortal sin; (4) the examples of the saints, of whom several have preferred to die rather than consent to one slight fault; (5) above all, the example of Jesus Christ.

Third Point: The third degree is the highest degree of Christian perfection. It consists of preferring, for the sole love of Jesus Christ, and from the wish to resemble Him more, poverty to riches, shame to honour, etc., even if on both sides your salvation and the glory of God were equally to be found.

To arrive at this third degree of humility, we may consider 1. *Its excellence*. It contains all that is most heroic in virtue, and the perfect imitation of Jesus Christ, who for love of us willingly embraced the ignominy of the Cross: "Having joy set before him, endured the cross, despising the shame and now sitteth on the right hand of the throne of God" (Heb. 12:2). 2. *Its happiness*. To this degree is attached (1) peace of heart, since nothing can trouble him who professes to love all that nature fears and abhors; (2) intimate union with Jesus Christ, who communicates Himself fully to those souls who give themselves to Him without reserve; (3) the choice graces and blessings of God on all that we undertake for His glory: "The foolish things of the world hath God chosen that He may confound the wise; and the weak things of the world hath God chosen, that He may confound the strong" (1 Cor. 1:27). 3. *Its utility*. This degree is the *most certain* way of salvation, because it snatches us away from all the dangers inseparable from fortune and honour; *the shortest*, because it delivers us at once from sin, and raises us to every virtue; finally, the most meritorious, because it is one uninterrupted course of sacrifices, and consequently of merits, for eternity.[17]

The aim of all the activities of the interior life is, as we have seen, the incorporation of the spirit in Christ, the putting on of the mind and will of God in love. As the soul progresses, it cannot resist the call to the restoration of all things in Christ. It must become a witness to Christ in the world, bring to realization those values which are most perfectly embodied in the God-Man. It is to these values, as they inform the Christian life, that we shall turn in the following section.

CHAPTER EIGHT

The Catholic Affirmation

So let your light shine before men.[1]

The life of the follower of Christ expresses a commitment as all-encompassing as the vision of God, as uncompromising as the Cross of Christ. The transformation of the person in Christ is a total transformation of his being, his relations and his actions. "With Christ I am nailed to the Cross; and I live, now not I, but Christ liveth in me" (Gal. 2:19-20).

The outpouring love of God, his creative and redemptive agape, is at once the power and the exemplar which calls the Christian to action just as it is the supreme value to which life is a response. To restore all things to Christ is to cooperate in bringing to birth in creation the truth, the goodness, the unity and the beauty of God, those values which most fully image the divine life. Christian action is incarnationism, the evocation in love of the God-likeness in all things.

Christian life is an integral life. There can be no compartmentalization. God is to be found everywhere; all things are to be restored to God. And it is a life of action, its supreme ideal the redemptive zeal of Christ. The sterile life is an un-Christian life.

THE VALUE OF EXAMPLE : ST. MATTHEW

You are the light of the world. A city seated on a mountain cannot be hid.

Neither do men light a candle and put it under a bushel,

but upon a candlestick, that it may shine to all that are in the house.

So let your light shine before men that they may see your good works and glory your Father who is in heaven.[2]

THE FOLLOWING OF CHRIST : ST. PAUL

But doing the truth in charity, we may in all things grow up in him who is the head, even Christ. . . .

And put on the new man, who according to God is created in justice and holiness of truth.

Be ye therefore followers of God, as most dear children:

And walk in Love, as Christ also hath loved us and hath delivered himself for us, an oblation and a sacrifice to God for an odour of sweetness.[3]

ACTION AND CONTEMPLATION : ST. AUGUSTINE

As concerning the three kinds of life, contemplative, active, one made up of each, although a man may live a life of unimpaired faith and attain to the eternal reward in any of them, yet there is a difference between what is held for love of the truth and what is expended in the duty of charity. One may not be so given up to contemplation as to neglect the good of his neighbour, nor so taken up with the active life as to omit the contemplation of God. . . . Wherefore the love of truth requires a holy retiredness, and the necessity of charity a just employment. And if this burden be not imposed on us we ought not to seek it but betake ourselves wholly to the search and perception of truth. But if it is imposed on us, the law and need of charity binds us to undertake it. Yet for all this may we not abandon our striving after the truth, lest we lose the sweetness of the one and be surcharged with the weight of the other.[4]

The values, then, which the Christian life incarnates are the values of God Himself as revealed in nature and supernature. As all values find their unity in the unity of the divine life, so man finds his identity in his relationship to God. The love of God in Christ is that which gives the Christian character its integrity.

We will exemplify several of these primary values here in extensive selections which will indicate not only the ideal of Christian action but its concrete implications in human living in the world.

INTELLECTUAL LIFE

KNOWLEDGE AND WISDOM : ST. AUGUSTINE

If therefore this is the right distinction between wisdom and knowledge, that the intellectual cognition of eternal things pertains to wisdom, but the rational cognition of temporal things to knowledge, it is not difficult to judge which is to be esteemed more and which less. But if another method of discrimination should be employed by which to know these two apart which the Apostle teaches are indubitably different, saying, "To one indeed, by the Spirit, is given the word of wisdom; and to another, the word of knowledge according to the same spirit" (1 Cor. xii, 8); still the difference between the two which we have laid down is a most evident one, in that the intellectual cognition of eternal things is one thing, the rational cognition of temporal things another; and no one doubts that the former is to be preferred to the latter.[5]

Whither do we go? To the Truth. By what path do we go? By faith. Whither do we go? To Christ. By what path do we go? By Christ. For He Himself hath said, "I am the way, and the truth, and the life" (John xiv, 6). But He had once said to those that believed in Him: "If you continue in my word, you shall be my disciples indeed. And you shall know the truth: and the truth shall set you free" (John viii, 31 *sq.*). And you shall know the truth, He saith, but only if you continue in my word. In what word? As the Apostle saith: "This is the word of faith, which we preach" (Rom. x, 8). First therefore is the word of faith, and if we continue in this word of faith, we shall know the truth, and the truth shall make us free. Truth is immortal, truth is immutable; Truth is that Word of which it was said, "In the beginning was the Word, and the Word was with God, and the Word was God" (John i, 1). And who can see this unless his heart be cleansed? How are hearts cleansed? "And the Word was made flesh,

and dwelt among us" (*id*. i, 14). In that therefore the Word
continueth in Itself, it is Truth to which we are coming, and
which will make us free. But inasmuch as the word of faith is
preached, in which the Lord wisheth us to continue, that we
may know the truth, it is this: "The Word was made flesh,
and dwelt among us." Thou believest in Christ born in the
flesh, and thus wilt come to Christ born of God, God with
God.[6]

CHRISTIAN EDUCATION : POPE PIUS XI

. . . Since education consists essentially in preparing man for
what he must be and for what he must do here below, in
order to attain the sublime end for which he was created, it is
clear that there can be no true education which is not wholly
directed to man's last end, and that in the present order of
Providence, since God has revealed Himself to us in the
Person of His Only Begotten Son, who alone is "the way,
the truth and the life," there can be no ideally perfect education which is not Christian education.

From this we see the supreme importance of Christian
education, not merely for each individual, but for families and
for the whole of human society, whose perfection comes from
the perfection of the elements that compose it. From these
same principles, the excellence, we may well call it the un-
surpassed excellence, of the work of Christian education becomes manifest and clear; for after all it aims at securing the
Supreme Good, that is, God, for the souls of those who are
being educated, and the maximum of well-being possible here
below for human society. And this it does as efficaciously as
man is capable of doing it, namely by co-operating with God
in the perfecting of individuals and of society. . . .

Education is essentially a social and not a mere individual
activity. Now there are three necessary societies, distinct from
one another and yet harmoniously combined by God, into
which man is born: two, namely the family and civil society,
belong to the natural order; the third, the Church, to the
supernatural order.

In the first place comes the family, instituted directly by
God for its peculiar purpose, the generation and formation
of offspring; for this reason it has priority of nature and therefore of rights over civil society. Nevertheless, the family is

an imperfect society, since it has not in itself all the means for its own complete development; whereas civil society is a perfect society, having in itself all the means for its peculiar end, which is the temporal well-being of the community; and so, in this respect, that is, in view of the common good, it has pre-eminence over the family, which finds its own suitable temporal perfection precisely in civil society.

The third society, into which man is born when through Baptism he reaches the divine life of grace, is the Church; a society of the supernatural order and of universal extent; a perfect society, because it has in itself all the means required for its own end, which is the eternal salvation of mankind; hence it is supreme in its own domain.

Consequently, education which is concerned with man as a whole, individually and socially, in the order of nature and in the order of grace, necessarily belongs to all these three societies, in due proportion, corresponding, according to the disposition of Divine Providence, to the co-ordination of their respective ends.

And first of all education belongs pre-eminently to the Church, by reason of a double title in the supernatural order, conferred exclusively upon her by God Himself; absolutely superior therefore to any other title in the natural order. . . .

Again it is the inalienable right as well as the indispensable duty of the Church to watch over the entire education of her children, in all institutions, public or private, not merely in regard to the religious instruction there given, but in regard to every other branch of learning and every regulation in so far as religion and morality are concerned. . . .

However, it is clear that in all these ways of promoting education and instruction, both public and private, the State should respect the inherent rights of the Church and of the family concerning Christian education, and moreover have regard for distributive justice. Accordingly, unjust and unlawful is any monopoly, educational or scholastic, which, physically or morally, forces families to make use of government schools, contrary to the dictates of their Christian conscience, or contrary even to their legitimate preferences.

This does not prevent the State from making due provision for the right administration of public affairs and for the protection of its peace, within or without the realm. These are things which directly concern the public good and call for special aptitudes and special preparation. The State may therefore reserve to itself the establishment and direction of schools intended to prepare for certain civic duties and especially for military service, provided it be careful not to injure the rights of the Church or of the family in what pertains to them. It is well to repeat this warning here; for in these days there is spreading a spirit of nationalism which is false and exaggerated, as well as dangerous to true peace and prosperity. Under its influence various excesses are committed in giving a military turn to the so-called physical training of boys (sometimes even for girls, contrary to the very instincts of human nature); or again in usurping unreasonably on Sunday, the time which should be devoted to religious duties and to family life at home. It is not our intention, however, to condemn what is good in the spirit of discipline and legitimate bravery promoted by these methods. We condemn only what is excessive, as for example violence, which must not be confounded with courage nor with the noble sentiment of military valour in defense of country and public order; or again exaltation of athleticism, which even in classic pagan times marked the decline and downfall of genuine physical training.

In general also it belongs to civil society and the State to provide what may be called civic education, not only for its youth, but for all ages and classes. This consists in the practice of presenting publicly to groups of individuals information having an intellectual, imaginative and emotional appeal, calculated to draw their wills to what is upright and honest, and to urge its practice by a sort of moral compulsion, positively by disseminating such knowledge, and negatively by suppressing what is opposed to it. . . .

Accordingly in the matter of education, it is the right, or to speak more correctly, it is the duty, of the State to protect in its legislation the prior rights, already described, of the family as regards the Christian education of its offspring, and consequently also to respect the supernatural rights of the Church in this same realm of Christian education.

It also belongs to the State to protect the rights of the child itself when the parents are found wanting either physically or morally in this respect, whether by default, incapacity or misconduct, since, as has been shown, their right to educate is not an absolute and despotic one, but dependent on the natural and divine law, and therefore subject alike to the authority and jurisdiction of the Church, and to the vigilance and administrative care of the State in view of the common good. Besides, the family is not a perfect society, that is, it has not in itself all the means necessary for its full development. In such cases, exceptional no doubt, the State does not put itself in the place of the family, but merely supplies deficiencies, and provides suitable means, always in conformity with the natural rights of the child and the supernatural rights of the Church.

In general, then, it is the right and duty of the State to protect, according to the rules of right reason and faith, the moral and religious education of youth, by removing public impediments that stand in the way.

In the first place it pertains to the State, in view of the common good, to promote in various ways the education and instruction of youth. It should begin by encouraging and assisting, of its own accord, the initiative and activity of the Church and the family, whose successes in this field have been clearly demonstrated by history and experience. It should, moreover, supplement their work whenever this falls short of what is necessary, even by means of its own schools and institutions. For the State more than any other society is provided with the means put at its disposal for the needs of all, and it is only right that it use these means to the advantage of those who have contributed them.

Over and above this, the State can exact, and take measures to secure that all its citizens have the necessary knowledge of their civic and political duties, and a certain degree of physical, intellectual and moral culture, which, considering the conditions of our times, is really necessary for the common good. . . .[7]

CHRISTIAN EDUCATION : THIRD PLENARY COUNCIL
OF BALTIMORE

. . . Few surely will deny that childhood and youth are the periods of life when the character ought especially to be subjected to religious influences. Nor can we ignore the palpable fact that the school is an important factor in the forming of childhood and youth—so important that its influence often outweighs that of home and church. It cannot, therefore, be desirable or advantageous that religion should be excluded from the school. On the contrary, it ought there to be one of the chief agencies for moulding the young life to all that is true and virtuous and holy. To shut religion out of the school and keep it for home and the church is, logically, to train up a generation that will consider religion good for home and the church, but not for the practical business of real life. But a more false and pernicious notion could not be imagined. Religion, in order to elevate a people, should inspire their whole life and rule their relations with one another. A life is not dwarfed, but ennobled by being lived in the presence of God. Therefore the school, which principally gives the knowledge fitting for practical life, ought to be preeminently under the holy influence of religion.

. . . The cry for religious education is going up from religious bodies all over the land. And this is no narrowness and sectarianism on their part; it is an honest and logical end to preserve Christian truth and morality among the people by fostering religion in the young. Nor is it any antagonism to the State; on the contrary, it is an honest end to give to the State better citizens by making them better Christians. The friends of Christian education do not condemn the State for not imparting religious instruction in the public schools because they well know it does not lie within the province of the State to teach religion. They simply follow their conscience by sending their children to denominational schools where religion can have its rightful place and influence.[8]

PRINCIPLES OF CATHOLIC PHILOSOPHY : POPE PIUS XII

It is well known how highly the Church regards human reason, for it falls to reason to demonstrate with certainty the existence of God, personal and one, to prove beyond doubt from divine signs the very foundations of the Christian faith: to express properly the law which the Creator has imprinted in the hearts of men; and finally to attain to some notion, indeed a very fruitful notion, of mysteries.

But reason can perform these functions safely and well only when properly trained. That is, when imbued with that sound philosophy which has long been, as it were, a patrimony handed down by earlier Christian ages, and which moreover possesses an authority of even higher order, since the teaching authority of the Church, in this light of divine revelation itself, has weighed its fundamental tenets, which have been elaborated and defined little by little by men of great genius. For this philosophy, acknowledged and accepted by the Church, safeguards the genuine validity of human knowledge, the unshakable metaphysical principles of sufficient reason, causality and finality, and finally the ability of the human mind to attain certain and unchangeable truth.

Of course this philosophy deals with much that neither directly nor indirectly touches faith or morals and which consequently the Church leaves to the free discussion of experts. But this does not hold for many other things, especially those principles and fundamental tenets to which we have just referred. However, even in these fundamental questions, we may clothe our philosophy in more convenient and richer dress, make it more vigorous with more effective terminology, divest it of certain scholastic aids found less useful, prudently enrich it with the fruits of the progress of the human mind, but never may we overthrow it or contaminate it with false principles or regard it as a great but obsolete relic. For truth and its philosophic expression cannot change from day to day, least of all where there is a question of the self-evident principles of the human mind or of those propositions which are supported by the wisdom of the ages and by divine revelation. Whatever new truth the sincere human mind is able to find certainly cannot be opposed to truth already acquired since God, the highest truth, has created and guides the human intellect, not that it may daily oppose new truths to rightly established ones but rather that, having eliminated errors which may have crept in, it may build truth upon truth in the same order and structure that exist in reality, the source of truth.

Let no Christian, therefore, whether philosopher or theologian, embrace eagerly and lightly whatever novelty happens to be thought up from day to day, but rather let him weigh it with painstaking care and a balanced judgment, lest he lose or corrupt the truth he already has, with grave danger and damage to his faith.[9]

In theology some want to reduce to a minimum the meaning of dogmas, and to free dogma itself from the terminology long established in the Church and from philosophical concepts held by Catholic teachers, and to return in the explanation of Catholic doctrine to the way of speaking used in Holy Scripture and by the fathers of the Church.

They cherish the hope that when dogma is stripped of the elements which they hold to be extrinsic to divine revelation, it will compare advantageously with the opinions of those who are separated from the unity of the Church and that in this way they will gradually arrive at a mutual assimilation of Catholic dogma and the tenets of the dissidents.

Moreover, they assert that when Catholic doctrine has been reduced to this condition, a way will be found to satisfy modern needs, that will permit of dogma being expressed also by the concepts of modern philosophy, whether of immanentism or idealism or existentialism or any other system. Some, more audacious, affirm that this can and must be done, because they hold that the mysteries of faith are never expressed by truly adequate concepts but only by approximate and ever changeable notions, in which the truth is to some extent expressed, but is necessarily distorted.

Wherefore, they do not consider it absurd but altogether necessary that theology should substitute new concepts in place of the old ones in keeping with the various philosophies which in the course of time it uses as its instruments, so that it should give human expression to divine truths in various ways which are even somewhat opposed, but still equivalent, as they say.

Unfortunately these advocates of novelty easily pass from despising scholastic theology to the neglect of and even contempt for the teaching authority of the Church itself, which gives such authoritative approval to scholastic theology. This teaching authority is represented by them as a hindrance to progress and an obstacle in the way of science.

. . . positive theology cannot be on a par with a merely historical science. For together with the sources of positive theology God has given to His church a living teaching authority to elucidate and explain what is contained in the deposit of faith only obscurely and implicitly. This deposit of faith our Divine Redeemer has given for authentic interpretation not to each of the faithful, not even to theologians, but only to the teaching authority of the Church. . . . Pius IX, teaching that the most noble office of theology is to show how a doctrine defined by the Church is contained in the sources of revelation, added these words, and with very good reason: "In that sense in which it has been defined by the Church."

. . . some go as far as to pervert the sense of the Vatican Council's definition that God is the author of holy Scripture, and they put forward again the opinion, often condemned, which asserts that immunity from error extends only to those parts of the Bible that treat of God or of moral and religious matters. They even wrongly speak of the human sense of the Scriptures, beneath which the divine sense, which they say is the only infallible meaning, lies hidden. In interpreting scripture, they will take no account of the analogy of faith and the tradition of the Church. Thus they judge the doctrine of the fathers and of the teaching Church by the norm of holy Scripture, interpreted by purely human reason of exegesis, instead of explaining holy Scripture according to the mind of the Church which Christ our Lord has appointed guardian and interpreter of the whole deposit of divinely revealed truth.

Further, according to their fictitious opinions, the literal sense of holy Scripture and its explanation, carefully worked out under the Church's vigilance by so many great exegetes, should yield now to a new exegesis which they are pleased to call symbolic or spiritual. By means of this new exegesis the Old Testament, which today in the Church is a sealed book, would finally be thrown open to all the faithful. By this method, they say, all difficulties vanish, difficulties which hinder only those who adhere to the literal meaning of the Scriptures.

Everyone sees how foreign all this is to the principles and norms of interpretation rightly fixed by our predecessors of happy memory.[10]

MORAL LIFE

GOD'S LAW, THE MEASURE OF MAN'S CONDUCT : STATEMENT OF THE ARCHBISHOPS AND BISHOPS OF U. S.

. . . By nature, man is a creature, subject to his Creator, and responsible to him for all his actions. By selfish inclination at times, he chooses to be something else, assuming the prerogatives of a Creator, establishing his own standard of conduct and making himself the measure of all things. This prideful folly on his part brings discord into his own life and profoundly affects the whole moral order. Frustration rather than fulfillment becomes his characteristic mark because he does not possess wholly within himself the way to fulfillment. That he can discover only by God's plan.

God's will, then, is the measure of man, it is the standard by which all human actions must meet the test of their rightness or wrongness. What conforms to God's will is right; and what goes counter to His will is wrong. This is the great and controlling rule of the moral order. Unless man recognizes and lives by this rule, he cannot come to that abundance of life destined for him by God.

How does he come to such knowledge? How can man know what is his place in the divine plan, and what is God's will in the moral decisions he is called upon to make? God had endowed man with intelligence. When rightly used and directed, the human intelligence can discover certain fundamental spiritual truths and moral principles which will give order and harmony to man's intelligence and moral life.

What are these truths which right reason can discover? First in importance is the existence of a personal God, all knowing and all-powerful, the eternal Source from whom all things derive their being. Next comes the spiritual and immortal nature of man's soul, its freedom, its responsibility and the duty of rendering to God reverence, obedience and all that is embraced under the name of religion.

From man's position as God's rational, free and responsible creature, destined for eternal life, springs the unique dignity of the human individual and his essential equality with his fellow man.

Out of the inherent demands of human nature arises the family as the fundamental unit of human society, based on a permanent and exclusive union of man and woman in marriage. From the essential characteristics of marriage come not only the right of parents to beget children, but also their primary right and duty to rear and educate them properly.

Since neither the individual nor the family is completely independent and self-sustaining, there arises the necessity of organized civil society and, in turn, the mutual responsibility of the individual and family on the one side and civil government on the other.

Man's social life becomes intolerable, if not impossible, unless justice and benevolence govern the operation of the state and relations between individual and groups. Without temperance, man can neither live in accordance with his human dignity nor fulfill his obligation to his fellow man. Without fortitude he cannot bear the trials of life or overcome the difficulties with which he is surrounded.

Furthermore, it is clear that the inherent dignity of the individual and the needs of the family and of society demand a code of sexual morality within the grasp of every mature mind.

These are some of the basic elements of natural law, a law based on human nature; a law which can be discovered by human intelligence and which governs man's relations with God, with himself and with the other creatures of God. The principles of the natural law, absolute, stable, and unchanging are applicable to all the changing conditions and circumstances in which man constantly finds himself.

These religious and moral truths of the natural order can be known by human reason; but God, in His goodness, through Divine Revelation has helped man to know better and to preserve the natural law. In the Old Testament this revelation was given to the chosen people of God. Completed and perfected in the New, it has been communicated to mankind by Jesus Christ and His Apostles and it has been entrusted to the church to teach all men.

While the natural law, taught and interpreted by the church, gives us a guide in many areas of human life, the perfection of human nature is revealed to us in Christ himself, God-become-Man, the Word-made-Flesh, "full of grace and truth," dwelling among us to be our Way, our Truth, our Life. Prayer and the sacraments are the channels through which the grace of Christ comes to elevate human nature until it becomes like unto Him who is true God and true man. In the supernatural order of grace, Christ, the God-man, is the measure of man.

Divine Revelation, then, not only includes the natural law, it complements it, and points the way to the supernatural order of grace. The natural moral law, however, remains the foundation of the supernatural order as it is the foundation of all man's relations to God, to himself, to his fellow man. . . .

Doing God's work means doing God's will. This requires the services of the whole man at every moment of every day he exists. There is all too frequently today the spectacle of men who divide their lives to suit their own convenience. Only when it serves their selfish purpose do they conform to God's will. Their business life, their professional life, their life in the home, at school and in the community occupy separate compartments unified by no central force. God's claims upon such men exist, but they are not honored. Expressions such as "My life is my own affair" or "I may do as I please" or "in politics, anything goes" are all too common today. They betray a gross misunderstanding of the moral order and the interlinking relationships which find their correct measure only in God's will.

We must be clear on one point. Man must either acknowledge that a personal God exists or he must deny His existence altogether. There is no middle course. Once he acknowledges that God exists, then the claims of God are coextensive with all the acts of His creatures. To pretend that any part of his life can be a private affair is to violate the most basic claim which God has on man. Man is a creature. As a creature, he is subject to the Creator in all that he does. There is no time in his life when he is excused from obeying the moral law.

The clergyman, the educator, doctor, lawyer, politician, employer, employee, husbands, wives, and children are alike strictly bound. All human rights and obligations have their source in God's law; otherwise they are meaningless.[11]

SOCIAL ORDER

CHRISTIAN MARRIAGE : POPE PIUS XI

How great is the dignity of chaste wedlock, Venerable Brethren, may be judged best from this that Christ Our Lord, Son of the Eternal Father, having assumed the nature of fallen man, not only, with His loving desire of compassing the redemption of our race, ordained it in an especial manner as the principle and foundation of domestic society and therefore of all human intercourse, but also raised it to the rank of a truly and great sacrament of the New Law, restored it to the original purity of its divine institution, and accordingly entrusted all its discipline and care to His spouse the Church. . . .

. . . And to begin with let it be repeated as an immutable and inviolable fundamental doctrine that matrimony was not instituted or restored by man but by God; not by man were the laws made to strengthen and confirm and elevate it but by God, the Author of nature, and by Christ Our Lord by Whom nature was redeemed, and hence these laws cannot be subject to any human decrees or to any contrary pact even of the spouses themselves. . . .

Yet although matrimony is of its very nature of divine institution, the human will, too, enters into it and performs a most noble part. For each individual marriage, inasmuch as it is a conjugal union of a particular man and woman, arises only from the free consent of each of the spouses; and this free act of the will, by which each party hands over and accepts those rights proper to the state of marriage, is so necessary to constitute true marriage that it cannot be supplied by any human power. This freedom, however, regards only the question whether the contracting parties really wish to enter upon matrimony or to marry this particular person; but the nature of matrimony is entirely independent of the free will of man, so that if one has once contracted matrimony he is thereby subject to its divinely made laws and its essential properties. For the Angelic Doctor, writing on conjugal honour and on the offspring which is the fruit of marriage, says: "These things are so contained in matrimony by the marriage pact itself that, if anything to the contrary were expressed in the consent which makes the marriage, it would not be a true marriage. . . ."

. . . [According to the teaching of Leo XIII,] "To take away from man the natural and primeval right of marriage, to circumscribe in any way the principal ends of marriage laid down in the beginning by God Himself in the words 'Increase and multiply,' is beyond the power of any human law."

Therefore the sacred partnership of true marriage is constituted both by the will of God and the will of man. From God comes the very institution of marriage, the ends for which it was instituted, the laws that govern it, the blessings that flow from it; while man, through generous surrender of his own person made to another for the whole span of life, becomes, with the help and co-operation of God, the author of each particular marriage, with the duties and blessings annexed thereto from divine institution. . . .

. . . That mutual familiar intercourse between the spouses themselves, if the blessing of conjugal faith is to shine with becoming splendour, must be distinguished by chastity so that husband and wife bear themselves in all things with the law of God and of nature, and endeavour always to follow the will of their most wise and holy Creator with the greatest reverence towards the work of God.

This conjugal faith, however, which is most aptly called by St. Augustine the "faith of chastity," blooms more freely, more beautifully and more nobly, when it is rooted in that more excellent soil, the love of husband and wife which pervades all the duties of married life and holds pride of place in Christian marriage. For matrimonial faith demands that husband and wife be joined in an especially holy and pure love, not as adulterers love each other, but as Christ loved the Church. This precept the Apostle laid down when he said: "Husbands, love your wives as Christ also loved the Church," that Church which of a truth He embraced with a boundless love not for the sake of His own advantage, but seeking only the good of His Spouse. The love, then, of which We are speaking is not that based on the passing lust of the moment nor does it consist in pleasing words only, but in the deep attachment of the heart which is expressed in action, since love is proved by deeds. This outward expression of love in the home demands not only mutual help but must go further; must have as its primary purpose that man and wife help each other day by day in forming and perfecting themselves in the interior life, so that through their partnership in life they may advance ever more and more in virtue, and above all that they may grow in true love towards God and their neighbour, on which indeed "dependeth the whole Law and the Prophets." . . .

By this same love it is necessary that all the other rights and duties of the marriage state be regulated as the words of the Apostle: "Let the husband render the debt to the wife, and the wife also in like manner to the husband," express not only a law of justice but of charity.

Domestic society being confirmed, therefore, by this bond of love, there should flourish in it that "order of love," as St. Augustine calls it. This order includes both the primacy of the husband with regard to the wife and children, the ready subjection of the wife and her willing obedience, which the Apostle commends in these words: "Let women be subject to their husbands as to the Lord, because the husband is the head of the wife, as Christ is the head of the Church."

This subjection, however, does not deny or take away the liberty which fully belongs to the woman both in view of her dignity as a human person, and in view of her most noble office as wife and mother and companion; nor does it bid her obey her husband's every request if not in harmony with right reason or with the dignity due to wife; nor, in fine, does it imply that the wife should be put on a level with those persons who in law are called minors, to whom it is not customary to allow free exercise of their rights on account of their lack of mature judgment, or of their ignorance of human affairs. But it forbids that exaggerated liberty which cares not for the good of the family; it forbids that in this body which is the family, the heart be separated from the head to the great detriment of the whole body and the proximate danger of ruin. For if the man is the head, the woman is the heart, and as he occupies the chief place in ruling, so she may and ought to claim for herself the chief place in love.

Again, this subjection of wife to husband in its degree and manner may vary according to the different conditions of persons, place and time. In fact, if the husband neglect his duty, it falls to the wife to take his place in directing the family. But the structure of the family and its fundamental law, established and confirmed by God, must always and everywhere be maintained intact. . . .

These, then, are the elements which compose the blessing of conjugal faith: unity, chastity, charity, honourable noble obedience, which are at the same time an enumeration of the benefits which are bestowed on husband and wife in their married state, benefits by which the peace, the dignity and the happiness of matrimony are securely preserved and fostered. Wherefore it is not surprising that this conjugal faith has always been counted amongst the most priceless and special blessings of matrimony.

But this accumulation of benefits is completed and, as it were, crowned by that blessing of Christian marriage which in the words of St. Augustine we have called the sacrament, by which is denoted both the indissolubility of the bond and the raising and hallowing of the contract by Christ Himself, whereby He made it an efficacious sign of grace. . . .

And since the valid matrimonial consent among the faithful was constituted by Christ as a sign of grace, the sacramental nature is so intimately bound up with Christian wedlock that there can be no true marriage between baptized persons "without it being by that very fact a sacrament. . . ."

And now, Venerable Brethren, we shall explain in detail the evils opposed to each of the benefits of matrimony. First consideration is due to the offspring, which many have the boldness to call the disagreeable burden of matrimony and which they say is to be carefully avoided by married people not through virtuous continence (which Christian law permits in matrimony when both parties consent) but by frustrating the marriage act. Some justify this criminal abuse on the ground that they are weary of children and wish to gratify their desires without their consequent burden. Others say that they cannot on the one hand remain continent nor on the other can they have children because of the difficulties whether on the part of the mother or on the part of family circumstances.

But no reason, however grave, may be put forward by which anything intrinsically against nature may become conformable to nature and morally good. Since, therefore, the conjugal act is destined primarily by nature for the begetting of children, those who in exercising it deliberately frustrate its natural power and purpose sin against nature and commit a deed which is shameful and intrinsically vicious. . . .

Since, therefore, openly departing from the uninterrupted Christian tradition, some recently have judged it possible solemnly to declare another doctrine regarding this question, the Catholic Church, to whom God has entrusted the defence of the integrity and purity of morals, standing erect in the midst of the moral ruin which surrounds her, in order that she may preserve the chastity of the nuptial union from being defiled by this foul stain, raises her voice in token of her divine ambassadorship and through Our mouth proclaims anew: any use whatsoever of matrimony exercised in such a way that the act is deliberately frustrated in its natural power to generate life is an offence against the law of God and of nature, and those who indulge in such are branded with the guilt of a grave sin. . . .

Holy Church knows well that not infrequently one of the parties is sinned against rather than sinning, when for a grave cause he or she reluctantly allows the perversion of the right order. In such a case, there is no sin, provided that, mindful of the law of charity, he or she does not neglect to seek to dissuade and to deter the partner from sin. Nor are those considered as acting against nature who in the married state use their right in the proper manner although on account of natural reasons either of time or of certain defects, new life cannot be brought forth. For in matrimony as well as in the use of the matrimonial rights there are also secondary ends, such as mutual aid, the cultivating of mutual love, and the quieting of concupiscence which husband and wife are not forbidden to consider so long as they are subordinated to the primary end and so long as the intrinsic nature of the act is preserved. . . .

But another very grave crime is to be noted, Venerable Brethren, which regards the taking of the life of the offspring hidden in the mother's womb. Some wish it to be allowed and left to the will of the father or the mother; others say it is unlawful unless there are weighty reasons which they call by the name of medical, social, or eugenic "indication." Because this matter falls under the penal laws of the state by which the destruction of the offspring begotten but unborn is forbidden, these people demand that the "indication," which in one form or another they defend, be recognized as such by the public law and in no way penalized. There are those, moreover, who ask that the public authorities provide aid for these death-dealing operations, a thing, which, sad to say, everyone knows is of very frequent occurrence in some places.

As to the "medical and therapeutic indication" to which, using their own words, we have made reference, Venerable Brethren, however much we may pity the mother whose health and even life is gravely imperiled in the performance of the duty allotted to her by nature, nevertheless what could ever be a sufficient reason for excusing in any way the direct murder of the innocent? This is precisely what we are dealing with here. Whether inflicted upon the mother or upon the child, it is against the precept of God and the law of nature: "Thou shalt not kill." The life of each is equally sacred, and no one has the power, not even the public authority, to destroy it. It is of no use to appeal to the right of taking away life for here it is a question of the innocent, whereas that right has regard only to the guilty; nor is there here question of defense by bloodshed against an unjust aggressor (for who would call an innocent child an unjust aggressor?); again there is no question here of what is called the "law of extreme necessity" which could even extend to the direct killing of the innocent. Upright and skilful doctors strive most praiseworthily to guard and preserve the lives of both mother and child; on the contrary, those show themselves most unworthy of the noble medical profession who encompass the death of one or the other, through a pretence at practicing medicine or through motives of misguided pity. . . .

Finally, that pernicious practice must be condemned which closely touches upon the natural right of man to enter matrimony but affects also in a real way the welfare of the offspring. For there are some who, oversolicitous for the cause of eugenics, not only give salutary counsel for more certainly procuring the strength and health of the future child—which, indeed, is not contrary to right reason—but put eugenics before aims of a higher order, and by public authority wish to prevent from marrying all those who, even though naturally fit for marriage, they consider, according to the norms and conjectures of their investigations, would, through hereditary transmission, bring forth defective offspring. And more, they wish to legislate to deprive these of that natural faculty by medical action despite their unwillingness; and this they do not propose as an infliction of grave punishment under the authority of the state for a crime committed, nor to prevent future crimes by guilty persons, but against every right and good they wish the civil authority to arrogate to itself a power over a faculty which it never had and can never legitimately possess. . . .

Public magistrates have no direct power over the bodies of their subjects; therefore, where no crime has taken place and there is no cause present for grave punishment, they can never directly harm, or tamper with the integrity of the body, either for the reasons of eugenics or for any other reason. . . .

Furthermore, Christian doctrine establishes, and the light of human reason makes it most clear, that private individuals have no other power over the members of their bodies than that which pertains to their natural ends; and they are not free to destroy or mutilate their members, or in any other way render themselves unfit for their natural functions, except when no other provision can be made for the good of the whole body. . . .

The advocates of the neo-paganism of to-day have learned nothing from the sad state of affairs, but instead, day by day, more and more vehemently, they continue by legislation to attack the indissolubility of the marriage bond, proclaiming that the lawfulness of divorce must be recognised, and that the antiquated laws should give place to a new and more humane legislation. Many and varied are the grounds put forward for divorce, some arising from the wickedness and the guilt of the persons concerned, others arising from the circumstances of the case; the former they describe as subjective, the latter as objective; in a word, whatever might make married life hard or unpleasant. . . .

Opposed to all these reckless opinions, Venerable Brethren, stands the unalterable law of God, fully confirmed by Christ, a law that can never be deprived of its force by the decrees of men, the ideas of a people or the will of any legislator: "What God hath joined together, let no man put asunder." And if any man, acting contrary to this law, shall have put asunder, his action is null and void, and the consequence remains, as Christ Himself has explicitly confirmed: "Everyone that putteth away his wife and marrieth another, committeth adultery: and he that marrieth her that is put away from her husband committeth adultery." Moreover, these words refer to every kind of marriage, even that which is natural and legitimate only; for, as has already been observed, that indissolubility by which the loosening of the bond is once and for all removed from the whim of the parties and from every secular power, is a property of every true marriage. . . .[12]

FAMILY LIFE : STATEMENT OF THE ARCHBISHOPS AND BISHOPS OF THE UNITED STATES

. . . Perhaps the most evident and devastating effect of the disregard of supernatural faith in human society is to be found in what it has done to family life. The world which discounts supernatural faith in God's revelation, praises family life, declaring its place and function essential to human well-being and speaks with high sentiment of the sacredness of the home. Yet by countless acts and agencies it moves steadily to disrupt family life and to destroy the home. It approves and facilitates divorce as a cure for domestic ills. It accepts multiple marriages which usually mean a hopeless entanglement of the infelicities of a plurality of broken homes. It sponsors planned parenthood by use of unnatural and morally degrading means, thus infusing poison into the heart of family life by destroying in husband and wife the self-respect and mutual reverence on which alone are built enduring love and patient fidelity. It is unconcerned, for the most part, about its manifest duty of removing the great difficulties that lie in the way of those who wish to marry and establish homes. Its social legislation in point of suitable housing, decent material facilities, security in income and prospects is slow, fumbling and inadequate.

. . . In the view of faith the family is, first of all, a divine institution. A divine institution is not within man's control to abrogate or alter. It is God's own work. Attack upon it is even humanly speaking disastrous. It strikes tragically at the even balance of right human relations and ends in calamitous disorder.

Faith merely confirms reason in holding that husband and wife constitute conjugal society. When their union is blessed with offspring, this society becomes a family. It is a divinely founded natural society. It is prior, in existence and in its nature, to every other human society, to every state or nation. It is the basic social unit. It has its own native rights which no civil power can take away or unduly limit. To serve and protect the family and its life, states are formed and governments established. . . .

Since family life is thus essential to the individual, to the State and to the church, it follows that whatever protects or promotes good family life is to be diligently fostered.

To exist in full effectiveness, family life must have permanence. This permanence depends chiefly on the permanence of marriage. Strictly requisite is marriage that is monogamous and indissoluble; the marriage of one man with one woman in divorceless union that is broken only by the death of one of the spouses. Such a marriage is requisite, not for the mere begetting of offspring, but for the rearing and training of children until they come to full maturity. Any marriage which looks to dissolution or divorce, even as a possibility, cannot give to children the security they need; cannot surround children with the enduring atmosphere of home; cannot breathe into children the spirit of true family life.

Further, family life must have freedom. There must be no undue interference of the civil power in the domain of husband and wife. This requirement involves two points of obligation. Freedom requires that rights be respected. The State must respect the rights of the family. It must not, therefore, fail to provide opportunity for the adequate housing of the family, for the required schooling of children, for the use of common benefits supplied through the taxing of citizens. On the other hand, the State must not oppose the family. It must not displace parental authority by invading the home and legislating upon matters which are of strictly domestic concern. It must not usurp the right which belongs to parents of educating their children. . . .

To the church belongs the pre-eminent right to guide the child's spiritual and moral formation; to the parent belongs the natural right to govern and supervise the child's nurture and general education; in society is vested the right to transmit, generally by means of schools, the cultural heritage of successive generations. . . . Again, the family, to exercise its good influence in full effectiveness, needs a just measure of economic security. When, in a wealthy and prosperous nation, diligent and willing parents are forced to live in grinding poverty; when parents have no opportunity of owning their own home; when the aid of government is extended to those who raise crops and build machinery but not to those who rear children; there exists a condition of inequality and even injustice. Social legislation and social action must concur to improve man's economic opportunity, to enable him to marry early, to free him from the peril of unnaturally limiting his family, and to afford some certainty of sufficient gainful employment and some assurance that death or accident will not reduce his dependents to the status of public charges.

Finally, the family needs religion. It requires the high morality and the unvarying standards of duty which only the spirit of religion can supply to family life. It needs the strong quality of staunch loyalty to God and to His commandments, to His church and her precepts. It needs the filial piety which has its source and support in piety toward God. It needs prayer and the growth of pious prayer in the home, the enthroning of the Sacred Heart, regular family prayer and the wide variety of Catholic devotions which have given to Christian homes the character of sacred sanctuaries.

The family needs to gather again round its hearths and rekindle there fires of religious fervour. The home must again become a shrine of fidelity, a place where God is the unseen Host. Family retreats, Cana conferences, courses on family life in schools and colleges, and study groups concerned with preparation for family life, should be widely encouraged and zealously promulgated throughout our country. The press, radio, motion pictures and all agencies of public opinion should give constant aid in emphasizing ideals of worthy family life. These forces should be an unfailing support for the virtues which safeguard the home and give nobility to the nation.[13]

POLITICAL ORDER

THE FUNCTION OF THE STATE : POPE PIUS XII

. . . What age has been, for all its technical and purely civic progress, more tormented than ours by spiritual emptiness and deep-felt interior poverty? . . .

The first of these pernicious errors, widespread today, is the forgetfulness of that law of human solidarity and charity which is dictated and imposed by our common origin and by the equality of rational nature in all men, to whatever people they belong, and by the redeeming Sacrifice offered by Jesus Christ on the Altar of the Cross to His Heavenly Father on behalf of sinful mankind. . . .

In the light of this unity of all mankind, which exists in law and in fact, individuals do not feel themselves isolated units, like grains of sand, but united by the very force of their nature and by their internal destiny, into an organic, harmonious mutual relationship which varies with the changing of times.

And the nations, despite a difference of development due to diverse conditions of life and of culture, are not destined to break the unity of the human race, but rather to enrich and embellish it by the sharing of their own peculiar gifts and by that reciprocal interchange of goods which can be possible and efficacious only when a mutual love and a lively sense of charity unite all the sons of the same Father and all those redeemed by the same Divine Blood. . . .

Nor is there any fear lest the consciousness of universal brotherhood aroused by the teaching of Christianity, and the spirit which it inspires, be in contrast with love of traditions or the glories of one's fatherland, or impede the progress of prosperity or legitimate interests. For that same Christianity teaches that in the exercise of charity we must follow a God-given order, yielding the place of honor in our affections and good works to those who are bound to us by special ties. Nay, the Divine Master Himself gave an example of this preference for His Own country and fatherland, as He wept over the coming destruction of the Holy City. But legitimate and well-ordered love of our native country should not make us close our eyes to the all-embracing nature of Christian charity, which calls for consideration of others and of their interests in the pacifying light of love. . . .

But there is yet another error no less pernicious to the well-being of the nations and to the prosperity of that great human society which gathers together and embraces within its confines all races. It is the error contained in those ideas which do not hesitate to divorce civil authority from every kind of dependence upon the Supreme Being—First Source and absolute Master of man and of society—and from every restraint of a Higher Law derived from God as from its First Source. Thus they accord the civil authority an unrestricted field of action that is at the mercy of the changeful tide of human will, or of the dictates of casual historical claims, and of the interests of a few.

Once the authority of God and the sway of His law are denied in this way, the civil authority as an inevitable result tends to attribute to itself that absolute autonomy which belongs exclusively to the Supreme Maker. It puts itself in the place of the Almighty and elevates the State or group into the last end of life, the supreme criterion of the moral and juridical order, and therefore forbids every appeal to the principles of natural reason and of the Christian conscience. . . .

. . . It is the noble prerogative and function of the State to control, aid and direct the private and individual activities of national life that they converge harmoniously towards the common good. That good can neither be defined according to arbitrary ideas nor can it accept for its standard primarily the material prosperity of society, but rather it should be defined according to the harmonious development and the natural perfection of man. It is for this perfection that society is designed by the Creator as a means.

To consider the State as something ultimate to which everything else should be subordinated and directed, cannot fail to harm the true and lasting prosperity of nations. This can happen either when unrestricted dominion comes to be conferred on the State as having a mandate from the nation, people, or even a social order, or when the State arrogates such dominion to itself as absolute master, despotically, without any mandate whatsoever. If, in fact, the State lays claim to and directs private enterprises, these, ruled as they are by delicate and complicated internal principles which guarantee and assure the realization of their special aims, may be damaged to the detriment of the public good, by being wrenched from their natural surroundings, that is, from responsible private action. . . .

The idea which credits the State with unlimited authority is not simply an error harmful to the internal life of nations, to their prosperity, and to the larger and well-ordered increase in their well-being, but likewise it injures the relations between peoples, for it breaks the unity of supranational society, robs the law of nations of its foundation and vigor, leads to violation of others' rights and impedes agreement and peaceful intercourse.

A disposition, in fact, of the divinely sanctioned natural order divides the human race into social groups, nations or States, which are mutually independent in organization and in the direction of their internal life. But for all that, the human race is bound together by reciprocal ties, moral and juridical, into a great commonwealth directed to the good of all nations and ruled by special laws which protect its unity and promote its prosperity.

Now no one can fail to see how the claim to absolute autonomy for the State stands in open opposition to this natural way that is inherent in man—nay, denies it utterly—and therefore leaves the stability of international relations at the mercy of the will of rulers, while it destroys the possibility of true union and fruitful collaboration directed to the general good.

So, Venerable Brethren, it is indispensable for the existence of harmonious and lasting contacts and of fruitful relations, that the peoples recognize and observe these principles of international natural law which regulate their normal development and activity. Such principles demand respect for corresponding rights to independence, to life and to the possibility of continuous development in the paths of civilization; they demand, further, fidelity to compacts agreed upon and sanctioned in conformity with the principles of the law of nations.

The indispensable presupposition, without doubt, of all peaceful intercourse between nations, and the very soul of the juridical relations in force among them, is mutual trust: the expectation and conviction that each party will respect its plighted word; the certainty that both sides are convinced that "Better is wisdom, than weapons of war" (*Ecclesiastes* ix:18), and are ready to enter into discussion and to avoid recourse to force or to threats of force in case of delays, hindrances, changes or disputes, because all these things can be the result not of bad-will, but of changed circumstances and of genuine interests in conflict.

But on the other hand, to tear the law of nations from its anchor in Divine law, to base it on the autonomous will of States, is to dethrone that very law and deprive it of its noblest and strongest qualities. Thus it would stand abandoned to the fatal drive of private interest and collective selfishness exclusively intent on the assertion of its own rights and ignoring those of others. . . .[14]

JURISDICTIONS OF CHURCH AND STATE :
JOHN HENRY CARDINAL NEWMAN

Certainly in the event of such a collision of jurisdictions, there are cases in which we should obey the Pope and disobey the State. Suppose, for instance, an Act was passed in Parliament, bidding Catholics to attend Protestant service every week, and the Pope distinctly told us not to do so, for it was to violate our duty to our faith:—I should obey the Pope and not the Law. It will be said by Mr. Gladstone, that such a case is impossible. I know it is: but why ask me for what I should do in extreme and utterly improbable cases such as this, if my answer cannot help bearing the character of an axiom? It is not my fault that I must deal in truisms. The circumferences of State jurisdiction and of Papal are for the most part quite apart from each other; there are just some few degrees out of the 360 in which they intersect, and Mr. Gladstone, instead of letting these cases of intersection alone, till they occur actually, asks me what I should do, if I found myself placed in the space intersected. If I must answer then, I should say distinctly that did the State tell me in a question of worship to do what the Pope told me not to do, I should obey the Pope, and should think it no sin, if I used all the power and influence I possessed as a citizen to prevent such a Bill passing the Legislature, and to effect its repeal if it did.

. . . But now, on the other hand, could the case ever occur, in which I should act with the Civil Power, and not with the Pope? . . . I know the Pope never can do what I am going to suppose; but then since it cannot possibly happen in fact, there is no harm in just saying what I should (hypothetically) do, if it did happen. I say then in certain (impossible) cases I should side, not with the Pope, but with the Civil Power. For instance, let us suppose members of Parliament, or of the Privy Council, took an oath that they would not acknowledge the right of succession of a Prince of Wales, if he became a Catholic: in that case I should not consider the Pope could release me from that oath, had I bound myself by it. . . . It should be clear that though the Pope bade all Catholics to stand firm in one phalanx for the Catholic Succession, still, while I remained in office, or in my place in Parliament, I could not do as he bade me.

. . . When, then, Mr. Gladstone asks Catholics how they can obey the Queen and yet obey the Pope, since it may happen that the commands of the two authorities may clash, I answer, that it is my rule, both to obey the one and to obey the other, but that there is no rule in this world without exceptions, and if either the Pope or the Queen demanded of me an "Absolute Obedience," he or she would be transgressing the laws of human society. I give an absolute obedience to neither. Further, if ever this double allegiance pulled me in contrary ways, which in this age of this world I think it never will, then I should decide according to the particular case, which is beyond all rule, and must be decided on its own merits. I should look to see what theologians could do for me, what the Bishops and clergy around me, what my confessor; what my friends whom I revered; and if, after all, I could not take their view of the matter, then I must rule myself by my own judgment and my own conscience. But all this is hypothetical and unreal.[15]

ECONOMIC ORDER

THE CATHOLIC CHURCH AND THE ECONOMIC ORDER :
POPE LEO XIII

The great mistake made in regard to the matter now under consideration is to take up with the notion that class is naturally hostile to class, and that the wealthy and the working-men are intended by nature to live in mutual conflict. So irrational and so false is this view, that the direct contrary is the truth. Just as the symmetry of the human frame is the resultant of the disposition of the bodily members, so in a State is it ordained by nature that these two classes should dwell in harmony and agreement, and should, as it were, groove into one another, so as to maintain the balance of the body politic. Each needs the other: Capital cannot do without Labor, nor Labor without Capital. Mutual agreement results in pleasantness of life and the beauty of good order; while perpetual conflict necessarily produces confusion and savage barbarity. Now, in preventing such strife as this, and in uprooting it, the efficacy of Christian institutions is marvellous and manifold. First of all, there is no intermediary more powerful than Religion (whereof the Church is the interpreter and guardian) in drawing the rich, and the poor bread-winners, together, by reminding each class of its duties to the other, and especially of the obligations of justice. Thus Religion teaches the laboring man and the artisan to carry out honestly and fairly all equitable agreements freely entered into; never to injure the property, nor to outrage the person, of an employer; never to resort to violence in defending their own cause, nor to engage in riot or disorder; and to have nothing to do with men of evil principles, who work upon the people with artful promises, and excite foolish hopes which usually end in useless regrets, followed by insolvency. Religion teaches the wealthy owner and the employer that their work-people are not to be accounted their bondsmen; that in every man they must respect his dignity and worth as a man and as a Christian; that labor is not a thing to be ashamed of, if we lend ear to right reason and to Christian philosophy, but is an honorable calling, enabling a man to sustain his life in a way upright and creditable; and that it is shameful and inhuman to treat men like chattels to make money by, or to look upon them merely as so much muscle or physical power. Again, therefore, the Church teaches that, as Religion and things spiritual and mental are among the workingman's main concerns, the employer is bound to see that the worker has time for his religious duties; that he be not exposed to corrupting influences and dangerous occasions; and that he be not led away to neglect his home and family, or to squander his earnings. Furthermore, the employer must never tax his work-people beyond their strength, or employ them in work unsuited to their sex or age. His great and principal duty is to give every one a fair wage. Doubtless, before deciding whether wages are adequate, many things have to be considered; but wealthy owners and all masters of labor should be mindful of this—that to exercise pressure upon the indigent and the destitute for the sake of gain, and to gather one's profit out of the need of another, is condemned by all laws, human and divine. To defraud any one of wages that are his due is a crime which cries to the avenging anger of Heaven. *Behold, the hire of the laborers . . . which by fraud hath been kept back by you, crieth aloud; and the cry of them hath entered into the ears of the Lord of Sabaoth.** Lastly, the rich must religiously refrain from cutting down the workmen's earnings, whether by force, by fraud, or by usurious dealing; and with all the greater reason because the laboring man is, as a rule, weak and unprotected, and because his slender means should in proportion to their scantiness be accounted sacred.

Were these precepts carefully obeyed and followed out, would they not be sufficient of themselves to keep under all strife and all its causes?

* St. James v. 4.

But the Church, with Jesus Christ as her Master and Guide, aims higher still. She lays down precepts yet more perfect, and tries to bind class to class in friendliness and good feeling. The things of earth cannot be understood or valued aright without taking into consideration the life to come, the life that will know no death.

... If Christian precepts prevail, the respective classes will not only be united in the bonds of friendship, but also in those of brotherly love. For they will understand and feel that all men are children of the same common Father, who is God; that all have alike the same last end, which is God Himself, who alone can make either men or angels absolutely and perfectly happy; that each and all are redeemed and made sons of God, by Jesus Christ, *the first-born among many brethren;* that the blessings of nature and the gifts of grace belong to the whole human race in common, and that from none except the unworthy is withheld the inheritance of the kingdom of heaven. *If sons, heirs also; heirs indeed of God, and co-heirs of Christ.*†[16]

† Rom. viii. 17.

The Last Things

Precious in the sight of the Lord is the death of His saints.[1]

The value of time and of life for the Christian is in the value of eternity. If eternity is not, time is meaningless. The fact that nature is the scene and the stuff of divine activity, the unfolding drama of the imaging of God in nature, renders to nature and time an intrinsic goodness in the eyes of God and of men. "And God saw all the things that he had made, and they were very good" (Genesis 1:31). Above all, the entrance of God Himself in the person of Christ at a unique moment of history redeemed time, gave it direction for man. Time and the things of time are, then, for the Christian good; they are to be loved as God loves them. The life of faith and charity is, in fact, the life of eternity in time.

Still, the vision which will fulfill faith is beyond time; the fulfillment of hope and the supreme realization of love are beyond. In time, man must live for eternity. So, too, is time the scene of the trial of man, the test of his worthiness for eternity. Through the infinite redemptive merit of Christ, man earns his eternity in time. The "state of term" follows "the state of trial." More real even than the things of time must be the "Last Thing."

Catholic belief specifies Four Last Things: Death, Judgment, Hell, Heaven. While treating of these, however, we shall add two other beliefs which fill out the vision of man's ultimate destiny: Purgatory and the Resurrection of the Body.

DEATH

The last moment, the moment of death, is a universal condition of man. It is an awesome moment even for the devout Christian, for it is that moment when loved ones are left, meriting ends, mercy becomes justice: for the greatest saint it can be the greatest moment of trial in a life of endless trial. For this reason, the Catholic is encouraged endlessly to meditate on the moment of his death and unceasingly to pray for "a happy death." In a real sense, the good life is a preparation for a good death.

DEATH : ST. AMBROSE

We know, however, that it [the soul] survives the body and that being set free from the bars of the body, it sees with clear gaze those things which before, dwelling in the body, it could not see.

. . . Let not my soul die in sin, nor admit sin into itself, but let it die in the soul of the righteous, that it may receive his righteousness. For He who dies in Christ is made a partaker of his grace.

Death is not, then, an object of dread, nor bitter to those in need, nor too bitter to the rich, nor unkind to the old, nor a mark of cowardice to the brave, nor everlasting to the faithful, nor unexpected to the wise. For how many have consecrated their lives by the renown of their death alone.

By the death of martyrs, religion has been defended, faith increased, the Church strengthened; the dead have conquered, the persecution been overcome. So we celebrate the death of those of whose lives we are ignorant. So, David rejoiced in prophecy at the departure of his own soul, saying "Precious in the sight of the Lord is the death of his saints" (Ps. 115:15). He esteemed death better than life.

But why should more be said? By the death of One the world was redeemed. For Christ had He willed, need not have died, but He neither thought that death should be shunned as though there were any cowardice in it, nor could He have saved us better than by dying. For His death is the life of

all. We are signed with the sign of His death, we show forth
His death when we pray; when we offer the Sacrifice we
declare His death, for His death is victory, His death is our
mystery, His death is the yearly recurring solemnity of the
world. What should we say concerning His death, since we
prove by this divine example that death alone found immortality and that death redeemed itself.[2]

DEATH : ST. BERNARD OF CLAIRVAUX ON THE DEATH
OF HIS BROTHER GERARD

You know, my children, what deep cause I have of sorrow;
for you knew that faithful companion who has now left me
alone in the path wherein we walked together; you know the
services he rendered to me; the care which he took of all
things; the diligence with which he performed all actions;
the sweetness which characterized all his conduct. Who can
be to me as he was? Who has ever loved me as he did? He
was my brother by ties of blood; but he was far more my
brother by bond of religion. Pity my lot, you who know all
this. I was weak in body and he supported me; I was timid
and he encouraged me; I was slow and he excited me to
action; I was wanting in memory and foresight and he re-
minded me. O my brother, why hast thou been torn from
me? O my well-beloved, why didst thou leave thy brother?
O man according to my own heart, why has death parted
us, who were so closely bound together during life? No, death
alone could have made this cruel separation. What else but
death, implacable death, the enemy of all things sweet, could
have broken this link of love so gentle, so tender, so lively,
so intense? Cruel death! by taking away one, thou hast killed
two at once; for the life which is left to me is heavier than
death. Yes, my Gerard, it would have been better for me to
die than lose thee. Thy zeal animated me in all my duties;
thy fidelity was my comfort at all times; thy prudence accompanied all my steps.

We rejoiced together in our fraternal union; our mutual
converse was dear to us both; but I alone have lost this
happiness, for thou hast found far greater consolation; thou
dost enjoy the immortal presence of Jesus Christ and the

company of angels; what have I to fill the void which thou hast left? O! I fain would know what are thy feelings toward the brother who was thine only beloved—if, now that thou art plunged in the floods of divine light and inebriated with eternal bliss, thou art yet permitted to think of our miseries, to concern thyself about our sorrows; for, perhaps, although thou hast known us according to the flesh, thou knowest us no more. *He who is attached to God is but one spirit with Him.* He has no longer any thought or care but for God and the things of God, because he is wholly filled with God. Now, *God is love;* and the more closely a soul is united with God, the fuller it is of love. It is true, that God is impassible; but He is not insensible; for the quality most proper to Him is to have compassion and to forgive. Therefore, thou must needs be merciful who art united to the source of mercy; and although thou art delivered from misery, thou hast not ceased to compassionate our suffering; and thy affection is not diminished by being transformed. Thou hast laid aside thy infirmities, but not thy charity; for *charity abideth*, says the Apostle. Ah no, thou wilt not forget us throughout eternity.

Alas, whom shall I now consult in my sorrow? To whom shall I have recourse in my difficulties? Who will bear with me the burden of my woes? . . .

Flow, then, my tears, since you must fall; let the fountains of my eyes open, and let the waters pour forth, abundantly to wash away the faults which have brought this chastisement upon me.

I mourn, but I murmur not. The divine justice hath dealt rightly with us both; one has been justly punished; the other deservedly crowned. I will say then—the Lord has shown Himself equally just and merciful; He gave him to us; He hath taken him away; and if we are made desolate by the loss, let us not forget the gift we so long enjoyed. I beseech you, bear patiently with my complaints. For my part, I regret not the things of the world, but I regret Gerard. My soul was so bound up in his that the two made but one. Doubtless the ties of blood contributed to this attraction; but our chief bond was the union of hearts, the conformity of thought, will and sentiment. And as we were in truth but one heart, the sword of death pierced both at once, and cut us in two parts—one in heaven, the other left in the dust of this world. Some one will, perhaps, tell me—your grief is carnal. I deny not that it is human, as I deny not that I am a man. Nay, more, I will grant that it is carnal, since I myself am carnal—the slave of sin, destined to die, subject to misery. What! Gerard is taken from me—my brother in blood, my son in religion, my father in his care of me, my only-beloved in his affection, my very soul in his love—he is taken from me and must I feel it not? I am wounded, wounded grievously. Forgive me, my children; compass the sorrow of your father. No! I murmur not against the judgment of God. He renders to every man according to his works; to Gerard the crown which he has won; to me the anguish which is good to me. God grant, my Gerard, that I may not have lost thee, but thou only mayest precede me, and that I may follow whither thou art gone! For, assuredly thou art gone to join those whom thou didst call upon to praise God with thee, when in the middle of that last night, to the astonishment of all present, thou didst suddenly intone, with a calm countenance, the verse of the psalm, "Praise the Lord, all ye in heaven" (Ps. 148:1). At that moment, oh my brother, it was already day with thee, notwithstanding the darkness of our night; and that night was full of light to thee. They called me to witness this miracle, to see a man rejoicing in death. O death, where is thy victory? O death, where is thy sting? To him thou art no sting but a song of jubilee. This man dies singing and sings as he is dying. And death, that mother of sorrow, becomes to him a source of joy! I had no sooner reached the bedside of the dying man, than I heard him pronounce aloud the words of the Psalmist, "Father, into thy hands I commend my spirit." Then, repeating that same verse and dwelling on the words "Father, Father," he turned to me and said with a smile "Oh, what goodness in God to be Father of men; and what glory for men to be children of God." Thus died he whom we all deplore; and I confess that it almost changed my affliction into rejoicing, so did his happiness make me forget my misery. . . . Lord, I beseech thee, stay these tears and moderate my grief.[3]

PARTICULAR JUDGMENT

At the moment of his death every man is judged according to his deserts. The time for merit is over; a man is either a friend or an enemy of God and so he remains for eternity.

PARTICULAR JUDGMENT : COUNCIL OF FLORENCE

And so if persons duly penitent die in the charity of God (i.e., in sanctifying grace) before they have satisfied by due works of penance for their sins and omissions, their souls are purified after death by the fires of purgatory . . . and the souls of those who have incurred no stain of sin after their Baptism, and those souls, too, who though stained have been duly purged whether with their bodies or after separation from their bodies as we mentioned above, are straightway received into heaven and clearly behold God Himself in three divine Persons. . . . And then the souls of those who die in actual mortal sin . . . straightway go down into hell.[4]

PURGATORY

Purgatory is a place or state in which are detained the souls of those who die in grace, in friendship with God, but with the blemish of venial sin or with temporal debt for sin unpaid. Here the soul is purged, cleansed, readied for eternal union with God in Heaven. The suffering of the soul in Purgatory is intense, yet it is a suffering in love: the souls in Purgatory are not turned from God; they are deprived of the vision of God but they are united with Him by love. Theirs is a twofold suffering, that of privation of God for a time and that of physical pain.

The logic of the existence of Purgatory for the Catholic is found in that fact that a person may die in the friendship of God, yet not be ready for the ultimate vision of God. He may have failed to do sufficient reparation

for his offenses, even though he has admitted them. It is
inconceivable to a Catholic that such a soul would, or
would want to, attain immediate presence of God.

The Catholic Church teaches as well that a person in
life may shorten his term in Purgatory or that of another
soul by application of indulgences which are given for
prayer and good works. To understand this, we must bear
in mind that all merit is derived ultimately from the
infinite satisfaction of Christ's sacrifice. In founding the
Church, Christ gave Her powers in earth and heaven and
placed in Her keeping the infinite merits of His life. Indulgences are the application by the Church of the infinite
merits of Christ in His suffering for the sins of men. The
power of the Church to grant indulgences follows from
the powers the Church claims as the Body of Christ on
earth.

PRAYER FOR THE DEAD : MACHABEES

And making a gathering, he [Judas Machabeus] sent twelve
thousand drachms of silver to Jerusalem for sacrifice to be
offered for the sins of the dead, thinking well and religiously
concerning the resurrection.

And because he considered that they who had fallen asleep
with godliness had great grace laid up for them.

It is therefore a holy and wholesome thought to pray for
the dead, that they may be loosed from sins.[5]

PURGATORY AND PRAYERS OF THE FAITHFUL : COUNCIL OF FLORENCE

If persons duly penitent die in the charity of God, before
they have satisfied by due works of penance for their sins
and omissions, their souls are purified after death by the fires
of purgatory: and unto the relief of such pains there avail
the prayers of the faithful on earth, that is to say the sacrifices
of the Mass, supplications and alms and other offices of piety
which the faithful have been accustomed to offer for each
other according to established customs of the Church.[6]

INDULGENCES AND SATISFACTION :
JACQUES BÉNIGNE BOSSUET

Catholics unanimously teach that Jesus Christ alone, true God and true man, was capable by the infinite dignity of his person fully to satisfy for our sins. But having offered up superabundant satisfaction for them, he might apply this for us in two different ways, either by abolishing them entirely without any punishment whatever or by changing a greater punishment to a lesser; that is, by changing eternal into temporal suffering. As the first way is more ample and more conformable to His goodness, He adopts it in baptism; but we believe that He makes use of the second method in the forgiveness granted to baptized persons, who fall back again into sin; being forced to it in some sort, by their ingratitude in the abuse of his first gifts, so that though the eternal punishment be forgiven them, they have still temporal suffering to endure.

From this it must not be concluded that Jesus Christ has not entirely satisfied for us; but on the contrary, that having acquired an absolute dominion over us, by the price which he paid for our salvation, He grants to us pardon, upon such terms, such conditions, and with such exceptions as He thinks proper.

We should do an injury and be ungrateful to our Saviour if we dared to dispute the infinite value of His merits under a pretext, that while He pardoned the sin of Adam, He doth not at the same time, free us from all its consequences, but leaves us still subject to death and to so many infirmities of body and soul, which this sin hath occasioned. It is sufficient that Jesus Christ has fully paid the price of that total emancipation from our evils which is one day to take place; in the meantime, it is ours to receive with humility and thanksgiving, every portion of His bounty, viewing the progress of our deliverance in the order His wisdom hath established for our advantage, and for a fuller manifestation of His own godliness and justice.

By the same rule, we should not be surprised if He who shows Himself so forgiving in baptism becomes more rigid toward us when we have violated these sacred promises. It is just, it is even advantageous for us, that in pardoning the sin, with the eternal punishment due to it, he requires some temporal punishment to hold us to the line of duty, lest being too speedily disengaged from the ties of justice, we abandon ourselves to a presumption of confidence, perverting in this manner to our own ruin His readiness to pardon.

It is therefore to fulfill this obligation that we are enjoined certain painful works, which should be performed in a spirit of humility and penance, and it is the necessity of performing such satisfactory works, that obliged the primitive church to impose upon converted sinners the penances which are called canonical.

Now, when she imposes those penances upon sinners, and when they submit humbly to them, that is what we call satisfaction. But when in consideration of the fervour of penitents, or in consideration of other good works performed by them, she remits a part of that punishment to them, this is called indulgence.

The Council of Trent proposes nothing more to our belief upon the subject of indulgences, than "that the power of granting them, hath been given by Jesus Christ to the church, and that the use of them is salutary"; adding "that it should be retained; with moderation, however, lest ecclesiastical discipline come to be enervated by an excess of mildness," which shows us that the manner of dispensing indulgences is an affair of mere discipline.

Those who depart this life in the state of grace and charity but without having discharged the debt of temporal punishment due by them to the divine justice suffer that punishment in the other life.

That is the reason why all Christians of antiquity offered up prayers, alms, and sacrifices, for the faithful who expired in the peace and communion of the church, in firm confidence that they were assisted and relieved by those suffrages. It is what the Council of Trent proposes to our belief concerning the souls in Purgatory, without determining the nature of their punishment nor many other things of the sort, upon which the greatest reserve is recommended by the Council, at the same time that all those are blamed by it, who advance what is either suspicious or uncertain upon the subject.

Such is the harmless and pious doctrine of the Catholic

Church on the subject of satisfactory works, which hath been imputed to her as so great a crime. If after this exposition, the gentlemen of the Reformation still object to us, that we do an injury to the satisfaction of Jesus Christ, they must forget our having already declared, that He hath paid the full price of our redemption, that nothing is wanting to the price; whereas it is infinite; and that these satisfactory works we have spoken of do not proceed from any deficiency in this matter, but from a certain order which He Himself hath established, the better to restrain us by the salutary discipline of reasonable apprehension. If they further impeach us with believing that of ourselves we are fully adequate to discharge a part of the punishment of our offences, we can truly say that the contrary is manifest from the maxims we have just laid down. They incontrovertibly show that our salvation is a mere work of mercy and of grace; that what we do by the grace of God is no less His, than what He does of Himself by His own absolute will; and that, in short, whatever we give Him, is as much His own already as what He is pleased to give to us. Let us also recall, that what we with the whole primitive church call satisfaction is nothing else after all than application of the infinite satisfaction of Jesus Christ.

This same consideration should quiet those who take offence at our saying that God holds fraternal charity and the communion of saints in so favourable a light, that He frequently accepts the satisfaction which we offer for each other. It would seem that these gentlemen do not comprehend how much our whole being is the property of God, nor how necessary a relation all His regards for the faithful bear to Jesus Christ who is their head. But surely those who have read and who have reflected that God Himself inspires His servants to mortify themselves with fasting and sackcloth and ashes, not only for their own sins, but for the sins of all the people, will not be astonished at our saying that, pleased with gratifying His friends, He mercifully accepts the humble sacrifice of their voluntary mortifications, in diminution of the chastisements which were to fall upon his people, which shows that, satisfied by some, He graciously relents toward others, honouring by these means His Son Jesus Christ in the communion of His members and in the holy society of His Mystical Body.[7]

Eternal rest grant unto them, O Lord: and perpetual light shine upon them.

Absolve, O Lord, the souls of all the faithful departed from all bond of sin, and by the assistance of Thy grace, may they deserve to escape the avenging judgment and enjoy the happiness of eternal light.

Grant, we beseech Thee, almighty God, that the soul of Thy servant which has this day departed out of this world, may be purified by this sacrifice, delivered from sins, and may receive forgiveness and eternal rest.[8]

SECOND COMING, GENERAL JUDGMENT, RESURRECTION OF THE BODY

At the end of the world, Christ will come again triumphant as judge of all men and all angels. This is the second coming and the general judgment to which Christ referred many times in speaking with his apostles. This belief is a firm part of the Catholic tradition.

The general judgment will manifest the mercy and the justice of God in the total history of creation. Scripture indicates that it will be preceded by the universal preaching of the gospel (Matt. 24:14), the conversion of the Jews (Romans 11:25), the great apostasy and the coming of anti-Christ (2 Thess. 2:3-4), and extraordinary disturbances of nature (Matt. 24:29).

At the second coming, the souls of all men will be reunited with their bodies. This resurrection of the dead is more than immortality of the soul: it is resurrection of man in the fullness of his nature. The human body will be glorified, according to Catholic belief, to prepare it for eternal life. "Then shall the just shine as the sun in the kingdom of the Father" (Matt. 13:43).

All men in their integral nature will at the Last Judgment find eternal destiny in Heaven or Hell.

THE SECOND COMING : CYRIL OF JERUSALEM

We preach not one advent only of Christ, but a second also, far more glorious than the former. For the former gave to view His patience but the latter brings with it the Crown of the divine kingdom. For all things, to speak generally, are twofold in Jesus Christ. His generation is twofold: the one, of God, before the worlds; the other, of the Virgin, in the end of the world. His descent is twofold: one was in obscurity, like the dew on the fleece; the second is His open coming, which is to be. In His former advent, He was wrapped in swaddling clothes in the manger; in the second, "he covereth Himself with light as with a garment" (Ps. 104:2). In His first coming, He endured the Cross, despising the shame (Heb. 12:2) but in his second, He comes attended by the Angel host, receiving glory. Let us not rest in His first advent, but look also for His second. . . .

The things then which are seen shall pass away and there shall come the things which are looked for, things fairer than these; but as to the time let no one be curious. "For it is not for you," he says "to know the times or moments, which the Father hath put in his own power" (Acts 1:7). And venture not to declare when these things shall be, nor on the other hand abandon thyself to slumber. For He saith, "Watch, for in such an hour as ye think not the Son of Man cometh" (Matt. 24:42,44). . . .

But what is the sign of His coming? Lest the hostile power dare to counterfeit it. "And there shall appear," he says "the sign of the Son of Man in Heaven" (Matt. 24:30). But Christ's own true sign is the Cross; a sign of a luminous cross shall go before the King, plainly declaring Him who was formerly crucified; that the Jews who before pierced Him and plotted against Him, when they see it, *may mourn tribe by tribe*, saying This is He who was smitten, this is He whose face they spat upon, this is He on whom they put chains, this is He whom of old they crucified, and set at naught; whither, they will say, shall we flee from the face of His wrath? But the Angel hosts shall encompass them so that they shall not be able to flee anywhere. The Sign of the Cross shall be a terror to His foes, but of joy to His friends who have believed in Him or preached him or suffered for His sake. Who then is that blessed man, who shall be found the friend of Christ? That King, so great and glorious, attended by trains of angels, the fellow of the Father's throne, will not despise His own servants. For, lest the elect be confused with his foes, He shall send his angels with a trumpet and a great voice: and they shall gather his elect from the four winds (Matt. 24:31). He despised no one, even Lot; how then shall he despise many righteous. *Come ye blessed of my Father*, will he say to them.

. . . Let us shudder lest God condemn us; who needs not enquiry or proofs, to condemn. Say not, in the night I committed fornication or wrought sorcery or did any other thing and there was no one by. Out of thine own conscience shalt thou be judged, "thy thoughts between themselves accusing or defending one another, In the day when God shall judge the secrets of men" (Rom. 2:15-16). The terrible countenance of the judge will force thee to speak the truth; or rather, even though thou speak not, it will convict thee. For thou shalt rise clothed with thy own sins or else thy righteousness. And this hath the Judge himself declared (for it is Christ who judges, "for the Father judgeth no man but hath committed all judgment to the Son" [John 5:22], not divesting Himself of His power, but judging through the Son; therefore the Son judgeth by the will of the Father; for the wills of the Father and the Son are not different, but one and the same). What then says the Judge, as to whether they shall have been thy works or no? "And before him all nations shall be gathered together; and he shall separate them one from another, as the shepherd separateth the sheep from the goats: and he shall set the sheep on his right hand, and the goats on his left" (Matt. 25:32-33). How does a shepherd make the separation? Does he examine out of a book which is a sheep and which a goat? or does he distinguish by their plain marks? In like manner, if thou hast been cleansed from thy sins, thy deeds shall be as pure wool.[9]

RESURRECTION OF THE DEAD : ST. PAUL

Now if Christ be preached, that he arose again from the dead, how do some among you say that there is no resurrection of the dead?

But if there be no resurrection of the dead, then Christ is not risen again.

And if Christ be not risen again, then is our preaching vain: and your faith is also vain.

Yea, and we are found false witnesses of God: because we have given testimony against God, that he hath raised up Christ, whom he hath not raised up, if the dead rise not again.

For if the dead rise not again, neither is Christ risen again.

And if Christ be not risen again, your faith is vain: for you are yet in your sins.

Then they also that are fallen asleep in Christ are perished. If in this life only we have hope in Christ, we are of all men most miserable.

But now Christ is risen from the dead, the firstfruits of them that sleep:

For by a man came death: and by a man the resurrection of the dead.

And as in Adam all die, so also in Christ all shall be made alive.[10]

RESURRECTION OF THE BODY : CLEMENT OF ROME

And let not any one of you say that this flesh is not judged and does not rise again. Understand: In what state were you saved, in what did you recover your sight, except in this flesh? We must, therefore, guard the flesh as a temple of God. Just as you were called in the flesh, so shall you come in the flesh. If Christ the Lord who called us, being spirit at first, became flesh and so saved us, so also shall we receive our reward in this flesh. Let us then love one another that we may all arrive at the Kingdom of God. While we have time to be healed, let us give ourselves to God the Healer, giving Him some recompense. What recompense? Repentance from a sincere heart. For He has foreknowledge of all things and knows what is in our hearts.[11]

HELL

Those who die in grave sin, deliberately turned from good as enemies of God will spend eternity in Hell: a place or state of eternal separation from God and of eternal punishment. In the sufferings of the damned, Catholic tradition holds that the most terrible is the insatiable hunger for God which will reach its keenest in Hell, a hunger which the damned will know as the fullest expression of his nature's needs and whose eternal unfulfillment he himself has brought about.

HELL : ST. AUGUSTINE

When God punishes sinners, He does not inflict His evil on them, but leaves them to their own evil. "Behold," saith the Psalmist, "he hath been in labour with injustice, he hath conceived toil; brought forth iniquity. He hath opened a pit and dug it: and he is fallen into the hole he made. His sorrow shall be turned on his own head: and his iniquity shall come down upon his crown" (Ps. vii, 15 *sqq.*).[12]

To be gone from the kingdom of God, to be an exile from God's city, to be cut off from the divine life, to be without the manifold sweetness of God . . . is so mighty a punishment that no torments that we know can be compared with it.[13]

HELL : ROBERT CARDINAL BELLARMINE

It remaineth that we consider the justice which God will use in punishing sinners in the uttermost depths of hell. Wherefore if we mark with attention and diligence, we shall indeed understand that it is most true which the Apostle teaches "It is a fearful thing to fall into the hands of the living God" (Heb. 10:31).

For God the just judge will punish all sins though ever so small, as, for example, an idle word, for so we read in the Gospel: "Every idle word that men shall speak, they shall render an account of it in the day of judgment" (Matt. 12:36).

Neither shall all sins be punished only, but so horribly punished that scarcely any man can imagine it. For as no eye hath seen, nor ear heard; neither hath it entered into the heart of man, what things God hath prepared for them that love him (1 Cor. 2:9), so no eye hath seen nor ear heard, neither has it entered into the heart of man what things God has prepared for those who hate him.

The punishments of sinners in hell shall be very great, very many and very pure, to wit, mixed with no comforts and which shall increase their misery everlasting. They shall be many because every power of the soul and every sense shall be tormented. Weigh the words of the highest Judge's sentence "Get ye away from me, ye cursed, into everlasting fire which has been prepared for the devil and his angels" (Matt. 25:41). Get ye away, He saith, depart ye from the company of the blessed, being forever deprived of the sight of God, which is the highest essential happiness and best end for which you were created. *Ye cursed*, He saith, that is, hope not hereafter for any benediction for ye are deprived of the life of grace and all hope of salvation; the water of wisdom and dew of divine inspiration shall not rain upon you; the beams of heavenly light shall not shine upon you; neither the grace of repentance nor the flower of charity, nor the fruits of good works shall grow in you. Neither shall ye lose only spiritual and eternal goods, but also corporal and temporal; ye shall have no riches, no delights, no comforts, but shall be like the fig tree which being cursed by me withered from the root all over (Matt. 21:19). *Into fire*, that is, into the furnace of burning and unquenchable fire (Matt. 13:42) which shall not consume one member alone but all the members together with horrible punishment. *Everlasting*, that is, into a fire which is blown by the breath of the Almighty and therefore needeth no fuel to make it always to burn, that as your fault shall still remain, so your punishment shall forever endure. Therefore I can truly exclaim "Which of you can dwell with devouring fire? Which of you shall dwell with everlasting burnings?" (Isa. 33:14). For there shall be the worm of conscience and remembrance of this life wherein they might easily, if they would, have escaped their punishment and obtained eternal joys. . . .

But if all these things which we have said of the loss of all goods both celestial and terrestrial and of most unsufferable dolours, ignominies and disgraces were to have end, or at least some kind of comfort or mitigation as all miseries in this life have, they might in some sort be thought tolerable; but since it is most certain and undeniable that the happiness of the blessed shall continue forever without mixture of misery, so likewise shall the unhappiness of the damned continue forever without mixture of comfort.

Lastly, if the sin of the damned were not eternal, we might marvel that the punishment thereof should be eternal but seeing that the obstinacy of the damned is eternal, why should we wonder if their punishment is also eternal? And this wilful obstinacy in wickedness, which is in both the damned and the devils, I say, this perverse will, which is in them averted from God the chief happiness, and shall so forever remain, maketh holy men more to fear a mortal sin than hell fire.[14]

HEAVEN

Those who die in the love and friendship of God enjoy forever the face-to-face vision of God. The soul and God are united in an act of love: vision fills the mind, love engages the will, there is born perfect and unceasing joy in union with the supreme Good for which all nature yearns. "Eye hath not seen, nor ear heard, neither hath it entered into the heart of man, what things God has prepared for them that love him" (1 Cor. 2:9).

THE JOY OF HEAVEN : POPE BENEDICT XII

Those who after the ascension of Our Savior Jesus Christ into heaven have died or shall have died, have been, are and shall be in heaven, in the kingdom of the heavens, in the celestial paradise with Christ and joined to the company of the holy angels . . . And they see the divine essence with intuitive, even with face-to-face vision, with no creature thrusting itself in between by means of which they might be able to see, but with the divine essence showing itself to them directly, unveiled and clear. And so, after this manner of vision, they enjoy the same divine essence. And moreover it is on account of this very vision and this very enjoyment that the souls of those who have passed from this life are truly happy; and they have rest and life everlasting.[15]

ETERNAL PEACE : ST. AUGUSTINE

Peace there will be there, perfect peace will be there. Where thou wishest thou shalt be, but from God thou wilt not depart. Where thou wishest thou shalt be, but wherever thou goest thou shalt have thy God. With Him, from whom thou art blessed, shalt thou ever be.[16]

THE VISION OF PARADISE : THE APOCALYPSE

And I saw a new heaven and a new earth. For the first heaven and the first earth was gone: and the sea is now no more.

And I, John, saw the holy city, the new Jerusalem, coming down out of heaven from God, prepared as a bride adorned for her husband.

And I heard a great voice from the throne, saying: Behold the tabernacle of God with men: and he will dwell with them. And they shall be his people: and God himself with them shall be their God.

And God shall wipe away all tears from their eyes: and death shall be no more. Nor mourning, nor crying, nor sorrow shall be any more: for the former things are passed away. . . .

And he said to me: It is done. I am Alpha and Omega: the Beginning and the End. To him that thirsteth I will give of the fountain of the water of life, freely.

He that shall overcome shall possess these things. And I will be his God: and he shall be my son. . . .

And there came one of the seven angels, who had the vials full of the seven last plagues, and spoke with me saying: Come and I will shew thee the bride, the wife of the Lamb.

And he took me up in spirit to a great and high mountain: and he shewed me the holy city Jerusalem, coming down out of heaven from God.

Having the glory of God. And the light thereof was like to a precious stone, as to the jasper stone even as crystal.

And it had a wall great and high, having twelve gates, and

in the gates twelve angels, and names written thereon, which are the names of the twelve tribes of the children of Israel. . . .

And the wall of the city had twelve foundations: and in them, the twelve names of the twelve apostles of the Lamb. . . .

And I saw no temple therein. For the Lord God Almighty is the temple thereof, and the Lamb.

And the city hath no need of the sun, nor of the moon, to shine in it. For the glory of God hath enlightened it: and the Lamb is the lamp thereof.

And the nations shall walk in the light of it: and the kings of the earth shall bring their glory and honor into it.

And the gates thereof shall not be shut by day: for there shall be no night there.

And they shall bring the glory and honour of nations into it.

There shall not enter into it any thing defiled or that worketh abomination or maketh a lie: but they that are written in the book of life of the Lamb. . . .

And they shall see his face: and his name shall be on their foreheads.[17]

References
and
Index of Sources

References

Standard references used in the preparation of this work are referred to in the references by the following symbols:

[LF] *Library of the Fathers of the Holy Catholic Church,* ed., E. P. Pusey, J. H. Newman, J. Keble, and C. Merriot (Oxford: J. H. Parker, 1838–85).

[AN] *The Anti-Nicene Fathers,* ed. Rev. Alexander Roberts, D.D., and James Donaldson, L.L.D. (Buffalo: The Christian Literature Publishing Company, 1885–96).

[NF] *A Select Library of the Nicene and Post-Nicene Fathers of the Christian Church,* ed. Philip Schaff (Buffalo: The Christian Literature Publishing Company, 1886–90).

[NF2] *A Select Library of the Nicene and Post-Nicene Fathers of the Christian Church,* ed., Philip Schaff, D.D. and Henry Wace, D.D. Second Series (Buffalo: The Christian Literature Publishing Company, 1890–94).

[TM] *St. Augustine,* Sir Toby Matthew's translation, ed. by Dom Roger Hudleston, O.S.B. (1620).

Biblical references are given from the Douay version.
Editor's translations are so indicated.

CHAPTER I

1. Wisdom 2:5.
2. Eccl. 3:1–9.
3. St. Augustine, *Enarationes in Psalmos,* XXXVIII, 7 (LF).
4. St. Augustine, *Sermo XVII,* vii, 7 (LF).
5. St. Augustine, *Enarrationes in Psalmos,* XLI, 13 (LF).
6. Eccl. 1:2–10, 14–15.
7. Job 8:11–15; 14:1–2.
8. Wisdom 3:11; 2:1–5.
9. St. John Chrysostom, *The Vanity of the World* (NF).
10. Ps. 41:2–5, 12.
11. St. Augustine, *Confessions,* I, i, 1; VII, viii, 16; X, xxvii, 38 (TM).

CHAPTER II

1. Ps. 18:1.
2. St. Anselm, *Proslogion,* 1, (ed. tr.).
3. Henry Edward Manning, *The Vatican Council* (New York, 1871) I, 209.
4. St. Anselm, *op. cit.*
5. St. Bonaventure, *Itinerarium* III (ed. tr.).
6. Wisdom 13:1–3.
7. Romans 1:20–25.

8. St. Augustine, *Sermo* CCXLI, ii, 2; iii, 3 (LF).
9. St. Thomas Aquinas, *Summa Theologiae,* I, q. 2, a. 3 (ed. tr.).
10. John Henry Newman, *A Grammar of Assent* (London, 1870), ch. V.
11. St. Augustine, *In Joannis Evangelium tractatus* XIII, 5 (LF).
12. St. Augustine, *Sermo* LII, vi, 16 (LF).
13. St. Augustine, *Confessions,* X, vi, 8 (TM).
14. Manning, *op. cit.,* Constitution *"Dei Filius,"* I.
15. St. Bonaventure, *Itinerarium,* V (ed. tr.).
16. St. Augustine, *Confessions,* XI, xiii, 16 (TM).
17. St. Augustine, *The City of God,* XI, 4–6 (NF).
18. Pius XII, Encyclical, *Humani Generis,* authorized English translation.
19. Matt. 6:25–34.
20. St. John Damascene, *Exposition of the Orthodox Faith* (NF2).

7. Gen. 3:22–24.
8. St. Anselm, *De conceptione virginis et peccato originali,* c. 27, cited in Chetwood, *op. cit.*
9. Cited in *ibid.*
10. St. Thomas Aquinas, *Summa theologiae* I, ii, q. 82, a. 3 (ed. tr.).
11. *The Canons and Decrees of the Sacred and Ecumenical Council of Trent* (London: Burns Oates; New York: Catholic Publication Society, 1848), Sess. V., D. 789.
12. John Henry Newman, *Apologia pro Vita Sua* (London, 1864), ch. V.
13. Lamentations 5:1–7, 15–22.
14. Romans 7:14–25.
15. Isa. 11:1–5.
16. Isa. 35:1–4.
17. Isa. 7:14.
18. Isa. 40:10–11.
19. Isa. 45:8.
20. Ps. 129.
21. Luke 3:2–6.
22. Selections from the Liturgy for Advent.

CHAPTER III

1. Isa. 11:1.
2. Pius XII, Encyclical, *Humani Generis,* authorized English translation.
3. John Henry Newman, *A Grammar of Assent,* ch. V.
4. Origen, *On Prayer* (AN).
5. Hugh of St. Victor, *Expositio in Hierarchiam caelestem* IV (ed. tr.).
6. St. John Damascene, *De Fide Orthodoxi,* L. 2, c. 30, cited in Thomas B. Chetwood, S. J., *God and Creation* (New York: Benziger Bros., 1928).

CHAPTER IV

1. John 1:1–14.
2. Martyrology for the Feast of the Nativity, *The Breviary* (Edinburgh and London: Wm. Blackwood and Sons, 1879).
3. Dionysius of Rome, *Quicumque vult* (AN).
4. St. Augustine, *Epistle* CCXXXII, 5, 6 (NF).
5. Pope Leo XIII, Encyclical "Divinum Illud," in John Wynne, *The Great Encyclical Letters of Pope Leo XIII* (New York, 1903).

6. Gen. 3:12–15.
7. Luke 1:46–55.
8. Apoc. 12:1–2; 5–9; 13–17.
9. St. Bernard, Homily on *"Missus Est,"* standard translation, cited in George N. Shuster, *Treasury of Catholic Literature* (New York, 1943).
10. Common Prayer of the Church.
11. St. Cyril of Alexandria, *Epistle to Bishop Nestorius with Twelve Anathematisms* (NF2).
12. Pius IX, Papal bull, *Ineffabilis Deus,* December 8, 1864.
13. Pius XII, Apostolic Constitution, *Munificentissimus Deus,* November 2, 1950.
14. St. Augustine, *Epistle* CII, ii, 12, 15 (NF).
15. St. Gregory Nazianzen, *Oration* XXVIII (NF2).
16. Luke 2:6–12.
17. St. Augustine, *Sermo* CXC, iii, 4 (LF).
18. St. Bernard, "Sermon for the Feast of the Nativity," *Oeuvres Complètes de St. Bernard,* trans. Abbés Dion et Charpentier (Paris, 1867), (ed. tr.).
19. Matt. 11:28.
20. Luke 21:16–19.
21. Mark 8:34–38.
22. Matt. 5:17–19.
23. *Ibid.,* 21–24.
24. *Ibid.,* 38–41.
25. *Ibid.,* 43–48.
26. *Ibid.,* 2–12.
27. Mark 14:61–62.
28. John 8:52–59.
29. John 14:8–10.
30. Matt. 27:41–43.
31. Mark 10:32–34.
32. Matt. 26:21–25.
33. Luke 19:41–44.
34. Matt. 9:2–7.
35. Mark 6:38–44.

36. Mark 14:22–25.
37. Isa. 53:2–7.
38. Matt. 27:31–54, *passim.*
39. "Reproaches sung on Good Friday," *The Breviary.*
40. St. Cyril of Jerusalem, *Catechetical Lecture* XIII (NF2).
41. Matt. 28:5–10.
42. *Exultet:* Hymn from the Blessing of the Paschal Candle.
43. St. John Vianney, Sermon for Easter Sunday, *Sermons for Sundays and Feasts of the Year* (New York: Joseph Wagner, 1901).

CHAPTER V

1. John 10:16.
2. John 15:5.
3. John 10:16.
4. Matt. 16:17–19.
5. Matt. 28:18–19.
6. Luke 10:16.
7. John 14:16–18.
8. John 14:26.
9. Acts 2:3–4.
10. I Cor. 12:12–31.
11. Pius XII, Encyclical, *Mystici Corporis,* Official English Version, Vatican Polyglot Edition, 1943.
12. Leo XIII, Encyclical, *Satis Cogitum,* in John Wynne, *Great Encyclical Letters of Pope Leo XIII* (New York, 1903).
13. Luke 12:33.
14. I Cor. 3:8.
15. Council of Trent, *op. cit.,* Sess. VI, ch. 16.
16. St. John Chrysostom, *Homily XXIII on Gospel of St. Matthew* (NF).
17. St. Augustine, *Enarrationes in Psalmos,* CXXX, 1 (LF).
18. John 3:3–5.

19. John 15:26.
20. Acts 8:14–17.
21. John 6:48–59.
22. Matt. 16:19.
23. John 20:22–23.
24. Rite of the Sacrament of Penance, *Roman Ritual.*
25. St. John Chrysostom, *On The Priesthood,* n. 6 (NF).
26. John Henry Newman, "Christ the High Priest," *Public and Parochial Sermons,* Vol. VI.
27. Mark 10:6–9.
28. Eph. 5:22–32.
29. St. Augustine, *De Civitate Dei,* X, vi (NF).
30. Council of Trent, *op. cit.,* Sess. XXII, ch. 1.
31. St. Cyprian, *Letter to Caecilius* (AN).
32. *Mass for the Feast of the Holy Trinity,* standard trans.
33. St. Chromatus, *Tracts on the Gospel of St. Matthew,* viii, cited in Joseph Berrington, *The Faith of Catholics* (New York, 1851), Vol. II.
34. St. John Chrysostom, *Homilies on First Epistle to the Corinthians* (NF).
35. St. Cyril of Jerusalem, *Catechetical Lecture* (NF2).
36. Manning, *op. cit.,* Vatican Council, Sess. IV, ch. iv.
37. Pope St. Leo I, *Sermon on Anniversary of His Elevation to the Episcopate* (NF).
38. St. Gregory Nazianzen, *Tract on Origen,* 26, cited in Berrington, *op. cit.*
39. Sacred Congregation of the Council, *Acta Apostolica Sedis* 38–401, authorized English translation, Oct. 14, 1946.
40. Supreme Sacred Congregation of the Holy Office, Decree of July 28, 1949, authorized English translation.

CHAPTER VI

1. I John 5:4.
2. Mark 16:15–16.
3. John 20:27–29.
4. Romans 1:16–17.
5. I John 5:3–5.
6. *Council of Trent, op. cit.,* Sess. VI, ch. 6.
7. St. Augustine, *Sermo* XXXVIII, ii, 3 (LF).
8. St. Augustine, *Sermo* XLIII, i, 1 (LF).
9. Hebr. 11:1–6.
10. Manning, *op. cit.* Vatican Council, Sess. III.
11. St. Augustine, *De ordini libri* II, ix, 26, 27 (TM).
12. Irenaeus, *Adversus Heresias,* I, i, 1 (AN).
13. *The Creed of the Apostles,* Common Prayer of the Church.
14. *The Creed of the Council of Nicaea,* 325 A.D., revised by Council of Constantinople, 381 A.D. (NF2).
15. John Henry Newman, "Faith Is a Gift of God," *Discourses to Mixed Congregations* (London, 1887).
16. St. Augustine, *De spiritu et littera,* xxi, 54; xxxiv, 60 (NF).
17. John Henry Newman, *Grammar of Assent,* ch. V.
18. Common Prayers of the Church.

CHAPTER VII

1. Gal. 2:20.
2. Matt. 7:13–14.
3. Matt. 6:20–21.

4. John 15:9-10; 12-14.
5. I Cor. 13.
6. St. Augustine, *De gratia Christi,* XXVI, 27 (NF).
7. St. Augustine, *Contra Julianum,* IV, iii, 33 (TM).
8. St. Augustine, *In Epistulam Joannis ad Parthos,* Tr. vii, 8 (LF).
9. St. Francis de Sales, *A Treatise on Love of God* (New York: P. O'Shea, 1868).
10. St. Augustine, *Enarrationes in Psalmos,* CI, i, 3 (LF).
11. St. Augustine, *Enarrationes in Psalmos,* XC, i, 1 (LF).
12. St. Augustine, *Sermo* CCV, 1 (LF).
13. John Henry Newman, "The Cross of Christ the Meaning of the World," *Parochial and Plain Sermons,* (London: 1870-73), Vol. VIII.
14. Phil. 2:5-8.
15. St. Ignatius Loyola, "Principle and Foundation," *Spiritual Exercises of St. Ignatius* (New York and Cincinnati: Fr. Pustet, 1894).
16. *Ibid.,* "Discernment of Spirits."
17. *Ibid.,* "The Three Degrees of Humility."

CHAPTER VIII

1. Matt. 5:16.
2. Matt. 5:13-16.
3. Ephesians 4:15, 4:24, 5:1-2.
4. St. Augustine, *De Civitate Dei,* XIX, xix (NF).
5. St. Augustine, *De Trinitate,* XII, xiv, 22-23; xv, 25 (NF).
6. St. Augustine, *Enarrationes in Psalmos,* CXXIII, 2 (LF).
7. Pius XI, Encyclical, *Rappresentanti in terra,* December 31, 1929, Official English Version, Vatican Polyglot Press.
8. Statement of the Third Plenary Council of Baltimore, 1884.
9. Pius XII, Encyclical, *Humani Generis.*
10. *Ibid.*
11. Statement of the Archbishops and Bishops of the United States, NCWC news release, November 18, 1951.
12. Pius XI, Encyclical, *Casti Connubi,* Official English Version, Vatican Polyglot Press, December 31, 1930.
13. Statement of the Archbishops and Bishops of the United States, NCWC news release, November 21, 1949.
14. Pius XII, Encyclical, *Summi Pontificatus,* Official English Version, Vatican Polyglot Press, October 20, 1939.
15. John Henry Newman, *Certain Difficulties Felt by Anglicans in Catholic Teaching Considered* (London: Longmans, Green and Co., 1900-01), Vol. II.
16. Leo XIII, Encyclical, *Rerum Novarum,* Official English Version, Vatican Polyglot Press, May 15, 1891.

CHAPTER IX

1. Ps. 115:15.
2. St. Ambrose, "On the Resurrection," in *Two Books on the Death of Satyrus* (NF2).
3. St. Bernard, "Sermon on the Death of His Brother Gerard," in Watkin Williams, *St. Bernard of Clairvaux* (London, 1867).
4. Council of Florence, 1415-45.

5. II Mach. 12:43–45, 56.
6. Council of Florence, 1415–45.
7. James Bénigne Bossuet, *An Exposition of the Doctrine of the Catholic Church,* trans. Rev. Wm. Coppinger (New York: B. Dornin, Bookseller, 1808).
8. From "Requiem Mass on the Day of Burial," *"Roman Missal.*
9. St. Cyril of Jerusalem, *Catechetical Lecture* XV (NF2).
10. I Cor. 15:12–22.
11. *So-called Second Letter of Clement of Rome* (NF).

12. St. Augustine, *Enarrationes in Psalmos,* V, 10 (LF).
13. St. Augustine, *Enchiridion, de fide, spe, et charitate* c. 112 (LF).
14. Robert Cardinal Bellarmine, *On the Ascent to God,* trans. T. G. Gent, 1616 (London, 1928).
15. Pope Benedict XII, cited in Thomas B. Chetwood, S.J., *God and Creation* (New York: Benziger Bros., 1928).
16. St. Augustine, *Sermo CCXLII,* viii, 11 (LF).
17. Apoc. 21:1–4, 6–7, 9–12, 22–27; 22:4.

Index of Sources